T0327651

Med Inc.

Sandy Lutz

Woodrin Grossman

John Bigalke

Med Inc.

How Consolidation Is Shaping Tomorrow's Healthcare System

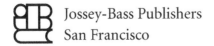 Jossey-Bass Publishers
San Francisco

Substantial discounts on bulk quantities of Jossey-Bass books are available to corporations, professional associations, and other organizations. For details and discount information, contact the special sales department at Jossey-Bass Inc., Publishers (415) 433-1740; Fax (800) 605-2665.

For sales outside the United States, please contact your local Simon & Schuster International Office.

Jossey-Bass Web address: http://www.josseybass.com

Library of Congress Cataloging-in-Publication Data

Lutz, Sandy.
    Med inc. : how consolidation is shaping tomorrow's healthcare
system / Sandy Lutz, Woodrin Grossman, John Bigalke.
      p. cm.
    Includes bibliographical references and index.
    ISBN 0-7879-4040-2
    1. Medical corporations—United States. 2. Integrated delivery of
health care—United States. 3. Hospital mergers—United States.
4. Physician management companies—Mergers—United States.
5. Managed care plans (Medical care)–United States. I. Grossman,
Woodrin. II. Bigalke, John. III. Title.
R728.2.L87 1998
362.1'068—dc21   97–40890

FIRST EDITION
HB Printing   10 9 8 7 6 5 4 3 2 1

Contents

I would like to extend my appreciation to several Price Waterhouse managers, especially Martha Garner in Dallas, who helped shepherd this project along. Also, thanks to Bridget Paige in Dallas, and Todd Hall, Mark Huppert, and William Lehman in New York.

Thanks so much to my infinitely patient husband, Larry, who read every page once and sometimes twice. His editing talents, writing suggestions, and encouragement are the lifeblood of this work. Thanks also to my daughters, Katie and Sarah, who endured as I wrote yet another book.

—Sandy Lutz

⟿ Preface

Money and medicine, profit and pain.

Whether we like it or not, money is generated from medicine, and profits actually flow from pain. The intertwining of these forces creates inevitable compromise and contradiction. This is a conundrum for today's healthcare managers, who are operating larger and larger medical organizations.

As in other parts of the business world, consolidation is rife. The once-independent threads of hospitals, physicians, clinics, and medical technology companies are rolling up into larger and larger corporate balls. Consolidation is one thing, but the true test for these companies is in making them cohesive and capable of managing the four critical factors of success: capital, information, risk, and government regulation.

This book explores the mighty corporations emerging in the ever-consolidating healthcare business, an archetypal class of company that we identify as Med Inc.

We describe what has led to this urge to merge. Some incentives are common to all segments of the healthcare landscape. In a climate of managed care, healthcare companies can no longer raise prices. They must cut costs, and to do so they must add volume to their organizations.

No one in healthcare—neither organization nor individual—is an island. Each segment has an impact on all others and responds to changes in the others. For example, as health maintenance organizations (HMOs) grow larger, physicians and hospitals feel dwarfed in contract negotiations. They, too, form larger organizations to match the health plans' clout.

Although many books have been written about the healthcare crisis—or, rather, the policy crisis in healthcare—this work details the business of the industry and why certain companies are succeeding. It's impossible for a single practitioner, hospital executive, or equipment manufacturer to see this trillion-dollar industry from all sides.

The audience for this book naturally includes those who work in or consult with the healthcare industry. However, investors and even patients also should be attuned to the machinations of America's new corporate medical giants. Many of the companies discussed in these pages are tucked away in the mutual funds as well as America's pension and retirement nest eggs.

Chapter One briefly describes the trends in healthcare consolidation; then Chapter Two steps back to show what has led to these trends.

Chapter Three addresses one of the biggest consolidation booms, the aggregation of physicians into large, publicly traded management companies. Chapter Four discusses the creation, strategy, and tribulations of the nation's largest healthcare consolidator, Columbia/HCA Healthcare Corp. The chapter that follows then gives an account of how tax-exempt hospital systems are also becoming consolidators in their own local markets. Chapter Six details the HMO consolidators, whose efforts to balance fiscal restraint will be watched by all consolidators entering the business of risk contracting.

Chapter Seven relates how the power of consolidation is spilling into all of the cracks of healthcare. Chapters Eight and Nine discuss the tools and methods of the consolidators, as they use smarter and cheaper machines to maximize profits. (In this vein, technology and the Internet are becoming ingrained in all of consolidation, as described in Chapter Twelve.) Chapters Ten and Eleven discuss how consolidators sell themselves and their products.

Finally, Chapter Thirteen tells why the future looks good. Although no one wants Big Brother looking over the physician's shoulder, Big Business is in fact adding much-needed accountability and predictability to the fragmented business of healthcare.

November 1997

SANDY LUTZ
Dallas, Texas

WOODRIN GROSSMAN
Dallas, Texas

JOHN BIGALKE
Orlando, Florida

⎯⎯ᴧᴧᴧ⎯ The Authors

Sandy Lutz is a writer and author who has covered the business of healthcare for nearly fifteen years. She has been a healthcare analyst at Rauscher Pierce Refsnes, a Dallas-based investment bank. Her first book, *The For-Profit Healthcare Revolution: The Growing Impact of Investor-Owned Health Systems* (1995) chronicled the rise, fall, and resurgence of the for-profit hospital industry. She was the Dallas bureau chief for *Modern Healthcare* magazine for almost ten years, covering the investor-owned hospital industry as well as a wide range of healthcare finance topics. Following that, she was a healthcare industry analyst for MDB Information Network in Dallas. She anchored and wrote a monthly TV news magazine, "Healthcare Business Update," for HSTN, the nation's largest healthcare satellite network. She has also worked for the *Memphis Business Journal,* the *Kansas City Times,* and the *Lincoln Journal* in Nebraska. Since 1996, she has been speaking extensively on the topic of investor-owned hospital chains. She is a journalism graduate of the University of Nebraska-Lincoln and lives in Arlington, Texas, with her husband and two daughters.

Woodrin Grossman is a partner and the chairman of Price Waterhouse's National Managed Healthcare Industry Services Group, Audit and Business Advisory Services in Dallas. He has thirty years of experience at Price Waterhouse in financial consulting, accounting, and SEC services. His experience covers a wide client base of investor-owned and nonprofit healthcare companies, including nationally recognized HMOs, hospital management companies, physician practice management companies and alternate site healthcare providers. Woody is a frequent speaker at national and regional healthcare meetings and symposiums, and he is a recognized facilitator for strategic planning and contract negotiations. He was chairman of the AICPA Healthcare Reform Committee and a member of the HFMA Principles and Practices Board, and recently completed serving a three-year term on the AICPA Healthcare Committee. He is currently serving on a Working Group of the FASB, Emerging Issues Task Force related to physician practice management companies. He received his MBA from the Wharton Graduate School, University of Pennylvania, and his BS from Moravian College.

John Bigalke is a partner and the East Region Leader of Price Waterhouse's National Managed Healthcare Industry Services Group, and is based in Orlando. He has twenty years of experience in auditing and consulting services to the managed healthcare industry. He has audited and provided business advisory services to all provider sectors and has extensive experience with health maintenance organizations, indemnity plans, third-party administrators, and other payors. He has been actively involved in mergers and acquisitions, negotiating managed care contracts, regulatory issues and securities filings, as well as expert litigation and defense of clients in healthcare claims. John is a frequent speaker at national and regional healthcare meetings and symposiums, and is recognized nationally as an expert in financial and regulatory matters in the healthcare industry. He is the immediate past chairman and current member of the AICPA Health Care Steering Committee, a member of the Board of Directors of the HFMA, and a former member of the HFMA Principles and Practices Board. He has a bachelor's degree in financial management from Clemson University and is a certified public accountant in Florida, North Carolina, South Carolina, Georgia, Maryland, and Virginia. He is a Fellow of the Healthcare Financial Management Association and a Certified Managed Care Professional.

Getting Bigger
to Get Better

P repare ye the way for the healthcare consolidators, a new league of financial giants rolling up and consolidating the business of medicine.

As this nearly trillion-dollar industry rushes ahead toward the new millennium, it resembles the rest of the corporate world. Think of these giant healthcare companies as a new genus of corporation: Med Inc. Tapping into the technological know-how of the banking and computer industries, consolidators are today's crash carts, disrupting healthcare's status quo and retooling an industry that has grown bloated and inefficient.

There are two parts to today's corporate retooling of healthcare businesses. The first is to consolidate providers to control markets, costs, and quality. The second, perhaps more crucial, phase is to make the delivery of patient care services work. After all, this second part suggests that the resulting healthcare businesses are something new and different. The task is to make healthcare work for patients, payers, and providers. It really hasn't worked well before, and that should be the point, shouldn't it? Through their actions, consolidators—be they big or small—are assembling a framework to make healthcare

1

work. The great consolidators of Med Inc. are on their way to shaping an industry that functions smoothly and efficiently.

What's behind this drive? In today's economy, healthcare businesses are losing their control of pricing. Therefore, they must control costs. Well, here's a pleasant surprise: the most cost-effective care is often the best-quality care. The unfortunate fact, though, is that care has historically been delivered for many wrong reasons. The conventional wisdom was that "we have to put you in the hospital for tests because that's the only place the insurance company will pay for them to be done." More recent conventional wisdom was that "we have to do these tests at the clinic because the insurance company won't pay for you to go into the hospital anymore." Now there is new wisdom: "we're not going to do all these tests because some of them aren't necessary. The rest of your care will be administered when it's most beneficial for you and wherever it's most cost-effective. We'll determine that through data gathered and analyzed through our partners in care."

As the industry approaches the twenty-first century, there is more emphasis on the process of care and controlling the cost of that process. Healthcare businesses, ranging as widely as a small community hospital in New Mexico and a national provider of posthospital services, are examining the process of care and how they can better manage the quality and cost. All of healthcare is becoming managed healthcare, as the lines blur among vendors, providers, and payers. The industry is converging; business rules dictate that traditionally separated segments are starting to resemble each other. However, a key strategy to controlling costs is increasing volume. This dictates growth and bequeaths a new class of economic giants: larger and larger health maintenance organizations (HMOs), hospital systems, physician practices, medical device makers, and so on.

Couple this consolidation theme with relatively high barriers to entry into the healthcare business, and what ensues is a rush of experienced and highly marketable entrepreneurs leaving one healthcare business to start another that can consolidate still other healthcare corporations.

The irresistible force behind this restructuring is Wall Street. Healthcare is an industry whose demographics, technology, and opportunity just keep growing and growing. Investors want a piece of it all. During 1995 alone, $18.8 billion in healthcare industry mergers were announced, according to Securities Data, a financial services firm in Newark. The mergers included providers such as hospitals and physician companies as well as vendors ranging from computer services to cardiac surgery set manufacturers. No wonder the mergers and acquisitions consultants and bankers are going crazy. This is all good for those folks' revenues streams, but once the deals are done healthcare companies are the ones that must make it work.

Med Inc. comprises hospitals along with physician, insurance, and supplier companies. As these companies develop more fiscal discipline, they have to maintain high quality. After all, no one wants to invest in a healthcare company that only thinks about the bottom line; in today's litigious environment, that could be one's financial demise. Who can make it work? Only certain healthcare companies will succeed in this dawning era of consolidation and rapid technological change. We discuss some of them, particularly in relation to what we see as four key success factors. The consolidators must excel at managing:

- Capital
- Information
- Risk
- Government regulation

Together, these factors point the way to just one path: operational efficiency and market dominance. The only question is the size and shape of the market that these consolidators choose.

America is witnessing one of the largest reindustrializations in history. Whereas healthcare profits and expansion ran relatively unchecked during much of the modern era, corporate America is taking over in a wave of mergers and acquisitions that stress cost effectiveness, customer satisfaction, and measurable quality of care. Like a bolt from the blue, healthcare providers and suppliers realize that a system that worked extremely well in the early 1900s grew unmanageable, bloated, and wasteful by the 1970s, 1980s, and 1990s.

Consolidation begets innovation. A fractious, uncommunicative industry cannot advance. It can only struggle alone, to no one's benefit. Healthcare is no longer immune from the corporate realities that have given birth to Wal-Mart, Citicorp, and Microsoft. Tomorrow's healthcare Goliaths, which we explore in this book, are companies the likes of HealthSouth, Medtronic, General Electric, U.S. Healthcare, and MedPartners, as well as some not yet imagined. Giants all, they have the capital, the strategic partnerships, and the propensity to take on risk so they can rule, and rule responsibly. The phrase *healthcare business* will no longer be an oxymoron.

The healthcare industry, fractionalized and oddly competitive, has been reviled for its lack of communication, foresight, and business principles. Those were valid criticisms. Instead of planning, historically the industry has acted, or reacted. Are the emerging corporate giants in healthcare who eye the quarterly earnings reports different? Or will they be reactors, not planners, as well? If they mirror the corporate giants in other industries, they will be different; they will dedicate resources to research and development, customer service, and new technologies, all of which favor both their customers and their bottom line. By gaining such girth, these medical Goliaths have the ways and means to tackle issues long ignored in the profession. The road to success follows these guideposts.

CAPITAL

Capital and access to capital are defining characteristics of the large corporate entities that are beginning to dominate the industry. For consolidators, access to capital may come with size, but managing it comes with experience. We discuss a few examples in the pages that follow. When Columbia/HCA Healthcare merged with another investor-owned hospital chain, Healthtrust, in 1995, access to capital was one of the simplest parts of completing the acquisition. Banks fell all over themselves trying to get in on the deal. Once the hospital chain crossed over into being a $10 billion-plus organization, its financial might fed on itself and it grew stronger and stronger. The Nashville-based healthcare company is one of the few corporations that has had the financial reputation to stand behind one-hundred-year bonds. Its ability to issue such long-term debt speaks volumes about investors' one-time confidence in Columbia's staying power. Additionally, Columbia often borrowed at interest rates lower than its tax-exempt competitors because of its strength as a consolidator.

Yes, Columbia mastered the art of raising capital. But that was its problem, as the company went through management turmoil and federal investigations in 1997. Given Columbia's example, we may guess that in the present acceleration of growth and consolidation in healthcare, mastering the capital part may be far easier than mastering the rest.

MedPartners—a company that didn't even exist four years prior to this writing—draws capital today from a $1 billion bank credit line.

The Birmingham, Alabama, firm started buying physician practices and is now the nation's largest physician company, having completed nearly $3 billion in mergers in 1996 and 1997. MedPartners is now leading the chorus of physician-companies-in-formation. Access to capital is one of the main reasons physicians are selling out to physician practice management companies like MedPartners.

Indeed, Wall Street's ability to raise capital is becoming addictive to physicians as well as vendors and other providers. To get it, organizations in every nook and cranny of the industry are consolidating into larger and larger balls of mass, tumbling faster and faster. Roll-ups are a type of consolidator that combines several smaller entities such as physician practices, for example, into a larger organization for the purpose of going public on the stock market. Consolidators are generally companies that combine several like entities into one big corporation in which the whole is greater than the sum of the individual parts. Roll-up activity has usually been seen in, say, auto dealerships or dry cleaning establishments. A roll-up of physician practices often goes on to be a consolidator, buying more practices and widening profit margins by leveraging its services into managed care contracting. Not all consolidators, it should be noted, start as roll-ups. Many take the good, old-fashioned path of starting small and slowly building.

The phenomenon isn't localized among physicians. Ambulance companies are being sopped up by American Medical Response, which in turn was absorbed by Laidlaw, a Canadian transportation company. Surgical instrument makers are being funneled into U.S. Surgical, rehabilitation clinics into HealthSouth Rehabilitation, and on and on. Also, from initially shopping only in their own niche, certain consolidators have had so much capital that they began hunting in related areas. (After all, how many times have consultants used the analogy of the railroads forgetting they were in the transportation business?) For example, in 1996, Beverly Enterprises acquired Hospice Preferred Choice, and Living Centers of America bought Heart of America Hospice in Kansas City, Missouri. Thus two nursing home chains bought hospice companies, a natural extension of services for individuals reaching the end of life.

It is grating for the little guys—in other words, those without capital—that inevitably they too will be swallowed up or crushed by healthcare monoliths. The mom-and-pop shops of the medical world (which may be multimillion-dollar businesses in their own rights) are challenged to match the cost efficiencies of their larger competitors. Capital-fed consolidators beat down marginal players, and they don't look back.

INFORMATION

In the United States, all healthcare companies must be healthcare information companies. If you can't measure something, you can't analyze it. Remember the old carpenter's axiom of measure twice, cut once? The irony is that healthcare providers often don't measure at all before they cut.

To make consolidation work, these healthcare companies must measure over and over and over again. Then analyze, and then cut. No one argues that there isn't room to cut, but collecting data is the first step to measuring. Consolidators are gathering data rapidly. Larry House, president and CEO of the nation's largest physician company, MedPartners, says, "We have the largest database of patient care knowledge in the industry." Talking about your dominion over data is the consolidator's machismo. Capital? That's powerful. But data amount to the holy grail. House, whose company was specifically designed to consolidate physician practices, knows that the time is right for medical giants. At a New York investment banking meeting in September 1996, he said, "We are seeing a very different approach in the way healthcare is delivered in this country. This fundamental change is bringing empowerment to physician groups."

Imagine a world in which consumers know not only who their family physician is, but why they picked him, where he went to medical school, and what group he was part of. This is a world where the options are crystallized into a handful of choices—doctors A, B, and C— rather than sifting through the names of hundreds of independent physicians. That world is now possible. Consumers are beginning to get a clue. For the first time, Americans are waking up to the fact that they have been spoon-fed a meager diet of information about the quality and cost of one of the highest-priced consumables, medical care.

Traditionally, healthcare businesses have relied on the federal government for much of their data because the Medicare program was the largest such depository. But Medicare information was always a year to two old even by the time it was released. Now, data are available in real-time format. In later chapters, we talk about how control over information gives providers a better grasp of costs and quality. The prices of medical procedures and treatments are becoming more standardized and, many providers believe, variation in price is narrowing. Through the Internet, consumers are learning more about medicine. Next, they'll demand meaningful data on their doctors and their hospitals. Examples abound as companies delve into "branding," a way of advertising their names so that they become recognizable to consumers. Kaiser Permanente is one of many companies using the Internet very effectively to get information into the hands of consumers so they can make decisions about their own healthcare.

Americans can access a wealth of medical information through the Internet, perhaps more information than any "patient advocate" could bestow in multiple office or hospital visits. That's just the first step. When data about costs follow, patients become their own best advocates and smart shoppers in a healthcare economy where the choices may be fewer but more precise.

Managed care started driving providers toward furnishing more information. HMOs couldn't control what they couldn't measure. This meant both the plans and the providers had to start filling disks with patient information that could spit out norms and outliers and efficiency ratios. Although the industry resisted for years, it quickly became a part of everyday business. Healthcare is not necessarily a community service; it is a commodity that can be valued in quality and quantity. Even the most complex procedure is broken down into manageable tasks and supplies that can be priced. More than a buzzword, "critical pathways" became a process of operation. The pathways were software based and data driven. As consolidation continues, payers use the Internet and intranets to extend their control over allocation of resources. Vendors such as Hewlett-Packard provide online training, through websites, to technicians who use their medical equipment.

Healthcare has outgrown its armor. It is being dragged into the information highway, where the physician's decision is not the be-all and end-all. In the next millennium, data will be shared, patients and practitioners will learn from one another, and the true "business" of healthcare will be better understood and appreciated.

It is said that fear and greed are the only true motivating factors. Money takes care of the greed factor for healthcare professionals. Fear lies in the information and what's done with it. If there is no fear behind how the information is used, it may not make a bit of difference to physicians, hospitals, or other practitioners. Consolidators must gather the information, and then take the next step; they must have the courage to act on it, or at least inspire their organizations to use it beneficially. "The crux of the problem continues to be the failure of people involved in the process—physicians and all providers—to receive, absorb, and act upon the information they have," according to Bruce Vladek, administrator of the federal Health Care Financing Administration (HCFA).[1] Vladek wasn't speaking about consolidators. He was addressing his concerns about Medicare's hospice benefit, and chronic problems with the way seriously ill patients are cared for. "Knowing what the patient wants and honoring his or her choices must be at least as important as identifying the source of payment for the services," he added. Even so, his point is applicable to consolidators. Gathering the information isn't enough; practice patterns based on that information must be changed.

Interestingly, many healthcare providers watching the consolidation phenomenon say it's not as much about controlling costs as about improving quality of care through improved information and communication. As healthcare is configured into more massive corporate bureaucracies, can the quality of information truly improve?

Information is vital to these giants as they are called on to deliver what amounts to an extremely customized product. After all, each American receives a highly individualized form of healthcare. The healthcare that one person receives during her lifetime is unlike anyone else's. In fact, it's highly improbable that any one person would follow the same medical pathway as anyone else. Even when it comes to what might be a fairly routine procedure—say, cataract removal or setting a broken finger—each patient's case is different. His age, family history, race, sex, circumstances surrounding the procedure, medications, and attitude toward the predicament all differ enough to consider the treatment a customized product.

Look at other industries where gigantic corporate organizations rule. In many cases, its products are stamped-out copies. A La Quinta motel room is virtually the same from city to city; a Buick is a Buick. A Blockbuster Video store buys thousands of the same tape of *Toy Story* to rent to customers in Lincoln, Nebraska, as well as Miami. Yet how a physician treats a screaming woman whose baby is breech may depend on where he received training, where the hospital is, how the mother's previous pregnancies proceeded, and dozens of other factors.

RISK

A pregnant woman in distress is a situation that has risk written all over it. The risks are clinical as well as financial. Managed care companies are in the business of analyzing that type of risk to sign contracts for hundreds or thousands or millions of "lives." Covered lives are the economic commodity of the future.

For years, healthcare was unique in economic enterprise because providers could simply raise prices and pass along the increase. There was no risk, and nobody really griped. Well, sometimes payers or patients or policy wonks groused, but nobody had enough control to do anything about it. Hospitals that wanted more ample profit margin hiked charges. Insurance companies that couldn't cover costs raised premiums. Vendors that developed a new high-tech whiz-bang gizmo didn't worry about the cost; their only worry was getting it through the Food and Drug Administration (FDA).

Now, to focus on just one segment of the industry, capital equipment and medical device makers are all concerned with making their products smaller, faster, and smarter. The game is different now; no turf is secure. Entrepreneurs turn threats into opportunities. Risk takers must assess the game board with new eyes.

In Texas, a group of podiatrists contract with an HMO for payment of 20 cents per member per month. What? Physicians can't even think in such small figures! But these doctors are making money off the contract; they pat themselves on the back because they know of a California podiatry group that's even more "underpaid," getting only a nickel per member per month. Yet through management of information, physicians can make money on such diminutive contracts through volume. This may sound like the old argument about losing money on each widget but expecting that "we'll make it up on volume," but it's not. Through risk contracting, physicians can assume risk for a group of individuals and be compensated for doing nothing if that population doesn't use their services.

Some physicians won't want to do business this way. So risk managers need to line up incentives to make it work. What other means of financial incentives can be used? Do the physicians invest in businesses together? What about paying bonuses for improved productivity? How is risk shared among provider, payer, and vendor?

More than 100 million Americans are enrolled in managed care plans in which some degree of risk is shared or shifted. All segments of the healthcare economy are learning to price services and budget costs based on risk formulas. The secret is to focus on something that is measurable. For example, Owen Healthcare, the nation's largest manager of hospital pharmacies, has so much experience in this area that it negotiates rates based on the number of hospital admissions. In 1997, Owen was gobbled up by a larger pharmaceutical medical supply company, Cardinal Health of Dublin, Ohio.

"You have to focus on exactly what you're going to do and what you're not going to do," says Vernon Loucks, chairman of Baxter International. The medical products company is focusing on four areas: cardiology, renal care, intravenous therapy systems, and biotechnology. Within each of these areas, Baxter plans to grow and make acquisitions (see Chapter Five). Loucks's strategy is to leverage its position as the number one player in each of those markets, in which Baxter knows the business inside out. Armed with that information, it can profitably contract on a risk basis.

Threatened by provider networks, HMOs are learning that taking risk entails more than being a middleman. They must add value, not cost. Risk is where the profit is; this prompts many healthcare businesses to charge down the risky road unfettered. However, many have found out that small errors in pricing can result in enormous losses. What's more, in an acquisitive industry, rapid growth can distort the numbers.

Patients have little tolerance for errors. If you make the financial incentives too severe, medical services may be withheld. Make the financial incentives too generous, and accusations of abuse flow. When some Medicaid HMOs began enrolling individuals in Chicago in the mid-1990s, the financial incentives to salespeople encouraged abuses. They were so busy signing people up, they didn't bother to help subscribers with the details of what they were enrolling in.

Hospitals are putting systems in place to take on risk. It began with Medicare's diagnosis-related groups (DRGs) in 1987. This amounted to a risk program in which Medicare abandoned cost reimbursement for inpatient stays. Instead, they paid for one full stay on a flat-rate basis. For the first time since the advent of Medicare, hospitals needed to hold the line on costs. Initially, each individual hospital's own costs were built into Medicare reimbursement, so the full effect of flat-fee pricing didn't really take effect until nearly 1990. By then, Medicaid had adopted DRGs in many states and physicians were being rolled into a fixed payment system, the resource-based relative value scale (RBRVS). For a while, it didn't matter if you were losing money on Medicare; you could make up the difference through commercial insurance payers. Now, that's over too. Managed care companies are telling providers how much they are going to pay, for everything from a hysterectomy to a cardiac bypass graft. Or they're telling hospitals what they'll pay to use a hospital bed for one day, or pediatricians what they'll pay to inoculate a baby. This means providers can no longer control prices; the marketplace is determining prices. Now healthcare is more like other industries.

Strengthening financial performance requires cutting costs. Back in the early 1900s, medical care was a cottage industry, small and localized. Patients knew what they were buying and paid in cash. As the industry evolved through the 1950s, 1960s, and 1970s, it became a complicated business paid through third-party agents and generating phenomenal cash flow. In the 1990s, the business is one of risk shifting, that is, keeping risk that is profitable and shifting the rest to somebody else. If you're the "shiftee," you must learn to manage the risk yourself.

GOVERNMENT REGULATION

Government regulation is the most vexing problem for consolidators who want to make their operations run well. Ironically, consolidators may find that it's not in their best interest to be the biggest. It may be better to fly below the government's radar, because to soar above is to become a target.

It is no accident that the government made the biggest consolidator, Columbia/HCA Healthcare, the target of a highly coordinated effort by several federal agencies. There are attractive financial incentives for reporting a consolidator's mistakes to government authorities. When SmithKline Beecham, the giant British drug company, agreed to pay the U.S. government $325 million to settle accusations of overcharging Medicare, the government shared the fine's proceeds with four whistle blowers. SmithKline executives said the company never intentionally broke the law and blamed the violations on "ambiguities over regulations and guidelines." Nevertheless, the company had to pay the largest civil settlement in the healthcare industry.

Because healthcare's biggest payer is the federal government, the industry is dotted with much more dangerous legal quagmires than most other businesses. How do consolidators work that out?

The Damoclean sword hanging over providers is fraud and abuse legislation. Several of the mighty have fallen, and many more will. In 1997, the U.S. Department of Health and Human Services (HHS) opened offices in six cities to investigate fraud. Eight more offices are planned in 1998. The government has found that the "return on investment" in healthcare fraud is extremely high. With criminal penalties now threatening executives at these providers, the stakes are much higher. This is particularly dangerous for the consolidators since the federal government shows a proclivity to target the biggest for investigations. Certainly, the threat hanging over Columbia/HCA Healthcare since its El Paso, Texas, hospitals were raided in 1997 will crimp its expansion plans and distract executives from other strategies.

It's no wonder that many of these organizations are hiring consultants and lawyers to ensure that details remain within the "safe harbors" of the law. Consolidators must seek out bright, honest, and diligent lawyers to navigate the various federal agencies, whether it be the FDA, the HCFA, the Federal Trade Commission (FTC), or other segments of HHS. Any healthcare company must eventually answer to these bureaucrats and learn how to succeed in spite of them.

That's just the federal side. Consolidating healthcare organizations also encounter a huge array of state regulations. HMOs in the Medicaid business find that each state has a different system with unique eligibility requirements, payments, covered services, and on and on. HMOs also have found that the states are developing a fondness for what they (the companies) view as anti-HMO legislation. "Any-willing-provider" laws are pushed by physicians who don't want to be locked out of managed care contracts. In recent years, several states have legislated twenty-four-hour maternity stays to prevent HMOs from performing "drive-thru" deliveries. Such HMO acts include a host of creative twists that govern advertising, utilization review, rate increases, consumer representation on boards, working capital requirements, and grievance mechanisms.

As the shadow of healthcare consolidators looms longer, patients may feel threatened and look to government to protect them. The feeling could be exacerbated as large consolidators grow in financial might. Their adherence to the dollar may be distorted by critics who feel powerless.

Interestingly, a study in late 1996 showed deep erosion of the public's trust in hospitals, saying that the hospitals were so interested in profits that they no longer act like patient advocates. "Hospitals are at risk of losing public support in maintaining their place at the table of healthcare decision-making," said a report commissioned by the American Hospital Association. "The full and frank report reveals that the public backlash against hospitals is largely due to the perception that hospitals and other segments of the healthcare industry are more interested in making money than caring for patients," reported *Modern Healthcare,* a weekly trade journal.[2] Hospital profitability and physician income levels were at an all-time high; obviously, the public thought these providers were more interested in money than patients. Some believed that Columbia's activities had a hand in this perception, as it snapped up community hospitals one by one.

The reality, of course, is that hospitals and all healthcare providers are businesses. Unless the public regards them as such, its members are living in a wonderland of unrealistic expectations.

CAN BIGGER MAKE HEALTHCARE'S BUSINESS BETTER?

In the past, the healthcare business tallied its own oddly configured income statement in which profits were often labeled "excess revenues," costs were whatever the doctor or hospital cared to spend, and value was a nebulous concept. For years, the laws of supply and demand didn't seem to apply to healthcare. There was an abundance of physician specialists. In most industries, abundance converts to low, competitive pricing. But in healthcare, it meant the highest-priced medical care.

A confluence of forces is skewing the market favorably toward consolidators. For one thing, consolidation brings some semblance of order. Let's face it: patients, physicians, and healthcare workers are frustrated by the sheer complexity of this unwieldy system. In fact, consolidators can take advantage of healthcare's unique economics. As technology makes delivery of healthcare services cheaper, the consolidators can usually outrun the payers, pocketing a wider profit for at least a few months and maybe a couple of years.

Market forces are bringing a convergence of trends that carry great benefits for patients. In the twenty-first century, patients will have more meaningful information about their doctors and hospitals than ever before. Despite arguments to the contrary, the advent of big organizations in healthcare may be a healthy turn of events for the nation that spends more on medical care than any other in the world.

This could challenge the holiest of healthcare commandments: that healthcare is a local business. But consider that we live in a mobile society and are employed by multinational corporations. Why is it that Americans can work anywhere using a laptop, cell phone, and a modem, yet when they need medical services, they're out of luck if they're not near home? Successful healthcare companies realize that *local* means having a strong orientation to the customer service, and recognizing the strengths, of local providers. However, they know that ideas are no longer localized. Through the Internet and vast information systems, data and outcomes are shared with unprecedented speed and access. Consolidators also have the capital to market to their ultimate audience, the consumer; this is another topic we explore later in the book.

Unquestionably, the consolidators are on a roll. Med Inc. is proliferating into all segments of the healthcare industry, whether consumers understand it or not. Who breaks up and who holds together as we begin the twenty-first century hinges on capital, information, risk, and government regulation.

To make it work: that's the ultimate prize for healthcare consolidators. Unless they make it work, this consolidation phase is nothing more than a giant multilevel marketing scheme, which only works if one keeps recruiting more members (in the case of healthcare, making more acquisitions). Wall Street will demand growth of the consolidators, and that growth must come from somewhere. The successful consolidators draw it from a combination of internal and external growth. What analysts refer to as "same-store sales" is internal growth; acquisitions are the external part.

Putting it together is the fun part, the exciting and lucrative part. There are proven leaders adept at doing the deals. However, innovation is in the execution; this is the litmus test for the consolidators.

CHAPTER TWO

A Climate
for Consolidation

Healthcare is experiencing a dramatic roll-up phenomenon. Hospitals, ambulance companies, HMOs, equipment manufacturers, and physician practices are marching to the beat of larger organizations that they perceive will better their future or that of patients.

In one sense, healthcare is simply keeping pace with the merger and acquisition frenzy of corporate America. It's the Med Inc. version of the business world. Healthcare deal making reached record heights in 1996, with 633 mergers announced, up 58 percent from the previous year, according to Irving Levin and Associates' press release. Physician groups announced 218 deals, an increase of 73 percent, and hospitals announced 169 deals, up 27 percent.

Medical device manufacturers were consolidated in mergers valued at $7 billion in 1995 and 1996, according to Piper Jaffray, a Minneapolis investment banking firm. That left so few "mid-cap" companies—companies with $500 million to $2 billion in revenues— that the acquirers soon became bait themselves. In other words, the large medical device companies that were doing the acquiring may now be gobbled up themselves.

What's behind all of this? The growing managed care environment coupled with an oversupply of providers produces an industry that is uniquely primed for a merger craze. Unlike retailers, even well-capitalized healthcare corporations are hard pressed to build from the ground up. Blockbuster Video can toss together new stores on every street corner, drawing managers and new employees by simply posting a "Now Hiring" sign. Blockbuster grows revenues by opening more stores. Healthcare companies can't do business that way.

This is an industry with an oversupply of hospitals, doctors, and device companies. There are already too many healthcare companies fighting over the same pie. That's why consolidators must truly consolidate when they're creating these giant roll-up companies.

To ferret out the healthcare providers or suppliers they want to buy, consolidators need capital. Through numerous sources, it has been funneled into the industry. Capital accelerates growth, which in healthcare is manifested through mergers. In some cases, it has become what some view as a voracious monster. Columbia/HCA Healthcare, for example, at one time considered buying nearly every hospital in America. "We're talking to everybody," was the mantra recited when executives were asked about their acquisition plans. Practically every healthcare services company was a potential takeover target. Tax-exempt hospitals in particular found this extremely unsettling.

By 1997, Columbia was the nation's largest healthcare services company, with $20 billion in sales; yet it still held only 7 percent of the hospital industry's revenues. Could a healthcare company become as dominant in its niche as Coca-Cola is in soft drinks or Microsoft in information technology? If a healthcare company took better care of patients than any other company, could it just keep growing? *Better* is really the question word. How do you make bigger better?

The way things are going, healthcare is going to get bigger. But will these organizations be better in terms of cost and quality? That's where information comes in. Quantifying *better* has always been difficult in healthcare, but today's consolidators have new tools (we discuss the use of information in later chapters).

CONSOLIDATORS SUBSIST ON VOLUME-DRIVEN DEALS

One of the factors driving consolidation—indeed, the entire industry today—is volume. The bigger the organization, the bigger the volume of business it can attract. To explain the consolidation phase, Josh

Nemzoff, a hospital mergers and acquisition consultant, posits that survival follows a kind of industrial food chain: market share, volume, revenue, cash flow, survival. One aspect simply is absorbed into the next larger one. If a hospital has market share, then it has volume. That leads to revenues, which cover expenses and create cash flow. With cash flow comes survival. When a hospital increases its market share, it enhances each segment along the chain.

Hospitals have notoriously high fixed expenses. Most industries are either capital intensive or labor intensive; hospitals are both. They must be both high-tech and high-touch, striking an equitable balance between both that doesn't cause costs to go through the roof. A hospital allots 40–50 percent of its expenses on such items as debt, supplies, equipment, and labor that must be there at all times. Regardless of how many patients walk in the door, the hospital must have a certain amount of nursing, technical, and administrative staff on site twenty-four hours a day, 365 days a year to fulfill federal, state, and other accrediting regulations.

Nemzoff recalls the story of a Florida hospital that hired him to work on a merger with another hospital in town. He told executives that they would save $40–45 million if they closed one of the two hospitals and consolidated services by moving all of the patients into just one building. The hospital he proposed closing reported operating expenses of about $100 million a year. Since nearly half of that was fixed costs—labor, supplies, administration—he figured the system would save $40 million a year. The executives said, "You're nuts." Instead, they contracted with another consultant for $300,000 to do a much broader study of the financial effects of such a merger. The consulting firm said Nemzoff was wrong; the correct figure was *even higher,* $52 million.

Even so, the hospital's trustees refused to consolidate. "They couldn't bring themselves to shut down that hospital," he said. They feared the public-relations problems generated by such a closure and resultant layoffs. This is no small concern to tax-exempt hospitals that may have been built, at least in part, through the donations of community benefactors and organizations. Although this particular not-for-profit hospital balked, other hospital systems will not hesitate to grab $50 million in savings through consolidation. Those are the systems that are driving the merger craze.

With too many hospitals and too many beds, consolidation is just getting started. Since hospitals claim 36 cents of every healthcare dollar, the potential savings are just too juicy for big consolidators to ignore. The median occupancy rate for hospitals dropped from 51 percent to 43 percent between 1990 and 1996, according to the annual statistical summary by HCIA, a healthcare information company in Baltimore.

At a Healthcare Financial Management Association meeting in the mid-1990s, William Cleverly, a healthcare finance professor at Ohio State University, asked a group of about one hundred hospital executives how many would lose business if they increased prices 10 percent. Only a handful raised their hands. That spoke volumes about the effect of competition on hospitals.

Until the consolidation of recent years, the industry was fractious and confused, multiplying at a rate that would embarrass rabbits. Everybody raised rates and worried nada. Sipping at the lemonade stand of the federal government, where everyone was assured a drink, healthcare businesses ballooned. By the 1990s, America simply had too many hospitals, too many heart monitor manufacturers, too many doctors, and too many nurses.

FRAGMENTED HOSPITALS RIPE
FOR CONSOLIDATORS' TOUCH

Considering the fractious nature of the healthcare industry, it's a wonder it works at all. Hospitals are frequently a sea of power struggles between departments and specialties, each jockeying for control, patients, budgets, and equipment. Yet as consolidation envelops whole hospitals, entrepreneurs spy out specialties within the hospital that can be merged. For example, one of the biggest trends in hospital management is outsourcing specific departments. Analysts estimate this is a $100 billion business and growing, as hospital CEOs believe they can more cost-effectively transfer the responsibility and the risk to an outside vendor.

For most of the 1970s and 1980s, outsourcing, also known as contract management, was primarily the domain of housekeeping firms like ServiceMaster and cafeteria companies like Morrison's. However, clinical and information systems broke into the market and now are the biggest future growth areas for consolidators. Take a health system with ten hospitals. It has ten human resource departments, ten labs, and ten radiology departments. How much time and money is being wasted? Savvy contract management can guide the system's consolidation of departments while making a hefty profit for its provider.

Consider Steris, a Mentor, Ohio, firm in the sterilization business. The company, whose worth on the stock market exceeds $1 billion, has grown with the market. In May 1996, Steris bought Amsco, another sterilization firm that was five times as big as Steris. In the next six months, Steris bought two other firms, so that by the end of 1997 it had more than one thousand sales and service people killing the bugs that cause diseases in healthcare facilities. Yet this company illustrates another trend in consolidation—decentralization of care. The volume of surgery is growing, but more and more are being done in surgery centers and other outpatient settings, such as doctor's offices. Decentralization increases the number of sites of surgery, which is good for Steris's business.

TOO MANY MEDICAL VENDORS

Not only are there too many hospitals, but too many vendors as well. At MDB Information Network in Dallas, a company that advises hospitals on medical equipment purchases, analysts try to keep track of as many as fifteen hundred medical equipment companies. In that kind of circus, it's nearly impossible for hospitals to sort out discrete differences among so many acts. How can buyers keep track of so many sales pitches? With dozens of companies peddling basically the same types of equipment, millions of dollars that could have been spent on research and development are instead spent on marketing.

Healthcare information systems managers often deal with myriad computer systems, none of which talk to each other. Laboratories have different systems than the billing area does, and the clinical information is sometimes kept on yet another system. Consolidators are finally tying systems together, a benefit to patients and providers. Protocol Systems, for example, sells patient monitoring systems that connect through simple telephone-type jacks to a central workstation. The monitors can be plugged in next to each patient's bed. That way, as a patient moves from department to department, her monitor and the record of her vital signs can move, too. This concept, which the Beaverton, Oregon–based firm, Protocol calls "flexible monitoring," frees up beds in the critical care and intensive care units and allows a patient to be moved to lower-cost settings.

Similarly, large medical equipment manufacturers are trying to become one-stop shops for hospitals. That kind of shopping is working for Marquette Medical Systems of Milwaukee and Physio-Control of Redmond, Washington. The latter dominates the external defibrillator industry, while Marquette is one of four manufacturers that control the patient monitoring sector. In a deal worked out in early 1997, Marquette agreed to discontinue making defibrillators in deference to Physio, while Physio makes its defibrillators connectable to Marquette's cardiovascular information system. The two will market a bundled product line to hospitals, hoping to unseat their main competitor, Hewlett-Packard. (HP has managed to muscle into the number two market-share position in defibrillators based on the strength of its top position in patient monitoring. Some hospitals lean on HP for all their capital equipment needs.)

Hospitals are likely to move toward larger one-stop corporations as they yearn for vendors with future stability with whom they can upgrade equipment. Although General Electric is known as a medical equipment manufacturer, it actually derives more revenue from leasing and servicing equipment. Its focus on service demonstrates how the company has achieved high profitability. The medical equipment service program, InSite, is the world's largest service organization. It provides remote diagnostics through online centers in Milwaukee, Paris, Tokyo, and Sydney.

From its nonmedical businesses, GE found the value and profit potential from servicing equipment. The company realizes that its hospital customers are making a long-term investment, expecting their equipment to last ten years or more. Upgrades may be necessary in the meantime, but hospitals can't afford to buy a replacement magnetic resonance imaging unit, for example, every twenty-four or thirty-six months. InSite support is available twenty-four hours a day, throughout the world—a challenge that competitors cannot meet.

The challenge for vendor consolidators, then, is the same as for provider consolidators: to make bigger better. Each day, GE battles the problems of bureaucracy yet remains innovative and moves with the marketplace. GE reaches out to other businesses to learn their best practices, an effort executives there describe as "overcoming NIH" (not invented here). For example, it uses a bonus structure that rewards employees and managers for finding and sharing new ideas. Stock options, which previously only went to a few hundred top employees, are now held by twenty-two thousand employees.

The results are in the products. More than 80 percent of GE's medical equipment sales come from products introduced within the past three years; the medical division has sales of $3.5 billion and more than fourteen thousand employees. The most profitable company in the United States, GE racked up net earnings of $7.25 billion in 1996. The company's operations yielded an amazing $9 billion in cash.

It's worth studying how GE got that way, and several hospital chains want to learn. For example, Columbia signed deals in which it buys nearly all of its capital equipment from GE. In addition, Columbia uses GE's EDI*EXPRESS service to send and receive electronic documents to and from more than two hundred national vendors. This means that Columbia's national vendors use GE's private value-added network exclusively in their dealings with Columbia. Although some of Columbia's employees chafed at being locked into the GE contracts, management saw financial synergies that make such moaning almost ineffectual. To get closer to hospitals, GE Medical spent much of 1996 beefing up its servicing capabilities by acquiring local firms; one significant purchase was National Medical Diagnostics, which services imaging equipment.

GE spent $80 million to build a state-of-the-art training center and TV studio to develop educational programming for its healthcare customers. TiP-TV (Training in Partnership Television) is a fully digital training network that provides the needed educational programs. For fees ranging from $3,000 to $20,000, hospitals can tune in live broadcasts on clinical and administrative techniques. Hospital executives receive tips on strategic planning and reengineering, topics in which GE is well versed and to which hospital executives give rapt attention so as to learn from a $70 billion giant that has successfully survived several industrial revolutions.

For example, Tenet Healthcare, a chain of 125 hospitals, saw value in aligning with GE and, in December 1996, agreed to buy computed tomography scanners only from GE. Tenet said the deal will save more than $2.6 million over the five-year life of the contract.

When hospital megasystems deal with megavendors, it changes the relationship between the two companies and cuts time and money spent on marketing. Large vendors must restructure sales efforts that were once built around regions. Consolidators don't cater to manufacturers' regional boundaries; the traditional territories are not useful in working with providers. In fact, manufacturers may see a diminishing need for "sales" people, and a growing need for technicians instead. Hype is eclipsed by the need for valuable information on price, performance, and outcomes.

DOCTORS FOR SALE

Consolidation among hospitals and medical vendors is much farther along than in some other segments of the healthcare industry. Take doctors, for example. Only in the past few years has the Med Inc. juggernaut rumbled in. Since then, the rolling up of physician practices has been likened to an oil boom. Lots of money is being thrown around, and lots of risk taken on in fledgling organizations. Hundreds, perhaps thousands, of physicians are making huge personal fortunes by selling their practices to physician practice management companies (PPMs). Some want to fund their retirement accounts. Others sell out of frustration, believing that the acquisition frees them to concentrate on practicing medicine. Still others believe that these consolidated organizations will finally begin to provide a framework for better quality and lower costs.

It is true that tremendous cost efficiencies lie in tying together physician clinics, and pooling billing and information systems. Yet the actual value is in controlling physicians' behavior since they have an impact on the costs incurred in hospitals, clinics, outpatient care, pharmaceuticals, and the whole range of medical purchases.

Consider a physician who works hard all his life: medical school, nights and weekends on call, hundreds of patients to keep track of. In the past, the physician would simply retire late in life, turn over dozens of boxes full of patient records to a fellow doctor, and move out to the lake with whatever savings he had accumulated. "Historically, the doctor has never been able to convert his practice assets into dollars," said Harris "Buddy" Miers, a former executive with a Dallas physician partnership who is helping other physician roll-ups get started.

Hello, Wall Street. Now, physicians find they can get value out of their practices, a maneuver that investment bankers refer to as monetization. In the process, physicians salt away money or stock options for the future. It's also frequently described as an exit strategy. Coupled with the need for capital to finance information systems, this phenomenon has made physician groups look like oilfields. In a $200 billion industry (which is what the physician sector amounts to), right now only 5 percent is consolidated through physician organizations. It spells a rush to market—the stock market, that is.

Doctors whose lexicon once centered on stents and keratotomy are becoming just as fluent in terms like take-out price, arbitrage, and EBITDA (earnings before interest, taxes, depreciation, and amortization). For roll-up experts, the field is so wide open, they're giddy with opportunity. It's like walking through a cornfield in late summer: money, money, money, everywhere you look. No wonder so many entrepreneurial executives travel from one roll-up to the next. They start with a small roll-up, move to a larger one, and then an even larger one. Or they sell their expertise to a "start-up roll-up" (an odd juxtaposition of words indeed).

Breaux Castleman is president and chief operating officer of Scripps Clinic, a leading physician organization in San Diego. Prior to Scripps, Castleman was with Caremark, another physician roll-up that was bought by the largest physician roll-up in the country, MedPartners. Before that, he was CEO of Kelsey-Seybold Clinic, Houston's premier doctor group that ended up selling to Caremark. Scripps is a PPM that drew private capital from investors interested in helping the clinic market its well-known name, which was recognized far beyond San Diego (it was founded in 1924), and brand it in other markets. Scripps's 290 physicians have weathered the managed-care storms of southern California and can share their "best practices" experience with the clinics that Scripps acquires.

A CLIMATE OF ACCOUNTABILITY

It may seem contradictory, but as physician and hospital organizations feed on each other and grow larger and larger, they become more, not less, accountable. They can measure costs more consistently, focus concern with price, and transform themselves into real businesses. "The era of limitless resources with no accountability or productivity measures has ended," noted Luis Marcos, M.D., president of New York Health and Hospitals.[1] Marcos was commenting on a radical new plan in which the public hospital agency linked its contract with Columbia University College of Physicians to specific productivity goals. The physicians must treat a certain number of patients and meet quality goals, such as improving the rates of prostate screening and mammograms.

This is a vision of the future of compensation for healthcare providers. What's more, for all of this, Columbia University will not be paid more. In fact, the institution will get less. Over the three-year contract, New York Hospitals estimates it will save nearly $31 million, costing Columbia a like amount. Although this kind of accountability is commonplace in many corporations, it's rare in healthcare. In reporting on the pact, the *New York Times* commented, "Doctors and administrators . . . have maintained that the public hospital agency was so poorly run that it was unfair to expect their employees to meet stringent productivity terms."[2] This has been a common argument in healthcare: "You don't know what you're doing, so why should we be held accountable to you?" How else to explain that hospitals and physicians are not the least bit regretful when they make money off Medicare? Why aren't consumers upset when their health insurance carrier doesn't ferret out shoddy or wasteful providers? If nobody else is striving to be efficient, why should we?

Such complacency is ending. In today's climate of consolidation, no one is complacent. In the world of corporate Med Inc. healthcare giants, the game is hardball. Accountability is one of the ground rules, and as the federal government turns over more of its health responsibilities to the private corporations, that is, to HMOs, the game will become even tougher.

Health systems and payers see value in physician practice consolidations. With physicians joining larger organizations, the chances of gaining access to valuable data increase. Large physician companies have the sheer numbers to produce such data on costs and outcomes. It is no coincidence that this consolidation began occurring during a time when healthcare cost inflation was moderating. After double-digit inflation rates in the 1980s, the rate dropped precipitously, and by 1994 and 1995 healthcare cost inflation rates were the lowest in more than three decades. Most shocking of all, the figure that many economists point to—healthcare spending as a percentage of the growth domestic product—stabilized between 1993 and 1995 at 13.6 percent. This may have put employers in a state of bliss that could unnerve them in the future. Healthcare costs have not been cutting into corporate profits for the last couple of years. This means CFOs haven't been storming into human resource offices with the fervor to attach healthcare costs that they had in the 1980s. If and when healthcare premiums start rising again, consolidators may find a new set of rules and players.

LEARNING FROM WITHIN

Healthcare may not suffer from the "brain drain" some industries have when good employees leave, but it is weakened by a sort of "brain cul-de-sac" by which great ideas are not shared widely and often do not receive the capital or marketing enjoyed by other segments of the population. Look at other industries that exploit their talent through the financial resources brought by a large corporation. In recent years, Xerox has funded new ideas through its own venture capital arm. It recently set up a company, called Xerox New Enterprises, which will help businesses financially and then launch them as publicly traded companies. Where did it get the idea? From a healthcare company.

Thermo Electron, of Waltham, Massachusetts, set the pattern. The company has been around since 1956 but really started humming in the 1990s, when the time was ripe for cost-efficient medical technology companies. Since going public in 1983, the company has spun out eighteen companies that raised capital through initial public offerings (IPOs). The strategy benefited this $3 billion conglomerate and its customers. Thermo has recorded a compound annual return of 28 percent since going public. Its spin-offs are companies such as ThermoLase (which makes hair removal lasers and operates spas) and Thermedics (equipment that detects explosives in airplanes and impurities in beverages). Thermo looks for companies that will ramp up 30 percent annual growth in emerging markets through new technologies.

As medical device makers get larger and stronger, they can pour more funds into research and technology, inventing products that strengthen providers as well. "I am often asked why other companies have not adopted Thermo Electron's strategy of spinning out its subsidiaries," said John N. Hatsopoulos, Thermo's president and CFO, in a letter to shareholders in early 1997. Brothers John and George Hatsopoulos were Greek immigrants who studied at the Massachusetts Institute of Technology before founding Thermo. George continued to lecture MIT graduate students on thermodynamics even while running the company, which licensed technology from the school. Now, Thermo is using its mass to strike accords with similar-sized giants. For example, its agreement with AT&T Capital gives Thermo customers an easy way to lease equipment from any of the Thermo companies.

Consolidation and corporate start-ups may appear to embody contradictory schools of thought, but they do not. In fact, one feeds the other, adding value to the whole. As healthcare segments consolidate, they build larger companies while deleting costly duplication. In turn, they spin off intelligent and aggressive managers who see other segments of the trillion-dollar industry that are ripe for their talents. All are chanting the hymn of value in healthcare: cheaper, smarter, faster, better.

One of Thermo's most recent IPOs is Trex Medical, itself a roll-up of four capital equipment manufacturers. The four companies dot the eastern half of the United States: Bennett X-Ray Technologies in Copiague, New York; XRE of Littleton, Massachusetts; Lorad in Danbury,

Connecticut; and Continental X-Ray of Broadview, Illinois. The con-
centration of Trex—with the financial backing of Thermo Electron—
allows the amalgamated companies to make a big leap from film
imaging to digital imaging. During the late 1980s and much of the
1990s, the imaging industry was not pushing the technology envelope.
Everyone was spending so much money on marketing and outma-
neuvering their competitors that dramatic leaps in technology were
not a priority.

Now that's starting to change. The days of physicians or technicians
holding up big films from X-ray or MRI machines are ending. Digital imaging and archival systems are already being used in other industries, where they're considered superior because they can be
manipulated and transmitted more easily. Hal Kirshner, president of
Trex, estimates that the $500 million worldwide market for mam-
mography will balloon because nearly every provider needs new digital equipment. Which vendors will hospitals and outpatient centers
go with? They are likely to choose consolidators with perceived staying power. That suits such companies as Trex and GE. Kirshner has
said he believes that some thirteen thousand digital mammography
units will be sold in the United States within a decade once the FDA
approves the technology. Another ten thousand will be sold overseas.
"So if you're looking at 20,000 units times an average price of
$300,000, you're talking about a $6 billion market over the next 10
years," he said.[3]

Thermo is a resident of Massachusetts, a state that hosts 160
biotech firms worth about $1.2 billion and another 160 medical de-
vice companies with a valuation of $2.6 billion. It is second only to
California in biotech firms. More than one-third of the fifty-one
Massachusetts companies that had IPOs in 1996 were either biotech
or medical device companies.[4]

By some estimates, 3 percent of the economy of Massachusetts is
dependent on medical device companies. Consolidation creates its
own dynamics. As the state's medical device companies grow larger,
they exert more pressure on their congressional representatives to address the slow progress that the FDA is making in approving new devices and therapies.

Another example is Texas, which has been a hotbed of PPM companies. In Dallas, Physician Reliance Network is a roll-up for cancer
specialists, OccuSystems focuses on occupational medicine, and American Physician Partners manages radiology practices. In Houston,
Physicians Trust and Integrated Orthopaedics both focus on ortho-

pedics. Both firms are targeting some twenty-thousand orthopedic physicians in the United States for their roll-ups. Also in Houston, American Oncology Resources is consolidating cancer-oriented physician practices, another huge market.

NASHVILLE, A HOTHOUSE FOR HEALTHCARE CONSOLIDATORS

On the banks of Tennessee's Cumberland River, Nashville is the nation's most prolific proving ground for healthcare consolidation. It is the birthplace of investor-owned hospitals, PPMs, and outpatient surgery center chains. In fact, it's sometimes referred to as "the Valley," a reference to Silicon Valley, only in this case it is the Tennessee Valley that has spawned literally hundreds of for-profit healthcare companies.

The city is home to more than one hundred healthcare companies. The number changes so fast with consolidations and new start-ups that it's difficult to keep count. However, the Nashville Health Care Council, a start-up itself that was founded in 1995 to organize, promote, and nurture the city's medical-related businesses, does keep tabs. In addition to working with the media to promote Nashville's healthcare companies, the council sponsors networking get-togethers and meetings like the Health Care Entrepreneurialism Conference in May 1997.

The council itself is a living example of the inbred nature of the healthcare business in the city of rolling hills, Opryland, and southern-style mansions. Laura Campbell Ortale, who once ran the council, is the daughter of Victor Campbell, who heads investor relations for Columbia/HCA Healthcare. Campbell was a long-time fixture at Hospital Corporation of America before it merged with Columbia in 1994. The council is so serious about hometown healthcare that its website (www.healthcarecouncil.com) maintains a family tree showing descendants of HCA and Hospital Affiliates (another former hospital company) and the sixty or more companies they have spawned. "Consolidators in healthcare do best when they're surrounded by like-minded individuals," said Al Kent, managing partner in the Nashville office of Price Waterhouse.

Nashville is a laboratory for that mingling, a pro-business home to a bunch of Junior Achievers who've grown into overachievers. At every turn, a new American dream for building a healthcare company blossoms. The city is governed by a former HMO executive, Phil Bredesen, and draws from two top-notch medical schools, Vanderbilt University Medical School and Meharry Medical College. Bredesen knows well the roll-up strategy. His HMO, Coventry, was started on his kitchen table and agreed to sell out to Principal Health Care in 1997. When Columbia was getting ready to merge with Healthtrust, an investor-owned chain of rural hospitals, and debating whether to stay in Louisville, Kentucky, or move to Healthtrust's home of Nashville, Bredesen was instrumental in designing a $26 million tax-incentive program to get Columbia to move.

It's no accident that the state has founded one of the nation's most innovative Medicaid programs, TennCare, which swept some 350,000 uninsured residents into the insurance program. Nashville is the state capital, and it was cited in *Plant Sites & Parks* magazine as one of the eight best places nationally to locate a business in 1994. After the article ran, the publication itself moved to the city.

Because the healthcare industry has been so segmented, there's no shortage of roll-up ideas for the well-funded, savvy entrepreneur. One roll-up often leads to another, which leads to another, and on and on. Obviously, investors and executives with stock options can ride this wave for years to come. Med Inc. is just getting started.

When Columbia bought HCA, some HCA executives left to start other companies. The same happened when Columbia bought Healthtrust. None of the talent pool was out of work for long. For example, Richard Francis, a former Healthtrust executive, founded a PPM company called UniPhy with funding from OrNda HealthCorp, a hospital management company that later sold out to Tenet Healthcare. Some roll-ups have made such big payouts to senior executives that they have gone on to fund other companies. Nashville is home to twelve venture capital firms that are dedicated to healthcare businesses. The newest, Clayton Associates, was founded by Clayton McWhorter, Jr., the former chairman of Healthtrust and Columbia/HCA. After making about $50 million from the sale of Healthtrust to Columbia, McWhorter left to feed the financing needs of younger upstarts.

One of the city's long-time capital partners, Massey-Burch, also has HCA roots. Jack Massey, who had already made a fortune taking Kentucky Fried Chicken public, was one of the four founders of HCA. Franklin Venture Capital is managed by three men who formerly managed HCA's venture capital subsidiary. Franklin has funded such companies as American Day Treatment Centers, an outpatient mental health firm, and Vitas Healthcare, a Miami-based hospice company. The list of interconnecting people and healthcare companies in

Nashville goes on and on. In nearly all cases, the companies are roll-ups in one form or another.

The rest of the country has gotten wind of this. New York, California, and Texas venture capitalists descend weekly on the airport and whoosh down West End Avenue, a kind of Music Row for many healthcare company stars. Although much of the nation knows Nashville for its country music names of Wynonna Judd, Merle Haggard, and the Grand Ole Opry, chamber of commerce executives talk about the city's other "record" industry: healthcare. Indeed, it takes a lot of sales of country music CDs to equal the revenue from just one cardiac bypass. The proof is in the phrase, "Show me the money." In 1995 and 1996, $300 million in private funding flowed to more than fifteen Nashville-based healthcare companies, according to the Nashville Health Care Council. Now, compare that figure to the $540 million that venture capital firms infused into medical businesses in 1995, and it tells you just how big Nashville's influence is.

"The talent pool that we will need to add to our company is certainly greater here than anywhere else," said Dana McLendon, when he and four other principals started New American Healthcare, a hospital company. "There are very few places where you find four or five or six law firms, all with staff experienced in healthcare deals." Rather than fight with the big boys like Columbia and Tenet to buy hospitals, New American sticks to America's back roads, looking for small-town hospitals without much of a future in a quickly consolidating healthcare economy. McLendon and CEO Rob Martin target hospitals in towns that are at least thirty-five minutes' travel time from the nearest alternative acute-care facility. The towns generally have fewer than forty thousand residents, and the hospitals' bed counts are typically under 200; in the range of 100 to 150 beds is perfect. They also look for hospitals in states without certificate-of-need requirements, so New American doesn't have to spend a lot on legal fees and regulatory hassles to either buy or upgrade the hospital.

But—surprise—New American isn't alone. Another company started by a former Healthtrust chief operating officer, Hud Connery, Jr., is also buying small-town healthcare facilities.

Nashville is bestrewn with not only healthcare providers and contractors but also the professionals needed to support them: ad agencies, law firms, architects, mergers and acquisitions consultants, and equipment planners well versed in the intricacies of conducting a healthcare business. "If we weren't already located in Nashville, we'd move here," McLendon said. After weighing several offers, McLendon and other former Healthtrust executives did a deal with Welsh, Carson, Anderson, and Stowe, a New York-based venture capital firm. Welsh, Carson, which also provided capital to Nashville hospital chain Quorum Health Group, put $50 million into New American. That kind of cash shows why the roll-up strategy works so well in healthcare. It's not cheap starting a healthcare company. If you want to buy hospitals, you can't do it with a couple thousand dollars in the bank. The high-stakes game of healthcare means that roll-ups are the most logical strategy for organizing the market, cutting costs, and building value.

Consolidators are flocking to Nashville, and other cities might want to learn from its bird-of-a-feather formula for economic growth. Cities that want to experience the growth of Nashville should pay attention to the way it treats businesses. The state has no income tax on wages or salaries, and its corporate excise tax of 6 percent is among the nation's lowest. In addition, Tennessee is a right-to-work state, which means it is not adversely affected by union activity.

By early 1997, fifteen publicly held healthcare companies with $33 billion in revenues were based in Nashville, but that figure could balloon with the dozens of start-ups now in early growth stages. Although known for its hospital companies, Nashville is quickly gaining a reputation for PPMs as well, with such firms as American Pathology Resources, MediSphere, PriCare, and Healthcare Resource Management.

JUST GETTING STARTED

As these examples demonstrate, consolidation and mergers are just the first step. These consolidators are on a journey toward better outcomes and better-valued healthcare services.

The real work begins when the ink dries. Then it is imperative to turn to the process of managing cash, information, risk, and government regulation—and do it all well. The biggest hospital company or the catheter maker around is likely to be judged on Wall Street by the standards of performance and success of the Microsofts and Citibanks of the world. Keeping Med Inc. going is not nearly as easy as growing it. The classic entrepreneurial drive is to build and build. Yet it often takes a different type of individual to operate this assembled group of assets and find a way to assimilate their services and products to market needs. As McWhorter says, "It's not fun being a captive in your office. It's more fun doing deals."[5]

CHAPTER THREE

Tapping the Rich Vein
of Physician Practices

P rospectuses stack up like term papers on the desks of Wall Street bankers, brokers, and analysts. Deals, deals and more deals. Ostensibly, they all look about the same: stylized corporate logo on the front, red lettering printed sideways along the spine saying "A registration statement relating to these securities has been filed with the Securities and Exchange Commission. This prospectus shall not constitute an offer to sell or the solicitation of an offer to buy nor shall there be any sales of these securities. . . ."

All that's missing is a terse message: "Millions of dollars in capital needed. Will trade for small ownership stake."

On slick white paper, each prospectus tells a story of one more company founder pursuing the American dream by writing a business plan, generating profits, and selling a portion of the business to potential investors. The latest installments in this dream are such entities as The Company Doctor, PhyMatrix, Physician Reliance Network, InPhyNet, American Oncology Resources, MedPartners, and Specialty Care Network.

Most of the dozens of such companies didn't exist five years ago. Now, they're so prolific that the industry has its own three-letter acronym, as we saw in Chapter Two: PPM, for physician practice management. Like birds of a feather, physicians and executives are flocking to Wall Street with their newly minted physician practice management companies. Investors feed them capital. Some soar, gathering speed and engendering a brood of wanna-bes; others plunge to the soil, bloodied and broken.

All of them initially predict success, and Joseph Hutts knows why. "We made it look too easy," explains the soft-spoken Southerner whose company, PhyCor, will be ten years old in 1998. Sitting in a starched white shirt and red-patterned tie, CEO Hutts talks about why he and three other hospital executives founded a physician company years before anyone else thought of it. The fundamental reason was healthcare costs; they wanted to contain them, and maybe bring them down.

Hutts's modest hand gestures and occasional smile belie his reputation as an impending invader, as many hospitals initially depicted him. They saw PhyCor as the Pied Piper who would lead their physicians away from their control. In fact, as head of the nation's first publicly held physicians' company, Hutts made the power and influence of Wall Street reachable for thousands of physicians and literally carved out an industry along the way.

The industry grew to $12 billion by 1996. It's made millionaires out of dozens of physicians and savvy healthcare executives who grasped the potential of physician roll-ups. The tale is compelling. Physicians account for an estimated $200 billion spent on medical services. That's just the start. What Hutts and others see is that physicians also wield the pen—the one that orders the pills and the rehabilitation sessions, the angiograms and the radiation therapy. Although hospitals generate some $400 billion in revenues, physicians decide how a great deal of that money is spent. By some estimates, physicians control as much as 85 percent of nearly $1 trillion spent annually on healthcare.

Remarkably, these highly trained professionals labor in isolated villages, far from the automation of the rest of the world. They want to concentrate on practicing medicine, yet they yearn to make their profession more effective.

What an opportunity for physicians and investors. By most estimates, less than 5 percent of the nation's nearly 700,000 physicians are affiliated with a PPM. That leaves hundreds of thousands of physicians out there to be organized, enticed with stock, and managed.

Physician companies, like all healthcare consolidators, struggle to manage the four critical factors discussed in Chapter One: capital, information, risk, and government regulation. What makes this niche exciting is that it's still so unorganized, and the potential is so large.

ORGANIZATION AWEIGH!

Since the mid-1990s, more than two dozen PPM companies have tapped Wall Street for initial public offerings, one-third in 1995 alone. In 1996, $785 million in venture capital dollars flowed into healthcare, much of it into physician companies, according to Price Waterhouse's National Venture Capital Survey. Venture-backed companies such as MedPartners and National Specialty Networks sprung into successful public stock offerings.

Physicians began funneling from private practices into PPMs dealing with oncology, cardiology, primary care, emergency medicine, orthopedics, and ophthalmology. Talk of PPMs monopolized conversation at medical staff meetings, in hospital hallways, and around the office coffee pot. "They're all getting deluged" with offers, says Robert Bohlmann, consulting service director of the Medical Group Management Association, an Englewood, Colorado, trade association. First venture capital firms and then Wall Street delivered unprecedented capital to a healthcare services niche that was unorganized and technologically lagging. In an age when teenagers manipulate graphic images and embed audio tracks on their own websites, physicians remained practically the only people still conducting business mostly on paper. While top-dollar consulting companies and software makers flocked to billion-dollar companies elsewhere with ideas for efficiency gains and information technology solutions, they largely ignored this cottage industry. There weren't enough collectively big entities to make it worth the time in fees.

Now, that is no longer true. Management and consulting talent is descending on PPM companies. They're telling doctors, "We can make you efficient, rich, and powerful. You'll be recognized for your business acumen as well as your clinical prowess. Your physician practice management company will soar exponentially once it's gone public, building you a nice nest egg for retirement. Wall Street will love your story. Best of all, you can focus on practicing medicine, and leave the business issues to us."

Not so fast. This is a consolidation story that's still learning its ABCs. Happily-ever-after may be years down the road.

Making it work financially is possible in these early stages. However, in the end, organizations need management and information systems so they can measure and analyze the cost and quality of how care is delivered, whether patients get healthier, and whether they're treated with the most effective combination of services, drugs, and procedures. Although most physicians still work in groups of five or fewer, the profession is rapidly hiving. During the 1990s, the number of doctors in practices with two or more physicians increased from 46 percent to 60 percent, groups with five or more doctors increased from 18 percent to 32 percent, and groups with ten or more increased from 8 percent to 16 percent, according to the American Medical Association's Council on Medical Service.[1]

The beauty of the PPM is that physicians can continue to practice in small, workable pods of five or ten but have access to information systems and outcomes reports of a national network of managed practices comprising hundreds or thousands of physicians. Still, there's a big price to pay. Physicians must give up some control. "Anybody going into medicine needs to understand it's a rapidly changing environment and you may not be your own boss," William F. Fogarty, M.D., chairman of the AMA Council on Medical Service, told *American Medical News* when the AMA released its report on the consolidation of physician practices.[2] Just as with other sectors of healthcare, consolidation of physicians was attributed to oversupply and pressures from managed care. The AMA noted that the number of physicians contracting with HMOs grew from 56 percent in 1986 to 83 percent in 1995, and the number of "non-federal, post-resident patient care physicians per 100,000 population" expanded from 150.5 in 1985 to 177.2 in 1994.

LOSING CONTROL

Everybody was trying to control the soaring cost of healthcare in the early 1990s, which led to creation of dozens of HMOs, preferred provider organizations (PPOs), and other managed care plans. This added a layer of managed care plans to the myriad insurance plans that doctors already had to deal with, not to mention Medicare and Medicaid. The plethora of payers meant that physicians were drowning administratively, scrambling to negotiate rates and reimbursement. Their overhead costs ballooned as they hired numerous clerks to keep up with all of the health plan paperwork.

Ira Korman, a former Dallas hospital CEO who now works with physician groups, cites the example of a group of eight surgeons who owned a surgery center. Imagine running a center that has agreements with sixty-six different health plans, each with its own copays, discounts, coverage limitations, and other reimbursement levels. "They've got Blue Cross, HMO Gold, HMO Seniors on a Thursday, and all these boutique plans. That's what's killing them," Korman noted.

Physicians felt they were losing control over their patients, their payments, and even their equipment. For most of the post-Medicare era, physicians had called the tune when it came time for hospitals to order the sutures or X-ray machines they wanted. It was called "physician preference," and hospital administrators blatantly bowed to it. Some vendors took advantage, bypassing the hospital's purchasing managers and primarily catering to physicians. However, by the late 1990s, physician preference was an outdated concept that no self-respecting hospital would permit. Nobody ordered equipment just because physicians wanted it. Cost and clinical efficacy had to be demonstrated.

Physicians typically want the latest technology, but their preference for certain instruments or equipment often steered them to brand preference, just as certain elite runners prefer Nike and others like Adidas. Managed care had a big impact on physician preferences because cost began overriding preferences.

Then, there's the matter of the paycheck. In 1994, physician incomes dropped for the first time in decades.[3] As physicians watched their paychecks and those of their colleagues drop, they looked for answers. They started considering other ways to practice. It used to be they just sent out the bills and collected their charges. But less and less was coming back. In 1992, physician practices collected 90 cents on each dollar of gross charges. By 1995, it had dropped to 73 cents thanks to bad debt and discounting, according to the Medical Group Management Association.

MGMA also compiles a fascinating study that compares physician "production" to compensation. Production is measured by gross charges, but that can be misleading because few physicians, or hospitals for that matter, collect the same amount as they charge. However, charges remain the yardstick used to gauge the volume of procedures performed. For the past five years, primary care physicians have seen greater increases in their pay than specialists have, but the contrast was especially interesting in 1995. In that year, diagnostic radiologists saw their income decline 6.4 percent and their production increase nearly 3 percent. Anesthesiologists saw their production increase 18 percent and their income drop 1.6 percent.

The financial prospects look particularly dim for some of these specialties. There are 9 radiologists per 100,000 population, but industry experts say that with the influence of managed care there is a need for only 4.4 per thousand. (We discuss why in Chapter Nine.) How quickly the other 4.6 radiologists per 100,000 are going to be looking for work is unclear, but it makes these specialists increasingly nervous.

In this collapsing environment, physicians today face four options:

1. Accept the status quo, which for many of them means practicing solo or in a limited partnership practice with a handful of other physicians.

2. Be acquired by a hospital.

3. Be acquired by a managed care plan.

4. Be acquired or affiliated with a PPM.

For many, the first option is unrealistic because they lack the capital to buy equipment and information systems and the clout to negotiate managed care contracts. They're caught in a squeeze play as costs rise and payments decline. The second and third options are unpalatable since physicians have spent much of their energies battling either the hospital at which they practice or the insurance company that pays them.

Also, the third option didn't turn out to be much of a long-term strategy, at least in the case of Aetna, which made the biggest foray into acquisition of managed care plans. Aetna began buying up doctor's practices in the early 1990s, saying that it would set up its own primary care network, called HealthWays Family Medical Centers. The company managed to set up forty-seven centers with 189 physicians in seven metropolitan markets: Atlanta, Baltimore and Washington, D.C., Philadelphia, Dallas, Akron, Chicago, and southern California. The insurer was also managing six independent physician associations that represented about eight hundred doctors. In early 1997, Aetna (now Aetna U.S. Healthcare, since it merged with another managed care company) decided it was more cost-effective to contract with a physician company than own one. It decided to sell its physician practices to MedPartners, the nation's largest PPM company. As part of the deal, Aetna's fourteen million enrollees gained access to MedPartners physicians, making it the first nationwide alliance between a physician company and an HMO.

With the solo practice being an impractical option and few managed care insurers buying physician practices anymore, the options became fewer but clearer. Accepting that they had to do something, physicians needed to ally with either a hospital or a physician corporation to survive. (Unfortunately, some physician practices bought by hospitals may end up feeling like free-agent baseball players as they go from owner to owner.) Many hospitals paid exorbitant prices for physician practices, later regretting the fact that they had married in haste.

Like Brer Rabbit with the tar baby, many hospitals didn't know what to do with these practices once they owned them. They wanted to get rid of them but had a hard time selling something for which they had overpaid. For one thing, the costs of managing the practice rose. Physicians are a thrifty lot who tend to pay their secretaries, techs, clerks, and nurses far less than hospitals do. When the hospital took over the practice, operating costs rose. "[It has been reported] that 82 percent of hospitals that own physician practices were losing money," Robert W. Daly, managing director of TA Associates, a Boston private equity investment firm, said wryly. "I consider that to be a boldfaced lie. There's no way 18 percent of those hospitals are making money."[4]

As if that were not bad enough, the IRS started scrutinizing the deals. This meant that tax-exempt hospitals couldn't use their cash reserves for the "inurement" of private individuals, which is to say, doctors. "The legal climate has changed," noted MGMA's Bohlmann, talking about the second half of the 1990s. Hospitals that overpaid relative to what the physicians produce "are going to get slammed," he noted.

Dallas-area attorney Scott Waters agreed that hospitals that haven't kept good records to justify the compensation of their physicians may be in trouble. "Unreasonable pay issues are all over the place," he warned. What is unreasonable? Compensation levels are a moving target—moving down, that is, because physician compensation levels were dropping.

In the late 1990s, many hospitals and physicians alike want to get out of their ownership or management agreements. The most interested buyers are investor-owned physician companies. "The calls I get are always the same," says PhyCor's Hutts, recalling conversations with hospital CEOs, who say, in effect, "We've bought some physician practices, and now we're losing money badly. Initially, we viewed PhyCor as a competitor, but now we want to come together with you in a long-term relationship where we [the hospital] won't get hurt."

For example, hospitals in Dayton, Ohio, ended up buying about one-third of all the city's primary care physician practices, paying "whatever it took," says a healthcare executive who formed an independent practice association-model PPM, or IPA. His group was formed to give physicians an alternative to selling out to the hospitals. The IPA was a compromise to get physicians used to working together without forcing them to sell their practices and sacrifice autonomy altogether.

Now, five years after the buying spree began, the hospitals are losing money on the practices and some of the acquired physicians want out, too. Yet the physicians have found that selling out leaves them few assets.

Many physicians see the business as a battle in which they must choose sides. Physicians-at-war is exactly the analogy that PhyCor uses in its website. It likens physicians to the Achaians in their fight against the Trojans in Homer's epic poem, *The Iliad.* Albeit overly dramatic, the analogy tells the story of how this group is rich in courage and resources but lacks a key element: "a leader who can inspire and unite them and achieve a position of strength against their adversary."[5] The website describes the role of Achilleus, who leads the Achaians to victory. Then, it connects the dots: "Today, uncertainty reigns concerning the future of healthcare delivery and the various roles that will be played. Only strong leadership can align market forces and resources necessary to create a successfully restructured healthcare system."

That makes option number four the strategy of choice.

GROUND ZERO FOR THE PPM

Until the early 1990s, Wall Street had not given much thought to the physician practice niche. The seeds were planted by Joe Hutts and three other executives from Hospital Corporation of America, a forerunner of Columbia/HCA. Hutts had spent nearly a decade at HCA, from 1977 to 1986; for part of that time he headed HCA Health Plans, the chain's managed care subsidiary. He followed that by heading up Equicor, which was a joint venture into managed care between HCA and the giant insurer Equitable.

"You can't spend your life in healthcare without understanding the fundamental issues, and what I had been concerned about was the cost of healthcare," Hutts said. He knew that control of cost rested with physicians. By organizing them and giving them the capital to build information-sharing systems, he believed healthcare costs and quality would improve. Even so, the idea was radical. "We had so many people tell us, 'You'll never do it,'" Hutts recalled, adding that "even good friends" told him so. "I finally stopped listening."

MGMA's Bohlmann, who has worked with dozens of physician groups, first heard about PhyCor at an MGMA meeting in Nashville in 1989, he says, as "these crazy guys that are going to buy physician practices." Though prohibited from outright ownership because of laws governing corporate practice of medicine, PhyCor could buy the assets of the physicians' clinics and then sign a long-term service agreement. Hutts knew he was on the right track. Holding up his cupped hands as if holding something precious, Hutts is clear: "What you know and I know is that the physician drives the costs. If you could hold down healthcare costs, it had to be through the physicians. Here was the opportunity that I had been waiting for all of my career."

Empowering physicians through corporate structures meant that "other things would happen," he says. "What's pleasantly surprised us [PhyCor's founders] was the huge value you could add to the equation." In 1988, PhyCor bought its first group, Green Clinic, a practice of thirty-five physicians based in Ruston, Louisiana. Four years later, the company went public.

However, the road to riches can be rocky, as PhyCor found out. Just a few months after the public offering, PhyCor was forced to announce bad news. Miller Medical Clinic, one of its first acquisitions, was bleeding red ink. It seemed that when PruCare, with which Miller had an exclusive contract, raised its rates, hundreds of members dropped the plan. Since the contract was bringing in 75 percent of Miller's revenues, the result was disastrous financially. One of the dangers in taking on risk is the prospect for unforeseeable change. Whether a risk-based contract is distributed through an employer group or an HMO, the provider may find that a huge block of business changes hands practically overnight. After attempts to recoup, PhyCor decided to sell the clinic to a local Nashville hospital and take an $18.6 million write-off.

That was not exactly the way to galvanize confidence in a concept that many had questioned from the beginning. Although the company's stock dipped momentarily, it rebounded quickly, and PhyCor went on demonstrating the ability to recover. Hutts takes this history in stride. "You can't come from nothing to be an organization that truly creates an industry without some stumbles," he says.

Just hearing the name PhyCor often struck fear in the hearts of hospital executives. When the Irving (Texas) Healthcare System heard that PhyCor was talking to some of its doctors in 1993, management scrambled to find out who this company was. PhyCor was seen as a divisive threat that would empower and possibly pit their doctors against them. But it was already too late for Irving's hospital executives. "One of the doctors leaked it, but it was almost a done deal by that time," recalls Scott Waters, who was the hospital system's attorney at the time.

Each physician received $225,000 and the clout to demand changes from the hospital administration. Without PhyCor, the physicians never would have been able to galvanize themselves into a cohesive, proactive group, Waters believes. "You need an outside expert—somebody with a suitcase, from out of town," he says. Not only did PhyCor give the doctors big checks, but the company also promised to increase revenues. Although the practice management firm took only about 13 percent of existing revenues, the split would be larger in the case of certain operating improvements, thanks to PhyCor's new management. "They had a whole litany of things," Waters says. The doctors wanted Irving Healthcare to build them a new medical office building and buy the present ones from their current owners, most of whom were the doctors themselves. The hospital ended up not bending to that demand, which would have made certain doctors even richer.

Any semblance of working together started to dissipate. "The hospital just battened down the hatches and said, 'We're going to war against you,'" Waters recalls. He says PhyCor's management had told hospital executives they would do joint ventures in certain outpatient service areas. However, nearly as soon as the deal was completed, the group snubbed the hospital by doing a deal with Medical Care International, at that time the nation's largest surgery center chain.

Interestingly, the relationship between PhyCor and Irving improved a great deal in later years. In 1997, PhyCor began working closely with Baylor University Medical Center, which is the current owner of the Irving hospital.

Savvy observers may have figured out that Hutts and company would bring to the physician industry what their Nashville colleagues had brought to hospitals. Through centralized management and purchasing, PhyCor would convince dozens of physicians to sell their practices to an investor-owned company. In exchange they would get stock and be allowed to concentrate on practicing medicine, leaving to somebody else the hassles of payers, lawyers, and administrators.

In each of the practices that PhyCor takes over, it sets up a policy board comprising three physicians and three PhyCor executives. Of the three executives, one is the clinic's executive director. The board decides strategic direction for the clinic, devises incentive plans that benefit both PhyCor and the doctors, and determines some clinical guidelines. The economic gains are obvious in such a cottage industry: administration, marketing, data management, raising capital, gaining access to managed care contracts.

One by one, clinics in Wichita Falls and Dallas also sold out to PhyCor.

ROLLING ALONG

No longer picking up small physician groups, PhyCor soon began aiming for larger and larger targets. In January 1997, the company cut a deal with the 152-physician Straub clinic in Honolulu. Wall Street analysts were consistently impressed with the amount of profit that PhyCor could squeeze out of existing clinics. In other words, after picking what bankers like to call the "low-hanging fruit" (cost cuts that are easy to make, such as lowering supply costs through group purchasing contracts or axing back-office personnel through shared services), PhyCor continued to increase profits. In announcing PhyCor's 1996 earnings, President and CEO Hutts said same-clinic revenues increased 16 percent for the year. PhyCor's revenues totaled three-fourths of a billion dollars, and profits were a record $59 million. During 1996, the company added thirteen medical groups with nine hundred physicians.

The machine churns away. At the same time it announced record financial results, PhyCor said it would sell another 6.4 million shares of stock, raising $200 million to repay bank debt. PhyCor's reputation and stability have won over many of its early skeptics. "I think PhyCor is a keeper," says Bohlmann, who is often hired to advise physician groups on which path to follow. He describes Hutts and his top executives as "highly ethical people, very Christian guys. I've heard a lot of people bad-mouth the concept, but not the individuals."

That reputation has helped propagate the hordes of followers. "It's a lot easier if the forerunner is setting high standards," says Ann James, a healthcare attorney who was involved in a PPM start-up herself. Hutts agrees that core values practiced by key individuals drive the organization. "I can make a mistake of the head and I won't get shot," Hutts said. "What I can't do is make a mistake of the heart." The attitude carries down through the ranks, which fact he describes as a "wonderfully refreshing empowerment." Yet Hutts is dubious about the values held by some of the people following in his footsteps: "The concern I have is so many PhyCor-style start-ups. Everybody wants to develop their organization, go public, and make a killing." He pauses and then adds, "And there have been some killings made."

THE KILLING FIELDS OF WALL STREET

When PhyCor started, Hutts and his team spent most of their time explaining what their company did, since it was such an oddball. Now, the oddball is rolling, which aids Hutts and every other PPM out there.

Making the idea a reality accelerated consolidation. Instead of spending time explaining the concept, PPMs can put their efforts into differentiating themselves from the rising tide of PPMs surrounding them. In addition, the physicians themselves can spend their time in due diligence on the PPMs rather than trying to figure out what's going on with these companies. Some of them, like Physician Resource Group, went from inception to managing hundreds of physicians in no time. They were part of a new breed of "poof" companies—and Wall Street loved them.

"Poof" companies (also known more familiarly as roll-ups) are created when a founder puts together several small companies at once. The companies, or physician practices in this case, are not consolidated into a single organization prior to going public. Instead of a small company growing into a bigger company, these companies seem to—"poof"—appear out of nowhere. There are distinct accounting advantages to these "poof" companies because the consolidator avoids generating goodwill, which has to be amortized against earnings. This gives the consolidator stronger earnings to report to Wall Street and a higher valuation.

One example is PhyMatrix, founded by Abe Gosman, a long-term-care entrepreneur with the Midas touch, who turned to physician practice management when that sector starting soaring in 1995. Although many healthcare consolidators have done exceedingly well, Gosman is one of the few who have been able to sell the same company twice for big gains. In 1986, he sold Mediplex, a subacute and long-term-care company that he founded, to the cosmetics giant Avon Products. Later, Avon decided to divest its healthcare businesses, Mediplex included; the New York-based corporation sold it back to Gosman for $42 million. Gosman took it public at $19 a share in 1991 and then sold it in 1994 to Sun Healthcare Group for $320 million, or $33 a share.

Gosman, who also runs one of the nation's largest owners of healthcare real estate at Meditrust, also hit a home run in physician practice management. His company, PhyMatrix, raised $100 million in its IPO, making it one of the largest healthcare offerings in 1996. After going public, the West Palm Beach, Florida, firm was soon managing the practices of two thousand affiliated physicians in the nation's southeast, mid-Atlantic, and northeast regions.

Gosman's golden touch with Wall Street brought capital to physicians who needed both the money to buy computers and the power to bargain in managed care contracts. Oddly enough, consolidation of physician practices into larger and larger corporations isn't generating nearly the outcry that arose with hospitals going in the same direction. In New England, overtures by Columbia/HCA to buy New England Medical Center were met with near horror by many local opinion leaders.

Yet, PhyMatrix waltzed into the Northeast and almost immediately started getting physicians on board. Within one year of the 1996 IPO, the company had purchased practices with about one thousand Northeastern physicians. Gosman announced a $500 million plan to develop, own, and operate medical malls and other facilities in five metropolitan New York counties in conjunction with North Shore Health System of Manhasset, New York. "The Northeast is where we'll have the greatest potential, because we feel it's a fairly fragmented market," said Gosman. "We're a young company in a young industry. I expect the physician practice management industry to go from $8 billion to $50 billion by the end of the decade."[6]

Gosman and other roll-up artists saw in the Northeast what early settlers saw in California: fertile turf. In terms of healthcare, the area was fragmented and expensive. Therein lay cause and effect; change the cause and you'll change the effect. PhyMatrix started out rolling up oncology practices and then spread to multispecialty PPMs.

It should be noted that PPMs sticking to only one specialty win points with certain doctor groups. Often founded by the specialists themselves, who are more comfortable with like-minded individuals, these companies claim that they can better manage a specialty they understand. For example, radiologists may have a tough time fitting in with multispecialty roll-ups that are dominated by primary care physicians. For one thing, primary care physicians are paid less than radiologists, who fear that the income levels of the "primes" will be raised at the expense of radiologists. Also, in the battle of dollars, radiologists may want to see the PPM invest in new imaging equipment. Instead, a multispecialty PPM may be more interested in spending money on buying more primary-care groups.

Specialty consolidators have been the most prolific among PPMs, however. In oncology, consolidators include Physician Reliance Network and American Oncology Resources, both of which tout their ability to efficiently manage a disease whose treatment is complex and expensive. They also cite savings through volume purchasing of drugs, one of the biggest cost drivers in oncology. Cancer is, unfortunately, a growth industry. The term covers hundreds of individual diseases, which generated expenditures of $35 billion in health services in 1995. Eventually, one-third of all Americans will be diagnosed with some type of cancer.[7]

Some investment analysts see value in a specialty consolidator called MedCath, which manages cardiologists and invests with them in new "heart hospitals." MedCath is an anomaly that many are watching because it is a physician company building hospitals. That's the mirror view of the usual situation of a hospital company buying physicians. Not surprisingly, this strategy has come under the scrutiny of journalists, investment bankers, and competitors who claim that their communities don't need any new hospitals.

MedCath's first facility was built in McAllen, Texas, a border community that is almost unlike any other healthcare market. The generous recipient of an oddly lucrative program called Medicaid disproportionate share (by which the government gives extra funding to hospitals that serve a disproportionate share of the poor), the hospital market is home to some of the most up-to-date facilities in the state.

Former hospital administrator and MedCath founder Stephen Puckett knows the hospital side of the business well, and he has tapped into its most lucrative artery. According to the American Heart Association, $115 billion was spent on cardiovascular disease in 1995. He believes the savings are huge. In a $40,000 bypass surgery, about 45 percent of the cost is in labor, he contends. Manage that cost better, and you can save big bucks.

By consolidating physician practices with hospitals, MedCath can make package deals with payers, better manage the continuum of care, and cut costs, Puckett says. This strategy is not widely embraced, however. Many question whether MedCath is adding to the overall cost of healthcare by building new hospitals, and whether new and minimally invasive heart surgery techniques are going to enable other hospitals to compete on price (see Chapter Eight).

THE CONSOLIDATION MACHINE OF MEDPARTNERS

One of the most incredible consolidators among physician companies is MedPartners. Specifically designed to consolidate physician practices, the company reported the biggest leap in revenue growth among the Fortune 500 firms in 1996, according to *Fortune* magazine, recording a 563 percent jump to $4.8 billion.

In less than three years, MedPartners went from start-up to the largest PPM company in the nation, with $5 billion in annual revenues. A decade ago, it would be hard to believe thousands of physicians could agree on anything. Yet, some ten thousand physicians are turning control of their practices over to MedPartners. The big gorilla in this industry, it also has managed care contracts in place with more than 1.7 million enrollees.

Despite its size, MedPartners has plenty of room for growth. At the end of 1996, MedPartners controlled just 6 percent of the patient population in Los Angeles, which, it is true, amounted to 11 percent of the prepaid population (those in HMOs or capitated plans). Yet its market share in Chicago was just 0.7 percent; in Houston, 2.4 percent. The company's goal is to gain 20 percent of a given local physician market and provide 95 percent of the types of physician services required by payers.

MedPartners grew out of another consolidator, HealthSouth Rehabilitation (which is described in Chapter Seven). Both HealthSouth and MedPartners are based in Birmingham, Alabama, which has long been regarded as an Old South industrial city. A blue-collar town humbled by the reindustrialization of manufacturing, Birmingham reared a native son who would resurrect it. He was Richard Scrushy, founder of HealthSouth, the nation's largest rehabilitation company.

MedPartners' founder, Larry House, learned from Scrushy as chief operating officer at HealthSouth for seven years before he went out on his own with a $1 million investment from HealthSouth and $20 million from venture capitalists who saw the company's potential. "We felt like there was a significant opportunity for a consolidator in the physician arena, and you'd really be able to define what this new industry looks like and feels like," House says.

If you had told physicians fifteen years ago that they would be selling their practices to someone who called himself a "consolidator," they'd have said you were crazy. Like many other consolidators, MedPartners started small, buying individual physician practices. Faster than most consolidators, however, MedPartners moved to acquire entire companies, such as Pacific Physician Services, Mullikin Medical Enterprises, and Caremark International. The Caremark merger pushed MedPartners ahead of PhyCor as the nation's largest PPM company. From the fall of 1995 until the end of 1996, MedPartners entered practice acquisition agreements valued at $3 billion.

Consolidators grow through dogged determination. MedPartners has thirty-five executives who do nothing but talk to prospective physician groups and craft deals with them. Although it's hard not to trip over MedPartners executives at physician meetings, House insists that "We rarely make calls [on potential physician groups] where we have not been invited first." MedPartners' House is one of an elite corps of consolidator pros. Scratch the surface of most successful PPMs and you'll find at least one executive who has done it before for someone else. Bringing a successful consolidator on board gives a start-up a significant edge.

For example, Houston's Integrated Orthopaedics is led Ron Pierce, who was vice president of operations at American Oncology Resources, also in Houston. Pierce's company hopes to consolidate the virtually untapped market of twenty-thousand orthopedic physicians across the country. "Everybody has access to capital, but what virtually none of these startup companies has is experienced management," Pierce says.[8]

Two other executives learned the ropes at Medical Care International, at one time the nation's largest surgery center chain; it was purchased by Columbia in 1994. Former executive John Carlyle leads OccuSystems, which is consolidating the highly fragmented business of occupational healthcare; another former executive, Emmett Moore, runs Physicians Resource Group, an ophthalmology roll-up. These managers (and the type they represent) are seasoned veterans in the intellectual and emotional capital of these new physician companies. The challenge of leading physicians has often been compared to herding cats, yet the PPM industry illustrates that it's not impossible. Still, forming the PPM is one thing, and nurturing and maintaining it is something else again. It demands human capital so that these companies don't "poof" away as suddenly as they appeared.

"The physician practice management company has to develop, foster, maintain, and nurture in order to have a successful partnering relationship with its affiliated physicians in most affiliation models," says Kurt Miller, formerly a partner with Price Waterhouse. "There is a tremendous cost to that human capital effort that tends to be overlooked or underestimated in the integration phase down the road."[9]

BUILDING THE RIGHT CONSTITUENCY

When asked about MedPartners, PhyCor's Hutts shakes his head and says, "They're a good company and I want them to do well. It's difficult to be objective." Then he adds: "They did what I would have done. They didn't have the size and were fairly late getting into it. They had to grow rapidly with some major deals," he says. All of the acquisitions that MedPartners made were ones that PhyCor considered, but "we looked at all of them and decided to pass."

PhyCor is sticking to its knitting, preferring to acquire medium-sized practices rather than large PPM companies. Even as MedPartners rises and surpasses PhyCor in size with its gigantic buys, Hutts stays the course. His formula is the best for physician groups that want to deal with hospitals and payers, he says. "To sit as equals, you have to have a lot of critical mass and a large primary care base," he notes. Plus, "we believe that managed care is going to be a dominant part of our future" and primary care physicians are needed to control that, he says.

A little over half of the physicians managed by PhyCor are in primary care. (That number includes obstetricians, whom some consider specialists.) Beyond 50 percent, "the economics are much more difficult," Hutts says, noting that specialists drive higher-dollar procedures and that primary care practices have higher overheads. "If you lower your revenues, you still have the same kind of fixed costs," he explains. Hutts seems careful not to upset the apple cart. PhyCor's stock climbed from less than $10 a share in 1994 to more than $40 in 1996.

Although many physician practice management stocks tanked in late 1996, PhyCor's shares performed well. It remains the old reliable, which is a tremendous marketing advantage. "Just as physicians want to go with a medication that's a proven winner, they want a company with a proven reputation," Hutts says. "If you fast-forward fifteen years, PhyCor will be one of the major entities in the health field."

THE ART OF THE DEAL

Although PPMs seem to be following a similar formula, the deals are structured in multiple ways. When you've seen one deal, you've seen one deal.

"Classically, the business model in physician practice management is where you have some smart money and some smart management that has a good business plan and then goes out and embarks upon a roll-up plan or consolidation plan," says Kurt Miller.

There are two basic models, the "acquisition" model and the "network" model. Under the former, the PPM acquires the hard assets of a physician's practice, which include the building and equipment. Physicians remain employees of their own professional corporation. Then they sign binding long-term contracts (typically for forty years) with the PPM.

Under the "network" model, a PPM doesn't acquire anything. It merely signs a contract with a physician group, which usually is organized as an individual practice association. The management company provides business function services for the IPA but exerts far less control over the physicians.

Network management can be a side door into an acquisition. For example, PhyCor began managing IPAs, which weren't willing to sell their practices but still wanted the management services of PhyCor. Many times, PhyCor would help a group of, say, five hundred physicians form smaller groups of fifty or so. Those groups could then unite to take capitated contracts or consider stronger attachments with Phy-Cor. Wall Street is more suspicious of these IPA arrangements because the PPM has less control.

In the acquisition model, the physician receives a combination of cash and stock. From there, the PPM adds information systems that can collect, bill, and collect clinical data for later outcomes studies. The PPM also begins signing managed care contracts, designed to bring in more revenue-paying patients, and considers adding locations or outpatient services, which is also designed to boost revenue. It's a business deal.

In the late 1990s, renowned medical schools such as Johns Hopkins and Duke University began offering courses in the business of medicine. It was good timing. Physicians need to find experts—not a brother-in-law who happens to be a CPA—to scrutinize these deals, recommends Ira Korman, the former hospital CEO who now helps physician groups. "I was looking at one that had a clause that if the doctor dies—which is a pretty safe bet—the stock reverts to the corporation. There's nothing left for his estate."

Getting started takes money, but for PPMs the requirement is not as much as for the capital-intensive consolidators of hospitals or HMOs. (When New American Healthcare, a rural hospital chain, was getting started, it received a $50 million infusion from venture capitalists.) However, consolidators should realize that it takes considerably more effort to assimilate physician practices into a roll-up. In addition, rolling up radiologists is far different from doing so with obstetricians, for example. "Ob/gyn offices operate differently than an office where you have less patient participation," said attorney James, the CEO of an ob/gyn consolidator that was not successful. Such offices do not lend themselves as much to consolidators, she says, because they need a long-term business partner, whereas a consolidator isn't able to squeeze short-term savings through the consolidation of such offices.

In musculoskeletal disease state management, one such consolidator is Specialty Care Network of Lakewood, Colorado, which went public in early 1997. It got started by raising just $2.5 million in private capital, of which $1.7 million was used to pay the physician-owners of the first five practices. In exchange, the physicians turned over management of the practices and agreed to pay Specialty 20–33 percent of pretax earnings. Also, Specialty agreed to develop a sports medicine center. Just four months after cutting its first deal with those practices, Specialty was selling stock in its initial public offering.

Initially, the PPM pays the physician a combination of cash and stock options. The ratio varies widely; some physicians only get stock, which usually carries restrictions about when physicians can sell it. If the stock appreciates in price, it's a great deal for the physicians. However, the reverse may be true. What if the PPM offers the physician one-third of the value of her practice's assets but pays the rest in stock? She could get fifty thousand shares of a PPM stock trading at $28 a share, and a year later, it's dropped to $5.

Poof companies don't have much margin for error. They roll up physician practices into a new company that doesn't even exist until its initial public offering. The executive may not have any track record in running these practices as a combined entity, yet investors demand that they deliver continued earnings growth. Even PPMs that aren't poof companies are vulnerable. The industry's most glaring instance is Coastal Physician Group, a once-high-flying physician company founded by Dr. Steven Scott. The Durham, North Carolina, company started out in the contract management business, persuading hospitals of the idea of letting Coastal run their emergency departments. Coastal hired the emergency physicians, managed billing and collections, and then realized it was on the crest of a wave to form physician management companies. Soon, Coastal was buying primary-care physician practices and diversifying in obstetrical services.

Scott, who owned about one-third of the company's stock, was leading a high flier. By 1994, it was trading in the $40 range. He crafted a relationship with Humana, a large HMO in Florida, and started buying physician practices to serve those patients in that relationship. Then, Coastal took another step, buying another Florida HMO called Health Enterprises. Soon the growth was too much, as Humana enrollees were using more services than Coastal had bargained for. The information systems weren't sophisticated enough to enable Coastal to manage the fixed payments for each managed care enrollee, and the physicians weren't part owners anymore, so they were distanced from the operation. Coastal's shares slipped to $14 and were set to dive further.

Keeping the physicians involved, both financially and clinically, is the PPM's most vexing problem. In the past, roll-up founders and other insiders, including venture capitalists, had to wait two years to sell their shares of stock. This provision reassured investors that the physicians would not jump ship and sell their stock after an initial run-up in its price. But in 1997, the SEC approved a rule slashing the holding period in half. This made it even more enticing for physicians to start new roll-ups or attract more venture capitalists to these companies, knowing that their investment would not be hanging out there for two years or more.

However, the fundamental issue that the market is looking for is sustainability. Investors don't back companies when it looks as if the founders will bail out quickly. The SEC rule was devised to ensure that a company's founders and key executives do not do so. Instead, venture capitalists, or even physician investors, may now take their money out of one roll-up and invest it in yet another. Because the physicians' reputation is tied to the company's value, executives can use other "platinum handcuffs" to ensure that the doctors stay. For example, they can penalize physicians financially if they don't meet certain quotas or specific revenue growth targets.

So, the physician agrees to take some cash and some stock. The question is, how much? Valuing physician practices is a wide-ranging, highly debatable topic that could be the subject of its own book. For example, American Oncology Resources, an oncology roll-up, pays about five times EBITDA (earnings before interest, taxes, depreciation, and amortization) for the physicians' practice. Using EBITDA as a measuring stick is common in buying healthcare enterprises. For example, Columbia/HCA typically tries to pay between three and five times first-year EBITDA for a hospital. In other words, Columbia figures what the hospital will earn and calculates a price based on the multiple.

EBITDA is always a higher amount than net profits because it excludes fixed expenses and gives a truer picture of the business's cash flow. For example, a physician's practice may be generating $10 million a year in revenues, but its profits may only be $500,000. Or maybe it's losing money. But taking out the debt and tax expenses—which the PPM company is bound to tinker with anyway—shows a truer picture of value.

Most of the PPMs look for a minimum earnings level. For example, American Oncology Resources looks at practices with more than $2 million in EBITDA. In sale agreements, the PPM buys the "hard assets." With radiologists, this may mean an imaging center or radiation therapy center. If the center is under the control of the PPM, the PPM reaps the profits or losses.

Valuing a physician practice isn't any more of an exact science than valuing a hospital or ambulance company. Another PPM, PhyCor, makes its offer based on return on capital over a ten–year period. From the other point of view, negotiating a sale price can be gut-wrenching for physicians.

THE EXCHANGE

Once in a PPM, physicians trade autonomy for a corporation that may tell them how much they get paid, when they work, what medical supplies they use, what patient base they treat, and what computer they use. However, the transaction does allow them to step out of the business office and focus on medicine.

The PPM usually takes a cut of the revenues or earnings. Then, depending on whether the physicians are employed with the PPM or merely under contract, the remainder of the earnings are split up. Phy-Cor doesn't employ physicians; it contracts with them. "When you make them an employee, you get an employee mentality," Joseph Hutts says. "The worst thing you can do is kill that entrepreneurial excitement." PhyCor also leaves it up to the physicians to determine the compensation split. PhyCor takes a predetermined percentage of funds available for compensation. Then the physician determines compensation, bonuses, and other income splits.

The amount of compensation that physicians receive after their practice is sold to a PPM varies, but it can drop by as much as 30–50 percent. The trade-off is in stock and stock options. When a PPM buys a practice, the physicians must sign a practice management agreement that binds them to the corporation for forty years—not a small amount of time in anyone's estimation. In fact, with all of the changes going on in the industry, this may be an eternity.

Some states make it illegal for nonphysicians to employ physicians because of statutes governing corporate practice of medicine. This means that corporations can't own physician practices. In those cases, the PPM usually signs a long-term service agreement with the physicians. The SEC is looking at this issue as it relates to control of the business itself. What is the shareholder really holding if the physician companies doesn't really own the business? The SEC questions how one PPM can merge with another when it doesn't really "own" the entire business.

In an era of partnerships, control is a troublesome issue. Problems arose in several deals that hospital chains such as Columbia/HCA Healthcare completed. When it entered a fifty-fifty joint venture with a hospital system, could it claim all of the hospital system's revenues and profits on its balance sheet? When it did, Columbia got a huge boost.

GROWING THE REVENUE LINE

Growing a physician practice management company isn't as much about controlling costs as it is about generating revenues. There isn't much money in simply managing physician practices. The revenues have to come from somewhere else: adding outpatient services, signing capitated contracts, buying more practices.

When physicians consolidate and hire more support staff, they may not decrease costs, but they increase revenues. That's the verdict from a Medical Group Management Association study that examined data from one thousand practices. The study found that increasing the ratio of support staff to physicians increased physician productivity more than it increased operating costs. The study found that the average multispecialty practice had 4.63 support staff for every full-time physician. Yet the groups with the best financial performance had a ratio of 5.37. It even noted that those "better performing" practices had more business office staff, fewer registered nurses, and more licensed practical nurses and medical assistants. This also gives credence to the theory that tomorrow's healthcare workers are more likely to have less training (see Chapter Eight).

The PPM has another selling point. It helps diversify the practice's revenues. If a physician group is garnering most its income from one HMO, or from indemnity insurers, its financial stability is poorer than that of one drawing from dozens of sources. The leading PPMs brag about their diversification of payment. MedPartners derives about 45 percent of its revenues from managed care, 25 percent from Medicare, 7 percent from Medicaid, 18 percent from indemnity, and 5 percent from private pay.

The PPM often receives a cut of the practices revenues, say, 20 percent. In addition, the PPM receives ancillary fees, although it passes a portion of the collections back to the physicians. Each physician usually receives a percentage of the clinic's profits; the specific amount may hinge on whether the physician meets certain performance goals. The physician management firm takes a percentage also.

PPMs brought fundamental change to running doctors' offices. In the past, doctors were happy if the amount of money coming in eclipsed the amount going out. It was that simple. Once public, though, the PPM must manage its capital and figure out how to raise more. After all, PPMs have to meet Wall Street expectations for earnings, and the only way to do that is to funnel down those same earnings expectations to the clinics themselves.

PhyCor's track record with clinics has been impressive. Growth is expressed in same-clinic revenues to make sure one is comparing apples to apples and not factoring in acquisitions as "growth." In 1992, same-clinic revenues grew 6 percent. The next year it was 8.5 percent, and in 1994 it jumped to 11.4 percent. Incredibly, the percentage hit 18.6 percent by early 1996.

Revenues are one thing, but profits are what really gets investors' attention. Operating margins at PhyCor went from 5 percent in 1991 to 8.8 percent in 1995, and many observers believe margins could grow to 10 percent by the end of the century. This flies in the face of cynics who say the physician companies can't continue to wring profits from these practices.

Since consolidation brings other costs—legal, marketing, and information systems—the movement boils down to one spurred by power rather than simply cost savings. "You're not going to save money," says Robert Bohlmann of the MGMA. "These consolidations are about who's controlling the market and what do we need to do to get the contracts."

Controlling the market often means working with others. Med-Partners does so through networks of local providers. For example, in southern California, the company linked its physicians with twenty-two hospitals owned by Tenet Healthcare to negotiate global capitation contracts (in which providers agree to meet all of the members' healthcare needs, like an HMO).

MANAGING RISK

PPM involves a simple principle: shared risks for shared rewards. "Healthcare has moved from a revenue business to a margin business," says Ira Korman. "You still hear physicians talk about what they get paid. That's irrelevant now. It's what they take home [that matters]." In risk contracting, physicians must get used to getting paid for patients they *don't see.* That's a hard transition for them to make. To address this, PPMs help physicians think in terms of a new tender: contracted lives.

Ultimately, managing physicians is about controlling risk and negotiating contracts. PPMs that can do that will prosper. When "Buddy" Miers was negotiating managed care contracts for physicians at Southwest Physician Associates in Dallas, he had strong experience to draw on. He's a former labor negotiator for Frito-Lay, a Pepsico company. "Labor negotiations, that's managed care," Miers said. "All the meanness and tough hardball negotiations. It's all about money." He added, "In labor contracts, the first year is always free, the second year is not bad, and the third year, they cash in."

Miers needed his background when he went to work in 1994 for the management company serving Southwest Physicians, a group that grew to one thousand Dallas-area physicians. About one-fourth of the physicians were primary care. Before throwing them into risk contracting, Southwest made them go through a mentoring program in which they met their colleagues and heard what was expected of them. As chief marketing and development officer, Miers said physicians couldn't enter into risk contracts until they had been through the program. "They saw exactly how they were going to be measured and what the incentives were," Miers comments.

Without that background, physicians can get badly burned when it comes to compensation because it is based on patient outcomes and economics. Miers recalls one primary care physician who had "three premature infants charged to his managed care capitation budget, and he never even saw the mothers." It's that type of thing that makes primary care physicians—the gatekeepers in most managed care plans—look to roll-up companies. "Your costs are up, your reimbursement is down, you're accountable for all kinds of mysterious things, and everyone wants to control you," Miers concludes.

A group of Houston physicians elicited the help of the Texas Medical Association in 1994 when Aetna "deselected" them from its preferred provider panel. With their medical society behind them, they sued, contending the managed care company dropped them without any reason or notice. Under the PPM model, physicians would have a resident ally for that kind of negotiation.

PPMs change the balance of power. In managed care negotiations, insurers and hospitals would battle it out, and physicians were usually the least organized and least powerful negotiator. The PPM gives them the power they lacked. If they win contracts, that's great. If they lose, physicians may see their revenue stream literally walk out the door. The bottom line for the PPM is quality and the ability to deliver high quality at a lower price to payers. First, it must be able to measure this quality through patient outcomes gathered through sophisticated information systems.

MedPartners helps physicians share best practices through its intranet. An intranet is simply a corporate network that uses Internet tools. In addition, it brings them together in meetings to discuss issues face to face. Through the acquisition of Caremark, MedPartners became the nation's largest independent prescription benefits management service, providing services to more than fifteen million people in all fifty states. It also got access to clinical data for those individuals, data that it can begin building on.

A few years ago, PhyCor opened the Institute for Healthcare Management, dedicated to designing tools that would demonstrate clinical outcomes. One of the studies involved asthma and how physicians were treating it. What percentage of patients were using inhalers? What kind of inhalers were physicians prescribing, and to what populations? What percentage of patients ended up in the emergency rooms, and how frequently? The next task is to show that these patients benefited, in terms of the quality or cost of their healthcare service. As physician groups take on risk-based contracts, they'll have to ensure that this kind of information is readily available to them. Without it, costs will creep into profits.

BOOM OR BUST?

So, what does the future hold?

Not all PPMs will make it. Some will go bust, just as some oil companies and computer companies went bust after hysterical periods of growing wealthy. Many of the first HMOs and hospital companies went belly-up. The same may happen with PPMs. "There are a lot of wildcatters out there," laughs MedPartners' Larry House when asked about an analogy to the oil boom. "When you see this much of the market move and the size and scale of what's moving, there are bound to be some hiccups."

Today's PPMs are the first generation. By the second or third generation, executives and physicians may have developed the instincts and knowledge to make this business work. Still few and far between are managers experienced in operating PPM companies. Acquiring a bunch of practices is the goal, but finding quality acquisitions is more difficult. PPMs often want to affiliate with practices that have strong local reputations that draw managed care contracts.

PPMs won't be able to lower costs appreciably simply through group purchasing and administration. Eventually, these practices have to consolidate personnel and real estate to achieve larger administrative savings. Since physicians or their IPA typically sign noncompete agreements of thirty to forty years with the PPM, bad agreements may destine some physicians to PPM hell. Having signed, they face staying or moving. Or else there's the alternative Miers tosses out: "I think it will be a struggle." He means a legal struggle. To avoid lawyers and equity exchanges, some physician groups are likely to engage in what is described as virtual integration, whereby the groups band together with a hospital or insurer but don't own each other.

The good news is that physician companies built on sticks tumble in the first winds. If they serve only as a means for physicians to cash out, this becomes apparent quickly because they won't be able to operate what they've created or acquired.

House insists MedPartners is here to stay as a physician company leader. "This is not a quick in and out; it's not a build it and sell it company," he contends. Hutts maintains the same; to his credit, PhyCor's founders have stayed on board since the beginning. "This was never an in-and-out thing for us," Hutts says. "We're here to make a fundamental impact. You see people getting involved just for the financial gains. We immediately pull back from them."

Both companies are identifying best practices—ways to efficiently and effectively deliver medical services—in their organizations. The question is, can they drive those best practices throughout their corporations? PPMs must ask themselves what their strategy is for operating the business. Is it to consolidate the physician groups into workable, efficient healthcare companies? Or is the strategy simply to sell out?

Those consolidators learning on the job are making only a cursory attempt to render their businesses operational. Disparate information systems are left to run, with no attempt to amalgamate the data into something meaningful. If roll-ups are just leveraging their size to roll into something bigger, then what differentiates them from a Ponzi scheme? That may be left for the regulators and the lawyers to sort out.

CHAPTER FOUR

Lessons from the Biggest Consolidator, Columbia/HCA

W hat does it say about consolidation when the biggest consolidator stumbles, shattering dozens of careers along the way?

In the summer of 1997, the mother lode of healthcare consolidators, Columbia/HCA Healthcare, began to implode. Just short of its tenth anniversary, Columbia had grown to be the nation's largest healthcare consolidator, the one that all healthcare consolidators watched. Watch and learn, some would say. In some cases, consolidators emulated its moves, and in others they did just the opposite.

Columbia's problems unfolded in July 1997, when teams of federal agents seized truckloads of documents from Columbia hospitals in seven states. The investigation reportedly centered on Medicare fraud, and in the succeeding weeks Columbia's founder, Richard Scott, and his top lieutenant, David Vandewater, were forced to resign under pressure from the board. Three Columbia executives responsible for filing Medicare cost reports in Florida were indicted. A month later, they pleaded innocent to the charges.

The detonation of Columbia was heard round the nation, chronicled almost daily in the *Wall Street Journal, The New York Times,* and dozens of newspapers across the country. For journalists, these are stories that can be career stepping stones. Like any such media target, Columbia would be guilty until proven innocent. Federal agents were tossing about charges of fraudulent behavior; that type of talk brought reverberating consequences in the form of lawsuits by payers and shareholders of all stripes.

But what really chilled healthcare consolidators was that the wideranging federal investigation had reached out and touched their counterparts. That is what stunned these people.

Facing a possible twenty-five years in prison if convicted on criminal fraud charges, Columbia reimbursement executive Robert Whiteside reportedly had never even met with federal agents. "He's never been interviewed or asked to be interviewed by anybody," Whiteside's lawyer, Hal Hardin told *The Tennessean.* "He was never even advised he was a target."[1]

Unfortunately, federal law dictates that executives of organizations contracting with the federal government can be sent to prison for terms ranging from twenty years to life if found guilty of fraud. That applies to hospital executives since hospitals contract with the Medicare system. The severity of the punishment is compounded by the fact that the guidelines provide specific and rather inflexible mathematical formulas and criteria that federal judges must follow. Suddenly, anyone who ever worked on a cost report written at Columbia had good reason to be nervous.

At the juncture when this book was being written, it was very difficult to predict the final outcome of Columbia's woes. Yet even without knowing the outcomes, healthcare consolidators were learning valuable lessons. To begin with, consolidation is creating larger and larger organizations, what we refer to as Med Inc. In nearly every segment, individual providers are giving way to larger ones as healthcare goes through a corporatization process. This new healthcare economy stresses formulas, templates of the individual components, consistency, and value rather than wide-open, free-for-all care in which cost isn't considered.

Consolidators seek economies of scale, often found in standardization in which individual decisions give way to corporate prescriptions. This takes the personalization out of much of the decision making in healthcare. Through decision support software, national contracts, and intranet-linked databanks, managers of today's consolidators can be more certain of their decisions because they're backed by experience and data-driven methodology. Yet, the newspaper photos of Columbia's indicted executives in the summer of 1997 brought a stark contrast to this picture of the corporatization movement. Medicine may be becoming more corporate, but the punitive aspects of this business are becoming more personal.

Who goes to jail if the corporation's templates are wrong or deemed to be fraudulent? Someone's colleagues, that's who. When Columbia is accused of breaking the law, does the corporation suffer consequences? Not really. The company may go through some restructuring, its stock may tumble, but it is likely to go on. Individuals suffer the consequences.

As organizations get larger, there may be a tendency to "Dilbertize" one's responsibilities. In the comic, "Dilbert" is often depicted as a cog in the corporate machinery. So, too, might healthcare executives feel like a cog in their consolidator/employers' business. Yet in healthcare this would be a gigantic mistake. Although healthcare consolidators grow larger and perhaps more faceless, the executives working there are becoming increasingly culpable for their subordinates' actions. When it comes to contracting with the federal government, any wrongdoing eventually zeroes in on certain "responsible" individuals—even though they may not have had personal knowledge of the wrongdoing.

Truly, Columbia/HCA Healthcare was the consolidators' Exhibit A. The nation's largest healthcare company, with more than $20 billion in revenues, sparked controversy in nearly every sector of healthcare. It came to be viewed as the Sheriff of Nottingham in this healthcare economy: shutting down hospitals where it saw fit, banking the profits, and often laying off surplus employees, all in the name of private sector healthcare reform.

Richard Scott, the young founder of Columbia who was forced to resign as its top executive in July 1997, was fond of talking about changing the status quo. It was his mission to change it. Doing so created untold numbers of enemies: hospital executives, labor unions, government officials, and even his own former managers. Indeed, Columbia's Medicare fraud charges were fueled by Columbia employees themselves who served as informants to the federal government. Columbia inevitably found the enemy; it came from within.

More than a dozen Columbia workers were reported to have filed lawsuits against the company under federal whistle-blower laws, giving the government a clear trail to follow in its investigation. "The federal whistle-blower laws," noted *The New York Times*, "are intended to encourage individuals to expose efforts to defraud the government, and offer those people who bring the suits rewards of as much as 15 percent to 30 percent of the total amount the government recovers. As a result, there are instances in which federal whistle-blowers have become multimillionaires for exposing wrongdoing to the government."[2]

The newspapers also noted that whistle-blower suits are most popular in healthcare. In fact, some have termed it a growth industry. Here's a challenge for would-be consolidators: factor a certain number of whistle-blowers into the business plan.

Allegations against Columbia ranged from improper Medicare coding, inflated expenses on Medicare cost reports and inducements to physicians, to billing payers for too many tests. So when Columbia's woes became too deep, Scott and his right-hand executive, David Vandewater, were both forced out. A cascade of other top executives followed: its top lawyer, Stephen T. Braun; Samuel A. Greco, vice president for financial operations; Herb Wong, vice president for strategic development; Jamie Hopping, who headed operations for seventeen Western states; and Lindy Richardson, senior vice president of marketing and public affairs. All were hired by Scott, and all followed him in his quest to change the healthcare world.

His ouster was engineered by Thomas Frist, Jr., who had merged his Hospital Corporation of America with Columbia in 1994, thus vaulting Scott's status as a megaconsolidator. Frist took over Columbia, saying he would remold it into a kinder, gentler company and assuage the federal authorities of Columbia's intentions. Getting the former Dallas lawyer out of the top spot at Columbia was critical to Frist's turnaround because Scott's name had become synonymous with Columbia and the turbulence it had wrought in city after city.

BEHIND THE MONOLITH

The early days of Rick Scott and Columbia Hospital are well chronicled. From day one, in 1987, the thirty-something Scott was probably a little overconfident as he entered the hospital business with a genuine conviction that he could make America's healthcare system more efficient. He thought he could make it work better. He had a plan that could rationalize the system's conflicting financial incentives and forge them into win-win situations. That's what consolidators do: they change the playing field, for better or worse.

From the beginning, Scott openly questioned the tax-exemptions enjoyed by 85 percent of the hospital industry. He also challenged the very moniker "not-for-profit hospital." "In fact, some of the most 'profitable' hospitals in the country are 'not-for-profit,' tax-exempt institutions," noted Scott in a memo to employees in late 1996. "He is their [not-for-profit hospitals'] worst nightmare," said Josh Nemzoff, a mergers and acquisitions consultant in Nashville. "The not-for-profits were very happy to coexist with each other and have healthcare costs go up 13 percent a year. Now, he has brought business issues into the healthcare arena."

In the early days, Scott made hundreds of cold calls from his office, nestled in one of two bluish-glass skyscrapers built by the billionaire Bass brothers of Fort Worth. Consolidators look for partners who can grow with them. Scott believed the best partners would be physicians. After months of frustration at breaking into a closed circle of hospital executives, Scott's Columbia Hospital Corporation and 110 physicians in El Paso bought two hospitals in 1987. In El Paso, Scott ingrained three principles that would be replicated time and time again over the next ten years: consolidation (closing underperforming facilities), networking (setting up a continuum of inpatient and outpatient providers), and physician partnerships (allowing doctors to buy minority stakes in the provider network).

By 1990, the fledgling company had $235 million in annual revenues, and Scott forecast that the company would add some $100 million each year through acquiring two or three hospitals. In retrospect, these goals were modest. By 1995, Columbia was adding two to three hospitals per month, and through a series of mergers, the company far eclipsed the projected annual growth rate.

Columbia's acquisition strategy fueled one of the most rapid merger and acquisition periods in hospital history. The giant hospital consolidator's entry into any market shook things up there, prompting mergers that likely would not otherwise have been contemplated. Hospital executives who had previously never dreamed of merging with a competitor or colleague entertained those thoughts for the first time. In many cities, an "ABC" mentality carried through: anybody but Columbia. For example, when Columbia announced a deal with Bishop Clarkson Memorial Hospital in Omaha, the resulting chaos resembled a game of Red Rover, with not-for-profits joining hands against the dreaded invader.

Columbia ended up pulling away from its $84 million bid for Clarkson, which subsequently merged with another suitor, the University of Nebraska Medical Center. (All along, UNMC contended it

had first refusal rights to buy Clarkson, and the legal struggle that en-
sued led to Columbia's dropping out of the bidding.)

Buying a not-for-profit hospital wasn't like buying a car or a house.
As the deals piled up, so did the questions. Was Columbia stealing
these hospitals away from their communities? Weren't these community hospitals financed by the philanthropy of its citizens? What were
they really worth? To whom should the proceeds of the sale go? The
issue became more and more complicated, a situation exacerbated by
increasing scrutiny from state attorneys general.

The stickiest questions centered on valuing hospital assets. For example, when the trustees of Cookeville General Hospital in Tennessee
decided to put the hospital up for sale, the bids were all over the map.
The highest, $100 million, came from Community Health Systems,
another Nashville investor-owned hospital chain. Columbia offered
$68.5 million. The lowest "bid" was nothing—in other words, free. It
was from St. Mary's Health System, which offered to affiliate with
Cookeville.

Such deals raised some obvious questions: Should a community
hospital take the highest price offered under the assumption that it
has a fiduciary duty to the community to maximize the value of the
community's collective investment? Or is the responsibility rather to
maintain provision of "control" over operations of the hospital, ensuring that medical services are always available to the community's
citizenry?

Scott's acquisitions team taught the industry a thing or two about
creatively structuring deals. Its fifty-fifty joint ventures strategically
benefited Columbia while giving the tax-exempt organization a continued ownership stake. Columbia's bid for one of San Diego's pre-
miere healthcare systems, Sharp Healthcare, exemplified the complex
financial questions that such deals can raise. How much was Sharp
Healthcare really worth? Was it an asset of declining value, as some
would argue, because the hospital business is overbuilt and utilization
is declining? Or was it an asset of increasing value because Sharp
Healthcare was a brand name in the local market? Many would argue
that the Sharp "franchise" was worth substantially more than the
average community hospital, and if it was losing money—which it
was—then management was to blame.

For Columbia, the deal flow began slowing in 1996. In 1996, the
company completed acquisitions or joint ventures with seventeen not-
for-profit hospitals. That was down from thirty-three in 1995, signaling

a drop in the momentum as the competition—predominantly the not-for-profit hospitals—became more organized.

TAKING THE EXCESS
OUT OF THE SYSTEM

As we've discussed in earlier chapters, putting together deals is one type of corporate skill. Making the deals work down the line takes an altogether different, but equally important, skill set. Unless it expands sales, an organization's cash flow can be increased in two ways: by raising prices or by lowering expenses. Since the managed care environment all but precludes raising prices, Columbia turned its attention to cutting costs.

Scott did this with a zeal that raised the hackles of many. By nature, he was as frugal as an Iowa farmer. As Columbia grew larger and larger, Scott demanded deeper and deeper discounts. Why should he pay the same as other hospitals, as other corporations, when they have the privilege of listing Columbia as one of their customers?

Getting hold of supply costs is crucial to a company that spends nearly $3 billion annually on things like sutures, bed linen, and medical lasers. So the company signed deals that locked its hospitals into purchasing from just one manufacturer for a given item, say, bone densitometers from Hologic, mammography units from Trex Medical, or radiologic systems from Continental X-Ray. About 95 percent of what Columbia hospitals bought was under a regional or national contract. The choices didn't always sit well, with Columbia employees or with the vendors. Some Columbia technicians griped about purchasing GE equipment when they'd rather work on equipment from the higher-priced Siemens.

On the other side of the deal, vendors cut deals with Columbia that they later simultaneously griped and bragged about, with equal zest. They griped because the margins were so small and bragged because they believed that as a favored Columbia vendor, they would draw additional business. Two multibillion-dollar medical suppliers credited—or blamed—Columbia's purchasing tactics for their merger in late 1996. "Columbia just couldn't squeeze us any harder than they were squeezing," Robert Martini, chairman of Bergen Brunswig, explained about his company's $1.4 billion merger with IVAX, the nation's largest generic drugmaker.[3] Bergen Brunswig, a medical distribution company with $9.9 billion in revenues, saw the merger as a way to cut more costs out of the system but that merger fell apart in 1997.

Scott cut costs in two ways: by shutting down inefficient facilities, and by stripping down the cost structure in those that remained. Closing facilities is controversial, and Columbia closed more hospitals than any other healthcare organization—thirty in eight years. The company closed more of its own acute-care hospitals in Texas during 1995 than closed in the entire state in the previous two years. Yet talk about downsizing or closing hospitals always brings an outcry. Indeed, such decisions are often based more on issues pertaining to employment or the economy than on cost-effectiveness or quality-of-care issues. This is because in most communities in America, hospitals are among the area's biggest employers. A report by the Pennsylvania Economy League in the early 1990s found that every $1 million in hospital payroll reductions would mean the loss of forty to fifty direct jobs and another forty to fifty jobs in businesses supported by the purchases of hospital employees. Therefore, downsizing or closing a hospital can have implications for the community far beyond merely requiring its citizens to drive farther to receive their medical care.

Traditionally, labor can amount to approximately 50 percent of a hospital's budget. Obviously, when it comes to trimming costs, that's going to be a primary target. In some markets, Columbia reduced labor costs to 32 percent of revenue. Overall, the company reduced the percentage of salaries and benefits from 41 percent in 1994 to 39.7 percent in 1996. This compares to a median of 43.5 percent for investor-owned hospitals overall. The difference is much greater when compared to not-for-profits, which spend a median of 52 percent on salary and benefits, according to the healthcare information company HCIA.

Because of its propensity to close hospitals, it's no surprise that some unions viewed Columbia as unfriendly. The California Nurses Association is one of the most vocal opponents of what it termed "slash and burn" staffing cuts. The association's website included a laundry list of the Columbia facilities that have either closed or been downsized and the toll on workers losing their jobs. "Community after community has been left stunned, bewildered, and feeling betrayed as facilities are closed or kept running according to the whim of those charged with maintaining corporate profitability," reported the website. (It should be noted that the association has also taken a hard line against other healthcare corporations, not the least of which is not-for-profit Kaiser Permanente, which proposed a 15 percent pay cut for half of its nurses in 1997.)

Columbia's labor problems were not limited to nurses. In 1997, the Service Employees International Union specifically targeted Columbia for unionization in an effort it calls "CODE Columbia." CODE stands for Caregivers Organized to Demand Excellence.

Some have questioned whether lowering labor costs has an effect on a hospital's quality of care. Unfortunately, it's difficult to make such comparisons because labor costs include those of far more people than nurses and other employees who have direct patient contact. It also includes employees staffing large marketing or food service departments.

On the subject of quality, Columbia bragged heavily about its quality ratings from the Joint Commission on the Accreditation of Healthcare Organizations. This organization, which doubles as a Medicare certifying body, is the only group that gives ratings to hospitals. That's why Columbia used those ratings to its advantage. All of its hospitals are commission accredited, although this is not unusual since only a minority of hospitals do not go through or pass the commission's standards. The bigger stick used by the corporation is the fact that 21 percent of its hospitals received accreditation with commendation, the organization's highest honor. Nationally, only 12 percent of hospitals receive it, Columbia points out.

The company also advertised the fact that a disproportionate share of its hospitals made the industry's "top 100 hospitals" list, a ranking based on financial management, operations, and clinical practices. In 1995, it had twenty-nine; in 1996, seventeen. These are pretty good percentages for a company that has only 5 percent of the nation's hospitals. (The top 100 list is compiled by HCIA in Baltimore and the Health Care Provider Consulting Practice of William M. Mercer, a human resources management firm based in New York.)

Scott's frugality wasn't imposed only on other organizations, however. It also carried over to the management suite. Columbia wasn't known for paying the industry's top salaries. He believed that talented executives would flock to the company just for the experience and notation on their resumes. He was right. In this age of consolidation, dozens of Columbia executives have used that experience to get jobs with consolidators in other healthcare niches.

As Columbia's name became tarnished after July 1997, the opposite became true. For years, Scott earned a salary that was much less than many not-for-profit health system CEOs. Not only was his salary smaller but his bureaucracy of high-paid executives was thinner. Scott's 1995 salary and bonus was $1.5 million. In comparison, the chairman and CEO of Citicorp, a company of similar revenues, received salary and bonus of $3.5 million in 1996, and three vice chairmen there earned more than $1 million in salary and bonuses.

However, Columbia's history of creating wealth for its management can't be discounted. Long-time managers of Hospital Corporation of America and Healthtrust, two hospital chains that were absorbed into Columbia, left as multimillionaires thanks to company stock programs. Even the rank and file had a chance for future wealth, albeit not in the millions of dollars. Employees could purchase stock through payroll deduction at a 15 percent discount to the market, which is fairly typical for a publicly held corporation.

Columbia's attitude with respect to compensation also rubbed some people the wrong way. Often, when making a pitch to hospital CEOs, Columbia executives stressed the stock options, the potential for riches. When it bought a not-for-profit hospital, it frequently hired the CEO to continue running the hospital. This led to accusations of buying loyalty to sway the board toward a sale. Even if a deal wasn't cut on the front end, the hospital CEO realized that he or she was more likely to stay than go. As for other members of management, the opposite was often true. Despite the prospect of future wealth, many questioned whether Scott pushed executives too hard, trying to squeeze 15–20 percent margins out of a business where admissions were flat and length of stay was dropping. Apparently, many former HCA executives complained to Frist about Scott's hard driving ways. Hospital CEOs quit rather than trying to meet what they viewed as unrealistic goals.

MANAGING INFORMATION, CAPITAL, AND RISK

Under Scott's leadership, Columbia's strengths were in managing information and capital. In those venues, the company was the pacesetter that other consolidators chased. Under Scott, Columbia became an integrated information company.

Once Columbia agreed to buy a hospital, managers moved quickly to get the information agenda in place. Usually, Columbia's financial systems were up and running before the deal even closed. As the hospital's purchasing contracts came up for renewal, they're quickly converted to Columbia contracts to track supply costs. The clinical information system was also added as soon as possible, giving physicians, nurses, and other professionals immediate access to patients' medical histories. Eventually, a patient treated at a Columbia hospital in Dallas who tears a tendon while surfing in California would be able to go to the Columbia hospital there and find his medical records, accessible through cyberspace.

In terms of capital, Columbia's reach may have exceeded its grasp—but not by much. As a corporation with $20 billion in revenues, it generated $3 billion in cash flow annually. The Nashville corporation was a favored client with commercial banks, investment banks, and private capital organizations. Considering that the company is only ten years old, that's pretty amazing. In comparison, it took twenty-three years for Fred Smith to build Federal Express, another "fast tracker," into a $10 billion business.

Less than 5 percent of Columbia's revenues come from risk contracting through capitated contracts, those in which the provider is paid a fixed amount per person to cover the full range of medical services required by a specified population, such as members of a health plan or employees of a large corporation. Because this is expected to be the predominant method of paying for healthcare in the future, Columbia was positioning itself to accept global capitation, providing hospital as well as nonhospital services. To do so, Columbia's goal was vertical consolidation, which meant acquiring companies in nearly every other provider segment, not just hospitals. Columbia deployed capital to assemble comprehensive provider systems that can provide a cradle-to-grave range of services. This helps it gain competitive advantage with major purchasers of health services such as managed care companies, large employers, and the Medicare program.

Several of Columbia's transactions illustrated this move to build comprehensive provider systems. The company made a huge splash when it acquired the nation's largest outpatient surgery chain, Medical Care America, in 1994. The purchase of Healthtrust in 1995 added a number of ancillary services such as home care, rehabilitation, and physical therapy. These transactions not only reduced contracting costs for purchasers but also achieved cost savings through better information and incentives. In addition, some of these services are reimbursed by Medicare on a cost basis, rather than prospectively (through DRGs). Inpatient hospital stays are reimbursed by Medicare based on diagnosis without regard to costs. However, certain services, such as rehabilitation and home healthcare, are reimbursed on cost. Since the costs of operating those businesses are being shared by the hospital, Columbia could shift them to the cost-based services. This meant that Columbia could run some of the costs of operating the hospitals through these other services.

Columbia's vertical integration strategy also included buying specific types of managed care expertise, as evidenced by its purchase in 1997 of Value Health, the country's largest provider of specialty managed benefit programs. Value Health, whose two main businesses are pharmaceutical benefit management (PBM) services and mental health managed care, has annual revenues of $1.9 billion. It is also involved in workers' compensation managed care activities and disease management.

The Avon, Connecticut, firm's subsidiary Value Rx, which manages some $2.2 billion of pharmaceutical purchases through its retail and mail-order pharmacy operations, and Columbia Pharmacy solutions will be combined, bringing total members to more than twenty-eight million and adding more than twenty-five hundred commercial and wholesale customers. Columbia, which purchases about $500 million of pharmaceuticals annually, was expected to leverage Value Rx's contracts into even greater discounts for its hospitals and other centers. Columbia executives estimated that Value Health's contracts would save Columbia as much as 5 percent on its drug costs.

However, those potential savings melted away as Frist announced plans to sell Value Health a month after he took over.

MANAGING REGULATION

There's a popular saying: don't sweat the details. Its corollary is that everything is a detail. The details are what tripped up Columbia—and there were oh so many.

Doing business with the government requires expertise in many details of reimbursement regulation and cost-reporting minutiae. Every hospital fills out a Medicare cost report that is filed first with a fiscal intermediary, which passes it on to the Health Care Financing Administration for payment. The fiscal intermediaries are third-party administrators; many of them are Blue Cross plans. They know and understand Medicare regulations and serve as a check to ensure that providers aren't cheating the government.

When Columbia officials were indicted for submitting false cost reports, it highlighted a new era in government oversight of hospitals. In the past, hospitals frequently filed cost reports that claimed reimbursement for items or services that might or might not eventually be paid. With this investigation, findings on a cost report became a criminal act. It certainly got attention. "I have never known in the history of this country where 35 search warrants have been served simultaneously on a New York Stock Exchange corporation," said John Cusack, a Chicago lawyer and ardent Columbia critic who frequently represented not-for-profit hospitals in litigation against Columbia.[4]

Columbia's stock lost about one-fourth its value in the months after the El Paso raid, and throughout the summer analysis of whether Columbia stock was undervalued or overvalued was renewed with each passing news story. Was Columbia big enough to withstand the blows? Was its past earnings power sustainable? Wasn't the acquisition program dead with the cloud of a federal investigation hanging over Columbia's head?

CAVEAT CONSOLIDATOR: THE RAMIFICATIONS OF CLOUT

Being a consolidator of Columbia's magnitude creates ripples. Sheer size alone can help a company the size of Columbia manage the capital, information, and risk. Yet in terms of regulation, size may be a huge disadvantage.

Columbia played hardball with competitors. In negotiations to buy Houston Northwest Medical Center in Texas, for example, where the hospital was owned in a joint venture by OrNda HealthCorp (another investor-owned chain) and the hospital's employees, the employee stock ownership plan had to get a predetermined price for its stock, which made negotiations more complicated than usual. OrNda, formerly known as Republic Health, had sold its half interest to employees amid frantic attempts to raise cash. Republic ended up going through a bankruptcy reorganization to lower its debt structure.

Anyway, the ESOP trustee held out for one price and Columbia said no. Instead, Columbia's Jay Grinney, who was in charge of the Houston market, simply announced that his company happened to buy land across the street from Houston Northwest. Columbia would build its own facility. Houston Northwest ended up selling itself to OrNda. "The for-profit hospitals need to handle their strength. I see a little bit of macho mentality," said PhyCor's Joe Hutts without naming names. "I don't think that plays well."

Columbia pursued the same hard line with federal regulators that it did with competitors. After Frist took over, he stopped throwing legal hurdles in the way of federal investigators and tried instead to show a demeanor of cooperation rather than confrontation. The latter certainly didn't play well to the feds. In fact, after Frist took over Columbia in July 1997, he busily started working with those authorities rather than against them.

Columbia's growing challenges with the media were an important lesson for fledgling consolidators. A journalist's inbred motto of "comforting the afflicted and afflicting the comfortable" produces a compelling situation for media types covering Columbia. Truly, Columbia had gone from somewhat "inflicted" (small, underdog hospital company takes on powerful not-for-profit health systems) to "comfortable" (multibillion-dollar conglomerate has resources to do just about anything). Columbia's press coverage changed from fawning to nasty when the company crossed the line from comfortable, to "corporate ogre" in the minds of some writers. The CBS news magazine "60 Minutes" spent months working on a report about the growing corporate giant. A major trade publication published an article comparing Columbia's contributions to the community with those of strip clubs, gun shops, and liquor stores.

Columbia spent nearly $200 million on advertising in 1995 and 1996, breaking most of the healthcare marketing commandments by a wide margin. Advertising is viewed as borderline taboo by most providers, although there are obvious exceptions in which large not-for-profit hospitals have launched billboard, print, and TV ad campaigns. Columbia spent 58 percent more in 1996 on a per-hospital basis than the average community hospital, according to *Modern Healthcare* magazine.[5]

Columbia found that it must create its own image, one other than what was created by an independent media. By appealing directly to consumers through advertising, the company hoped to overcome what it viewed as a negative press. However, the media always hope to puncture the biggest balloon, and there's a lesson for consolidators here. As an organization becomes bigger and more aggressive, its propensity to run into antiaircraft fire increases proportionately.

While the media regaled in the fact that the Columbia machine was under federal regulators' floodlights, many hospital executives knew that any one of them could also come under the third degree. No hospital financial officer is safe because the complexity of Medicare reimbursement leaves so many holes into which she can stumble. Medicare reimbursement consists of volumes of laws enacted by Congress, regulations promulgated by the Health Care Financing Administration, and administrative interpretations written by Medicare program administrators for use by their auditors and field agents. Rarely are these complex rules black and white; many times, provisions seem open to interpretation. The opportunity for maximization of reimbursement afforded by "gray areas" in these rules creates an incentive for providers to aggressively interpret the laws and regulations in their favor. It becomes a thorny matter to maintain a distinction between "interpretations within the parameters of the law" and "intent to defraud."

Regulators alleged that Columbia kept two sets of books, a somewhat common practice in the industry. The fact that federal agents may view that as criminal makes hospital executives tremble. Providers may assert an aggressive position by including costs related to a valid gray area in their annual Medicare cost report, even if they know in advance that the Medicare fiscal intermediary is likely to disallow them. Inclusion of the disputed costs is necessary in order to establish the provider's right to appeal the issue to a higher authority, should it become necessary to do so. To protect itself against the appearance of fraudulent intent, the provider usually will flag these "appeal items" with explanatory footnotes.

When the cost report is settled, the provider may owe money to Medicare, or, sometimes, Medicare owes money to the provider. There may be a lag of up to three years between the time a cost report is filed and when it is considered closed and the final settling up takes place. This is because cost reports are tentatively settled on the basis of a desk review, but many require a later onsite examination by Medicare.

Such examinations are standard practice and hardly an indication of suspected wrongdoing. The final settlement amount usually lies somewhere between what was originally submitted by the hospital in the cost report and the amount Medicare computes after desk review and/or audit adjustments. Therefore, a balance-sheet reserve is customarily established in the provider's financial statements (similar to a bad-debt reserve) to adjust the actual receivable/payable shown on the cost report to what management estimates will eventually be realized or incurred.

In the context of Columbia's situation, it seems that its hospitals may have filed cost reports that included costs in the gray areas, hoping to resolve some of them in its favor. Was that abuse? If so, does that constitute fraud? This was the turning point in the Columbia story.

Can a healthcare consolidator become too big for its own good? Columbia's problems were exacerbated by its sheer size. The quantity and complexity of its cost reports were vast, making errors mathematically more likely. The U.S. Office of the Inspector General, which investigates fraud at the federal level, estimates the Medicare insurance system made $23.2 billion in improper payments last year. Was all of that fraud? For how much of it will Columbia be held accountable?

We said earlier that Columbia was Exhibit A for consolidators. In 1997 it became Exhibit A for all healthcare providers.

CHAPTER FIVE

Hospital Consolidators of the "Not-for-Profit" Breed

‹‹‹

I n Houston, Texas, a healthcare company sits on nearly $1 billion in cash. The Methodist Hospital System is building a network of healthcare providers powerful enough to dominate the southern Texas market as well as attract cash-paying patients from Mexico and Latin America. Yet this company is a "not-for-profit" hospital system.

Not-for-profit is a term of tax status, not a description of the organization's financial status. Methodist is one of dozens of tax-exempt Med Inc. companies that are amassing market strength and financial power in local markets. The system is buying hospitals, physicians, and clinics, investing hundreds of millions of dollars to set up a comprehensive network that can overpower its competitors. Consolidators are not limited by tax status, especially in the hospital business. In fact, hospitals are the only healthcare segment that is mostly tax-exempt (85 percent to be exact).

This situation creates its own logic and lore. Despite the sale of several dozen not-for-profit hospitals to tax-paying companies such as Columbia/HCA Healthcare and Tenet Healthcare, a backlash remains against these "for-profit" corporations. Many Americans simply don't want to cut the umbilical cord with charitable hospitals, whose marquees imply the values of the Catholic, Methodist, or Baptist system that owns them. Communities view these facilities as hospitals of last resort, just as Blue Cross and Blue Shield plans were viewed as insurers of last resort. Although there are a handful of cities in which all of the hospitals are for-profit, many communities fear this prospect. What if Columbia or Tenet simply pulls the plug, they cry?

This is why most markets will be ruled by large not-for-profit hospital systems, which are getting larger each year as they gain the economies of companies the likes of Columbia. Hospital consolidators, like Methodist, eventually will rule all of the nation's markets. Several already dominate metropolitan markets: Baylor Health Care System in Dallas, Henry Ford Health System in Detroit, BJC Health System in St. Louis, and Intermountain Health Care in Salt Lake City.

For example, BJC, which generated $1.5 billion in 1996 revenues, is a consolidator controlling one-third of the St. Louis market. The system is run by Fred L. Brown, who joined Christian Health Services in 1982 when it had nine hundred hospital beds and one nursing home. A decade later, he had expanded it to a 2,277-bed system of two St. Louis hospitals, seven Missouri and Illinois feeder hospitals, and six nursing homes. In an era when hospitals were king, Christian's integrated delivery system was virtually unknown, but viewed as the future. But this was just the start. Like dominoes, in 1993 the St. Louis hospitals began to fall in line, either with BJC or against it. During a five-month period in 1993, St. Louis changed from a fragmented market of approximately forty hospitals to a market composed of three dominant health care systems.

The catalyst for this seemingly overnight transition was a blockbuster merger announced in early April 1993. The surprise merger of Barnes Hospital, Jewish Hospital, and Christian Health Services united some of the area's largest hospitals and created a mammoth system with 3,900 hospital beds and 570 nursing home beds in Missouri and Illinois. It united two of the area's largest teaching hospitals, Barnes and Jewish, with a system of community hospitals.

The previous fall, Barnes and Jewish, which sat right next door to each other at 700 and 800 Kingshighway, had negotiated an affiliation agreement. Both were major teaching hospitals affiliated with the Washington University School of Medicine. Like most of the nation's teaching hospitals, they were anchored in the heart of the city but needed access to the health-insurance-rich suburban markets.

The deal with Christian fit like a glove. The merger provided Barnes and Jewish with access to an established network of suburban and out-state feeder hospitals, a large network of highly qualified primary care physicians, and six nursing homes. They would also benefit from Christian's understanding of how to organize, manage, and grow a healthcare system and its knowledge of working in multiple markets. In return, Christian was linked to superior specialists, state-of-the-art diagnostic equipment, and established transplant and cardiac surgery programs at Barnes and Jewish.

Because of his experience in building an integrated system, Brown was selected to head the new BJC Health System with its eighteen thousand employees and forty-one hundred physicians. The BJC merger started a chain reaction among other providers in the St. Louis area. Doctors at every hospital in the metro area began to ask, How will this affect me? Hospitals quickly began scheduling strategic planning retreats. At the time, industry watchers predicted that the marriage could signal the beginning of an era of megamergers in the St. Louis area, which might result in six or seven large affiliated groups. Little did they know how fast the consolidation would occur.

Five months later, in August 1993, eight other hospitals announced plans to form a second billion-dollar healthcare system in the area. This system, to be known as the St. Louis Health Care Network, comprised five hospitals affiliated with the SSM Health Care System, plus the 494-bed Missouri Baptist Hospital in the western suburbs, DePaul Health Center (424 beds) in the northern suburbs, and SLU Health Sciences Center, another major teaching hospital, with 315 beds. The eight-hospital alliance represented 2,855 licensed beds, four thousand physicians, twelve thousand employees, and more than $1 billion in revenues.

One week later, three major suburban players—St. Anthony's Medical Center (746 beds), 871-bed St. John's Mercy Medical Center, and St. Luke's Hospital with its 369 beds—announced plans for creating a third major network, Unity Health System. St. John's and St. Luke's were powerful presences in the booming western suburbs, while St. Anthony's had a stronghold in the southern part of the county.

Things stayed pretty quiet for a few months, until the spring of 1994. BJC's biggest need was for a facility in the booming, wealthier western suburbs. That area was dominated by Missouri Baptist and St. John's Mercy, two of the area's biggest baby factories, and St. Luke's. The previous year, all three had been approached by BJC about a merger, and all three refused. BJC officials were quoted as saying that if they couldn't sign up one of those facilities, they would build their own facility in West County.

That didn't prove necessary. In April 1994, amid great controversy, Missouri Baptist defected from the St. Louis Health Care Network to join BJC, giving the latter the west county presence it needed, particularly in obstetrics. The alliance was strengthened in June when BJC signed another merger agreement, this one with St. Louis Children's Hospital, a highly regarded pediatric facility. The acquisition of its main competitor forced the hand of Cardinal Glennon Children's Hospital. Although it formally belonged to St. Louis Health Care Network, in July 1994 it signed a collaboration agreement with the 871-bed obstetric powerhouse St. John's Mercy Medical Center. This loosely tied Glennon to Unity as well as the St. Louis Health Care Network.

The for-profits weren't totally left out in the cold, however. In early 1997, Tenet Healthcare agreed to acquire Deaconess-Incarnate Word Health System, a small three-hospital system. The deal gave Tenet four hospitals in the area, plus three in outlying Missouri. Tenet's acquisition came after merger talks between Deaconess and Unity fell apart over differences between the two organizations' contracts with physician groups. The Deaconess primary-care component provided Tenet with access to most of the major managed care contracts in the area and established Tenet as a legitimate fourth player in the market, albeit a small one.

While Tenet was announcing its merger, BJC took further strides toward its goal of becoming a fully integrated delivery system. It agreed to buy nine physician medical centers from the Coventry Group, a Nashville HMO company that operated Group Health Plan of St. Louis. The deal gave BJC seventy-five primary care physicians and specialists whose offices had laboratory, radiology, pharmacy, and eye care services. As part of the agreement, nearly 100,000 Group Health beneficiaries continued to receive care from these physicians, and BJC received a portion of Group Health's capitated premium.

Next, BJC began talking merger with Blue Cross and Blue Shield of Missouri, the state's largest insurer with nearly two million enrollees and an 80 percent stake in RightChoice Managed Care, the Blues' publicly traded for-profit subsidiary. Combined, BJC and the Blues would create a giant, vertically integrated healthcare powerhouse that could dominate the St. Louis metro area and the state. Interestingly, Columbia/HCA was at the same time trying to buy Blue Cross and Blue Shield of Ohio.

The St. Louis negotiations were fraught with problems, however, starting with executive changes, reports of a federal investigation, and a Missouri circuit court judge's decision that the Blues violated their not-for-profit status when they moved too much of their business into RightChoice.

In March 1997, the deal fell apart. The national Blue Cross association said it would no longer recognize the Missouri insurer as a Blues plan if it went ahead with its BJC deal. The decision mirrored another one in which the association stripped the Ohio Blues of national membership after the plan's proposed sale to Columbia.

Indeed, consolidation is not an easy road, particularly when the consolidator is reaching into unchartered territories. Yet what has happened in St. Louis will be replicated in market after market. Strong systems, whether they be not-for-profit like BJC or for-profit like Columbia, will consolidate the inpatient and outpatient sides of the healthcare business into larger entities. Those that don't get into one of these forward-looking systems could be left out in the cold. (In mid-1997, the city's indigent hospital, St. Louis Regional Medical Center, was in the process of shutting its doors. One of the few remaining unaffiliated hospitals, St. Louis University Hospital, was beginning to sweat and actively look for a partner. It eventually sided with Tenet.) After that, the consolidator will start to take on insurance products and risk contracts as it corrals segments of the payer market.

The lesson in this is that these hospital consolidators need leadership that isn't necessarily grounded in the inpatient business. Or, at least, leaders like Brown, who can make the transition. "These system leaders will need different skills," says Grant Wicklund, a partner who specializes in healthcare searches at Heidrick and Struggles, a national executive search firm. "That's not to say that current hospital CEOs are unqualified. However, they have to understand healthcare insurance."

The leaders of these healthcare consolidators are more likely to be health insurance executives rather than traditional hospital executives, Wicklund believes. They need to operate systems in which revenues come from risk pools rather than from inpatient revenues, because that's where control of market share will be derived. "If you're not part of a system, you're going to get squeezed out even if you are a standalone prestigious hospital," Wicklund adds.

Federal regulators won't let any one hospital system control more than 40 percent of a competitive market, but some consolidators are already bumping up against that limit. In fact, the giant Utah system Intermountain controls more than that. Its market share in Salt Lake City doesn't run afoul of federal regulators, however, because the system grew from within, rather than through mergers that require federal antitrust approval.

Although Intermountain is grounded in the Mormon church, some of the hospital industry's largest consolidators are Catholic-sponsored. Today, one in every six hospital admissions is to a Catholic hospital. Although they generate billions in revenues, their financial strength is not public knowledge since they are private organizations. An analysis of *Modern Healthcare* magazine's annual surveys of hospital systems shows that Catholic hospital systems are the only sector of the industry that has added beds during the past ten years. The overall number of U.S. hospital beds has dropped 13 percent from 1985 to 1995, but the number of beds controlled by Catholic health systems actually increased by 7 percent. Investor-owned hospital systems reported a drop of 13 percent, which matched the overall rate.

This makes the Catholic systems probably the biggest Med Inc. consolidator of all. "The Pope himself has acknowledged the importance of Catholic healthcare here in the United States," said Bruce Japsen, who covers healthcare economics and hospital companies for *Modern Healthcare* magazine. "He warned against healthcare being used to turn a profit. If Rick Scott's company is healthcare's eight-hundred-pound gorilla, the Roman Catholic church has the potential to be King Kong."

Catholic systems began to put their money where their mouths were, becoming active acquirers in 1996. Catholic Healthcare West, a San Francisco system, acquired ten hospitals in California in 1996 and agreed to acquire Samaritan Health Systems in Phoenix, a $1.2 billion revenues system that would control 40 percent of the Phoenix market.

In 1996, 768 hospitals were involved in mergers or acquisitions, up from 735 in 1995. Only a fraction of those involved the nation's most notorious hospital acquirer, Columbia/HCA Healthcare. In fact, the Nashville firm added fewer hospitals in 1996 than in the year before, completing twenty-eight acquisitions or joint ventures.[1]

During 1995 and 1996, not-for-profit systems consolidated more rapidly than the investor-owned ones in terms of sheer numbers. These systems have preached for years about how they must wrench costs out of their systems, and the reality may finally be coming. However, if there's a lesson in healthcare, it is that nothing changes as quickly as one plans or hopes for. In the late 1980s, healthcare experts predicted a monumental shift to outpatient treatments and home healthcare, but it took a decade for that change to really unfold.

Changes in the "standards of care" in medicine must ebb and flow through entire systems, converting physicians, administrators, payers, policy officials, and finally consumers themselves before the changes can truly be accepted. Even then, one region of the country—often the West Coast—typically accepts change years before the rest of the nation. The Minneapolis market was also at the forefront of change, thanks to an extremely active business community and leadership by a handful of tax-exempt hospital systems. In 1994, the city's largest hospital system merged with an equally large HMO to form Allina Health System, a fully integrated healthcare company. Allina, with $2.3 billion in annual revenues, provides managed care coverage to one in every four Minnesota residents.

Minneapolis has been regarded as prescient to upcoming changes in the healthcare industry, and Allina's recent developments bear watching. In late 1996, the system cut $37 million in overhead and asked two thousand employees to consider a voluntary severance package.[2] Allina's CEO Gordon Sprenger told *Modern Healthcare* magazine that one of the biggest challenges was getting doctors to cooperate in controlling utilization. "The point is to get better relationships with physicians so we can determine a better way to take care of patients," said the former American Hospital Association president. "We've been through this command-and-control approach. Now, the physicians really need to get engaged and incentivized."[3]

Minnesota has no for-profit hospitals because they're prohibited by law. However, in many markets, it took the fear of Columbia to instill a tax-exempt board with the desire to move ahead into mergers and integrated delivery systems. There's no such thing as a hostile takeover in the tax-exempt hospital industry. Boards must get together, discuss the mutual advantages of a merger, and anticipate the public relations fallout. Hospital trustees often don't, or won't, move very quickly.

When they do move, the community definitely benefits. For example, in Boston, three nearby cancer providers linked together to provide services in a more reasonable and cost-effective way. Dana-Farber Cancer Institute closed its inpatient unit and began renovating its building for more outpatient care. Brigham and Women's Hospital and Massachusetts General Hospital will continue to provide inpatient cancer care, but all three operations are managed under a single entity, Dana-Farber Partners CancerCare.

As not-for-profit providers ally under larger systems, residents want to see results. "We're approaching a time when mergers should be beginning to demonstrate real benefit for employees and the public," said James Stutz, executive director of the St. Louis Area Business Health Coalition. "Absent that, we should discourage further mergers and perhaps dismantle ones that have occurred. If we're going to have a private sector approach to health reform, we must preserve competition and choices."[4]

TAX-EXEMPT HOSPITALS AND THE CONSOLIDATOR'S ADVANTAGE

Not-for-profits have already achieved the first stage of integration. They've formed networks in which they purchase in bulk, gaining economies of scale to buy sutures, IV fluids, and the like. Alliances of not-for-profit hospitals began forming in the 1980s, and those groups have gone through their own consolidations. The nation's largest hospital alliance, Premier, resulted from the merger of three large hospital purchasing groups. In fact, nearly 85 percent of hospitals' medical, surgical, and pharmaceutical supplies were purchased through a group purchasing organization, according to Amerinet, a St. Louis purchasing group. That's given the tax-exempt hospital industry the volume to achieve discounts similar to those enjoyed by investor-owned hospital chains.

In 1995, hospitals achieved record profitability. Although investor-owned hospitals proved to be more than twice as profitable as tax-exempt, the latter systems were reinforcing their financial security. Investor-owned hospitals carried more debt, but tax-exempt ones managed to keep storing more cash; hence Methodist's nearly $1 billion store in Houston. But tax-exempt hospitals were keeping prices lower, according to William Cleverley, who tracks hospital performance and heads the Center for Health Industry Performance Studies at Ohio State University, Columbus. Even so, the promised land of hospital consolidation has not been reached. "There's been no substantial reduction in costs through merger activity," Cleverley told a group at the Health Industry Manufacturers Association meeting in late 1996.

Higher profits, little cost savings through consolidation. Still, managed care is turning the screws on reimbursement. Does this add up? There's a "tremendous ability in the industry to adapt," Cleverley concludes. In fact, Cleverley notes that hospitals in high managed care markets realized bigger profitability improvements in 1995 than those in low or medium managed care markets. He attributes this to hospitals' remarkable ability to deal with economic pressures. Since the overwhelming majority of the hospital industry is tax-exempt, this would suggest that the hospitals can lower their internal cost structure if pressed to do so. They may not lay off employees or make tough consolidation decisions, however, unless managed care plans start squeezing them to the breaking point.

Cleverley notes something else that speaks to consolidators' management. Up to now, most of the cost savings have been achieved by lowering the length of stay, a quick fix to cutting costs. Yet Cleverley points out that lowering costs by improving operations still needs to be addressed. "A tremendous opportunity for cost reduction still exists in the hospital industry," he notes. He also says that the differences between the haves and have-nots of the tax-exempt hospital industry are widening. Large not-for-profit consolidators, like Methodist, have the financial resources and market share to take them into the new millennium. Smaller, stand-alone hospitals do not.

Those have-not hospitals are on the precipice of a decision, however. They must align with a healthcare consolidator, but the decision as to whether to stay not-for-profit or go with a for-profit company is a controversial one, though less controversial when the hospital looks as if it's about to go out of business otherwise. For example, when the Quorum Health Group bought a rundown, inner city hospital in Columbus, Ohio, some local residents told the new CEO of the for-profit chain, Neil Serle, that he should rent his house "because I wasn't going to be staying long." Five years later, the hospital, Park Medical Center, is making money. Turned around by Quorum's strong management, the hospital has gained respect from the community.

All hospitals are aligning into systems of care. As they do, they inevitably must decide between not-for-profit and for-profit. The momentum was with Columbia and the for-profits in 1994 and 1995, but it began to shift halfway through 1996 as state officials started challenging the conversion of tax-exempt hospitals. When Columbia encountered problems with government regulators over the physician ownership structure of its El Paso operations in 1997, not-for-profits stopped throwing themselves at the giant's feet. When the indictments of Medicare fraud against certain Columbia executives were unsealed in July 1997, Columbia's hopes of acquiring more not-for-profit hospitals were dead.

For-profits bought hospitals by offering money, but sometimes that wasn't what hospital trustees wanted. This is a war in some communities, and money isn't the issue. It's interesting to consider what happened in Dallas in 1995 when St. Paul Medical Center, a Catholic hospital, decided to merge with Harris Methodist Health System, the largest hospital system in neighboring Fort Worth. St. Paul executives explained that Columbia had offered to buy the hospital but the board had decided instead to give it to Harris—for free.

It's kind of like a game of Monopoly. Your brother is winning and you're about to get wiped out. But you'd rather die than see your brother win, so you give all of your properties to his friend, who's also playing.

HERE COME THE REGULATORS

The hotel conference room in Columbus, Ohio, is standing room only, as some 250 attorneys, consultants, and hospital executives listen intently to discussion of what some view as a frightening trend. Many in the room work for state attorneys general, protecting the charitable trusts of tax-exempt organizations. As companies like Columbia/HCA have swept in and bought more tax-exempt hospitals, questions are raised about the deals. This deal-making can "no longer be relegated to the few power brokers," says Betty Montgomery, Ohio's attorney general, at the opening session of the 1997 Symposium on Nonprofit Health Care Conversions. "There are far-reaching consequences that affect almost every corner of society."

During 1996 and early 1997, her office was involved in the conversion of nine hospitals with $400 million in assets and two HMOs that wanted to convert to for-profit from not-for-profit status. If the deals had gone smoothly, the conference would never had taken place. They didn't. Montgomery's office identified several problems:

1. An attempt to channel charitable proceeds to a for-profit purchaser
2. An offer by a for-profit hospital chain to hire a hospital's chairman of the board before the deal was closed
3. Gross undervaluation of assets
4. Failure by a not-for-profit hospital board to do a valuation
5. Refusal to provide documents to the attorney general's office
6. Alteration of future budget projections to reduce a hospital's valuation

In the wake of these allegations, a premier deal of Columbia's to acquire the state's biggest insurer, the not-for-profit Blue Cross and Blue Shield of Ohio, was halted by the state amid problems and allegations of clandestine payments and arrangements.

Valuations are the most incendiary issue in the sale of a not-for-profit hospital to a for-profit company. When Columbia agreed to buy Blue Cross of Ohio for $299.5 million, the state noted that the insurer's managed care business had been valued at $405 million just eighteen months earlier. The problem is that most states don't have clear laws about how tax-exempt healthcare organizations should be valued or sold. The tax-exempt status of these assets stems from their organization as charities. State attorneys general typically oversee the use of those charitable assets, and when they're sold, the law enforcer may get involved.

Not all conversions present problems, the attorney general's office pointed out at the conference. Quorum Health Group, the investor-owned chain from Brentwood, Tennessee, bought two hospitals in Ohio without incident. One of those hospitals was owned by the city of Barberton, which put the issue to a vote. In that case, the price of $75 million and the benefits of putting the money into a charitable foundation were spelled out to voters. The city approved the deal by a three-to-one decision.

SELLING OUT TO A FOR-PROFIT SYSTEM

"We have come to the conclusion that the most economic and sensible way to maintain our mission of providing high-quality, cost-effective care to our area, including our medically indigent, is for the city to get out of the high-risk business of running a healthcare enterprise."[5] That was the statement from Jim Simms, board chairman of Northwest Texas Healthcare System, when the public hospital decided to sell to Universal Health Services, a for-profit hospital consolidator, in September 1995. The hospital system had talked at length with Columbia, but when the board decided to put it up for bid, the winner was Universal, owner of thirty-one hospitals, from King of Prussia, Pennsylvania. It meant that the community no longer paid some $8.5 million in local taxes to support the hospital, and as a bonus the now-tax-paying hospital began turning over $3 million in new taxes annually.

Evidence shows that the charitable assets of tax-exempt hospitals can be effectively deployed elsewhere in the community. Karen Wolk

Feinstein, president of the Jewish Healthcare Foundation in Pitts-burgh, tells how the Jewish community in her city started their own hospital at the turn of the century because of anti-Semitism. Jewish doctors couldn't practice at other hospitals in town, and Jewish pa-tients couldn't get kosher meals at other hospitals. The 1990s tell a dif-ferent story. "Now every hospital in Pittsburgh has kosher meals. Every hospital in Pittsburgh has a rabbi. Every hospital in Pittsburgh claims to be a Jewish hospital," she relates.

In 1990, the Jewish foundation that she now heads decided that in-stead of plowing money into its hospital each year, it would sell the facility to the local medical center with which it had affiliated. Instead, the foundation put its funds into other causes, including building a continuum of care for the aged: a nursing home, home healthcare agency, hospice, and assisted living facility.

There are cases in which the requirements for capital may outstrip the fundraising abilities of its faith-based owners, Feinstein says. That's a quandary other religious hospitals will face. In some cases, religious systems must sell to other consolidators; in others, they must become consolidators themselves in order to raise the capital and gain the economies of scale needed to compete with other consolidators.

This is not to say there aren't emotional issues along the way in hos-pitals where several generations of family members have memories of births, deaths, and everything in between. "Everything was a source of scrutiny, conflict, and comment," Feinstein relates. For example, the Jewish hospital was awash in memorial plaques. The foundation ended up calling in local rabbis and holding a formal burial for those plaques. "The disconnect of owning a hospital has many positive outcomes," she adds. "The issue is not who controls these facilities, but how do we reach our religious aspirations."

Experienced foundation professionals know that the work does not stop once the foundation is established. Foundation executives must focus beyond the deal and determine how to make the money pro-ductive for the community. Feinstein said her foundation learned that once it sold the hospital, it has no further hold on it. The new owners might promise to keep some traditions or make other guarantees; but then, they might not.

That's the problem with sales to for-profits as well. Many of these deals include strict covenants about maintaining a specific amount of charity care or not discontinuing certain services such as obstetrics or trauma. However, unless the new owner makes such convenants, all bets are off. This leads to the issue of trust. Deals are often based on trust in the people who forge them. However, in the for-profit world, more so than the not-for-profit world, those people will change. There's no doubt about that. So, a city that sells its hospital to a for-profit chain may negotiate with an acquisitions executive and work with an operations executive. However, chances are those people will advance in the company, or simply quit. The individuals that a community trusted during negotiations may not be present two or three years later when problems arise.

What's more, the ownership of the hospital may shift again thanks to mergers and acquisitions among hospital companies. Hospitals that were owned by Humana got bought by Columbia, and then sold because of antitrust problems. Hospitals owned by American Healthcare Management were bought by OrNda HealthCorp, which was bought by Tenet Healthcare. Did the not-for-profit hospitals that sold to OrNda—such as those in Massachusetts and Arizona—realize that they would be owned by Tenet, a hospital chain from Santa Barbara, California?

This is even more troubling for hospital boards that craft fifty-fifty joint ventures with for-profit companies. Such deals have been increasingly popular because local boards feel that they're not completely losing control of their hospitals. Even so, their partner may change.

HOSPITAL CONSOLIDATORS SLOWLY BUILD

In the mid-1980s, hospitals were regarded as lousy business opportunities. The figures tell a far different story. The hospital business, while shrinking in the number of patient beds, nearly doubled in revenues. According to a ten-year comparison of *Modern Healthcare* surveys, hospital systems reported $98.5 billion in revenues in 1995, compared with $48.2 billion in 1985. Profits also doubled, by the way.

Today, hospitals may still be regarded as lousy business opportunities as they face pricing pressures from managed care, Medicare, and Medicaid. Yet the tax-exempt consolidators are rolling out systems designed to handle these pricing pressures. The question is, can they can manage physicians and contract for risk?

In terms of capital, not-for-profit systems continue to benefit from philanthropy, which brings in about $4 billion a year, and tax-exempt bonds, which bring in at least that much but have to be repaid. Hospitals are using their capital to purchase needed information systems at a rapid rate.

However, reimbursement will be volatile. In 1998, hospital inpatient reimbursement rates are frozen by Medicare. Medicare may be the oxygen tent that keeps inefficient hospitals breathing. If it paid at a comparable rate to some HMOs, dozens—perhaps scores—of hospitals would be forced to close. But Medicare hasn't caught up yet with the discounted rates of HMOs and other aggressive payers. That will change in the years ahead.

Any massive cut in federal reimbursement is likely to be accompanied by wails and moans. The problem is that Medicare is the lifeblood of America's hospitals, and America's hospitals are not a monolithic body. Some are extremely well-managed and efficient, and others are poorly managed and wasteful. Similarly, the upper 20 percent or so will derive double-digit profit rates off Medicare while about the same percent will lose money off Medicare. When weighing reimbursement rates, Congress and Medicare administrators must figure out how to reasonably reimburse hospitals without pushing the badly managed ones into bankruptcy.

As a taxpayer, one might say, oh heck, if they're badly managed, let them close. But they may be vital hospitals to a community, without which the community's health is jeopardized. This problem may be solved through consolidation. Those stand-alone hospitals that are struggling will eventually be brought into a larger system where they can enjoy the economies of scale and the management expertise of those who are making the double-digit profit margins. In this way, consolidation can bring measurable results. It also brings Med Inc. closer to reality for thousands of not-for-profit hospitals.

CHAPTER SIX

Managing Managed Care

Integration among all providers is happening, but consumers are not very happy," says Vicki Baldwin, an executive with the HMO, Oxford Health Plan. That just about hits the nail on the head for healthcare consolidators, but coming from an HMO executive, it's especially relevant. Yet Oxford is striving to be what some consider an oxymoron: a consumer-friendly HMO.

Like other growing Med Inc. companies, HMO consolidators must strive to manage capital, information, risk, and government regulation. But they have an additional distraction: consumer groups that regularly rise up to decry the HMOs' very existence. Speaking to a group of Price Waterhouse healthcare consultants in 1997, Baldwin bluntly questioned whether the "monoliths are really thinking about how they're going to serve the needs of their increasingly vocal customer base." When HMOs get bigger, the thinking is, they often don't get better.

HMOs became the penny-pinching landlord of the healthcare comfort inns. They are powerful and a big, easy target. "Health plans ought to exist to add value," says George Crowling, who, as manager of managed care, negotiates contracts for the telecommunications giant GTE. "But the main value they add is contracting and financial pressure. There are very few that add information. They've had ten to fifteen years to establish themselves in the public's view as superior-quality products, and few of them have done that."

By 1995, nearly three-fourths of all covered employees were in some form of managed care plan, up from 63 percent just one year earlier.[1] Many of the traditional insurers have cast off their other operations just to concentrate on healthcare. This means they must manage that business because they can't rely on other segments. For example, Aetna made a strategic decision in 1995 to focus on managed healthcare. It sold its property casualty business, Travelers Insurance Group, for $4.1 billion, using most of the proceeds of the acquisition to buy U.S. Healthcare in 1996. The acquisition made Aetna U.S. Healthcare the nation's third largest HMO after Kaiser Permanente of Oakland, California, and United Healthcare of Minneapolis.

Aetna U.S. Healthcare was one of dozens of HMO consolidations in 1996. The granddaddy of the industry, Kaiser Permanente, entered into its first deals in 1988, adding about one million enrollees through the purchase of Community Health Plan of Albany, New York, and Group Health Cooperative of Seattle. Kaiser also consolidated its northern and southern California operations into one statewide organization.

Much like another consolidator (Columbia/HCA), Kaiser, with 7.4 million members in seventeen states, was busy fighting off inquiries from state officials in California and Texas about the quality of its services and claims of denied emergency care.

To a certain degree, such highly publicized incidents demonstrate a law of averages in the consolidation game. Bad stuff happens. Even so, HMOs are now controlling what prompted the most complaints: that, until recently, HMOs exhibited an almost complete lack of flexibility. The old wisdom is that one size fits all. Every HMO enrollee gets a static set of benefits, and there are no exceptions. The new conventional wisdom is that health plan members can select from a variety of plans at a variety of prices with a variety of provider networks. In the vernacular, this is called choice. "We want to stop trying to fit everything into a single solution," says Arthur Ryan, chairman and CEO of Prudential, one of the nation's largest healthcare companies. "There are going to be different prices for different networks. Most consumers are pretty knowledgeable with these kinds of cost-benefit trade-offs."

This is a big leap, involving the proper management of capital, information, and risk. Early on, HMOs figured they couldn't manage risk by offering choice. Now, they're learning that they can. Consolidators in all healthcare niches should heed the HMOs' experience because they're all becoming managed healthcare organizations in one way or another. The tribulations of HMOs may be repeated by every other consolidator that attempts to balance financial goals with patient care.

The charter of HMOs and other managed care companies is to deliver healthcare services for a finite amount of dollars, called a capitated payment. If an HMO receives $100 a month to cover a member's care, it must live within that budget, or at least average it out among all of the other members. As the lines among consolidators blur, more companies are taking on capitation and trying to solve that equation. It's a problem that healthcare companies must solve for themselves.

Lessons in other industries can't really help. Does the grocer worry about whether a customer can afford the steak she's buying? Does a car manufacturer worry whether the buyer will be able to pay for gasoline a month later? Until recently, hospitals, physicians, and medical vendors operated the same way. They supplied the services, charged for it, and didn't worry about whether there was enough money at the end of the rainbow. Now, more of them are contracting to take care of populations of patients. They have to balance the budget.

HMOs have dared to experiment with financial incentives. Initially, many of them used "withholds" as incentive for physicians. Physician compensation schedules were set up so that part of their reimbursement was held in a money pool. If the physician or his group met certain financial targets, the pot of money would be released. If not, the financial pool would have to fund the higher costs caused by the physicians' practice patterns. But this led to allegations of withholding care for financial motives. This type of negative incentive system is giving way to positive incentives in which physicians can earn bonuses for helping the managed care plan be profitable.

The degree to which managed care has kept costs down is most evident in statistics from the pharmaceutical industry. In 1995, price increases accounted for just 1.7 percent of the industry's growth, compared with 7.3 percent five years earlier. About one-half of all prescriptions go through a managed care company; that's twice as much as in 1990. Under the old system, the incentive was to do more to make more money. Under capitation, the incentive is to do less to make more money. Although this raises questions of rationing care, a system that does too much can be at fault as well.

Like other consolidators, HMOs can make this equation work and provide a model for managed healthcare consolidators in other niches. Again, they must manage the four critical factors of consolidation: capital, information, risk, and government regulation.

Capital flows from volume contracting, a concept that HMO consolidators understand. Volume makes risk bearable, or at least calculable, as long as one understands the population's characteristics. Yet insurers have learned that volume alone isn't enough. It has to be *local* volume. This is different from other businesses because HMOs can't stand alone; they need hospitals, physicians, home care agencies, and outpatient centers to do business, and they can't negotiate favorable rates from them without delivering volume. "You have to be number one, two, or three to survive in a market," Prudential's Ryan warns.

NATIONAL GROWTH
TO MEET EMPLOYER NEEDS

By having access to Wall Street capital, HMOs can buy other managed care plans to fill in gaps in their national networks. This is the way to tap into billion-dollar national contracts. Large employers want a single network that can serve their companies throughout the country, which gives HMOs and insurers an incentive to consolidate. "We want to use our economic leverage by selecting a single baseline provider," says Daniel P. O'Connell, corporate director of employee benefits and human resource systems for United Technologies in Hartford, Connecticut, a firm with seventy thousand domestic employees. In 1994, it signed just such a three-year agreement with CIGNA and renewed it in 1997. By negotiating with a single network, United Technologies has the clout to determine cost structure and quality indicators. For example, the company demands that CIGNA and its forty HMOs in different markets go through the accreditation process of the National Committee on Quality Assurance.

Although thirty thousand of the company's employees are in Connecticut, O'Connell says executives wanted a national insurer that could guarantee "that our couple of employees in Wyoming got the same level of care and service as those in Connecticut." O'Connell declined to provide figures, but he says the CIGNA contract delivered a "substantive reduction" in what United Technologies was paying for healthcare. In exchange for attractive rates, United Technologies delivers volume to CIGNA. Although employees are offered a choice of some forty other HMOs, the contributions paid by the employees themselves for the CIGNA plan are the baseline. This puts an incentive before the other HMOs to keep their costs competitive with CIGNA's in marketing to United Technologies employees. About two-thirds of United Technologies' salaried employees receive care through the CIGNA plan.

Offering the same plan throughout the company helped United Technologies in labor negotiations. In fact, all of its domestic hourly workforce is in a managed care plan wherever such a plan is available. In collective bargaining negotiations, O'Connell adds, "we have designed a very good plan that the chairman and all the operating unit presidents are in. It is that same very good plan that we believe all the bargaining units should be in as well."

Having cut the deal with CIGNA, United Technologies leaves contracting with local providers up to CIGNA. "We say to them, you need to use the dynamics of the competitive marketplace to make sure you get the best deal," O'Connell says. Of course, those decisions can impact United. For example, in Hartford CIGNA decided to select just one of the city's two largest hospitals for its network. "It was a no-fun deal," O'Connell says, noting the pressure from both hospitals to get a contract to treat employees of the state's largest private employer. "It altered forever the marketplace around here because there was a much more rapid introduction of managed care."

Before managed care's negotiated reimbursement became reality, insurance companies paid what they were billed. Hospitals and physicians sent bills, and insurers paid them, unless they suspected there was something awry. By and large, they didn't question the amount of reimbursement. As HMOs like CIGNA flexed their muscle, the situation swiveled 180 degrees. "You will be paid this amount. Take it, or we'll go next door," HMOs said to providers. This prompted price wars.

Now, yet another organization is telling physicians and hospitals what to do. Previously, the hospital and the physician coexisted in a somewhat adversarial relationship. But here was a relationship that gripped providers by the bank account.

HMO consolidators are struggling with the same operational problems of other consolidators. They're busy rolling things up, and they haven't figured out how to run it smoothly.

Deal-making takes time. The most visible megamerger was Aetna's $9 billion acquisition of U.S. Healthcare in 1996, a deal expected to bring substantial savings in administrative costs and give Aetna strong leverage to lower payments to providers. Aetna, a life insurance company founded in 1843, was anxious to learn from what was considered one of the best-managed HMOs in the country. U.S. Healthcare boasted the lowest medical loss ratio in the industry while Aetna's was one of the highest because of its lack of managed care experience. (Medical loss ratios are the percentage of premium revenues spent on medical services. It does not include administrative expenses. Obviously, the more an HMO spends on medical services, the less profit it generates.) In addition, although Aetna was a recognized name in larger corporations, it lacked the recognition among small and medium-sized employers that U.S. Healthcare had.

Although half of Aetna's insured population was already in managed care, it was continuously challenged to deliver a better-quality product. (As one of the fastest growing HMOs, Oxford faced that dilemma as well.) Yet, nearly a year after the merger, U.S. Healthcare and Aetna were still shaking things out, as the megacompany figured out its marketing message and information systems.

Insurers are "buying business" when they consolidate with other insurers, a strategy that's good but still requires that they figure out how to run what they own. Like other components of the healthcare continuum, in the past insurers spent much of their lives passing on price increases. The buck never stopped. Now they are like other healthcare consolidators; HMOs can't keep raising prices. They must control costs and generate profits through volume. One strategy is to gobble up other HMOs to gain economies of scale and volume to better manage risk. At the same time, these medical moguls are trying to act more customer friendly. They want to operate like a small company within a big-company framework. This is the true test of all healthcare consolidators.

INFORMATION-DRIVEN CONSOLIDATION

To position itself for the future, Oxford formed a data-driven company, Oxford Specialty Management Initiatives, with three goals: equip patients with critical information, reward physicians for better solutions, and empower the specialist to coordinate care. But weren't specialists the ones who had been blamed for driving up the cost of healthcare during most of the 1980s and 1990s?

Oxford, which is based in Norwalk, Connecticut, is an HMO with 1.7 million members in six states. It set the system on its head in a plan that would create better outcomes, better patient satisfaction, and—finally—more cost savings. With 1996 revenues of about $800 million and a market capitalization of $5 billion, this plan is one of the nation's fastest growing, adding nearly forty-four thousand members per month in 1996. But Oxford realized that 75 percent of what it spent on care was in the specialty area, and it was asking primary-care physicians to manage that extremely complex area.

Gathering claims data from its own patient population, Oxford determined how much it cost to take care of a patient with a specific type of case in twelve carved-out specialties. (Some plans call this case-rate reimbursement because it covers the costs of an entire individual case of care.) A panel of between six and eight physician experts met regularly, debating each of the steps in each case from a patient's workup, through treatment into recovery. For example, in obstetrics and gynecology the teams developed cases for maternity, neonatology, hysterectomy, and infertility. Then, Oxford took bids from physician specialty groups. But here's the kicker. It required that the bids be 20 percent below what Oxford currently was spending. That's a pretty steep discount; after all, Medicare only shaves 5 percent off what it's paying the managed care groups.

Oxford was sending a message that groups could take risk, manage care, and still make a profit. The specialty groups are reimbursed on an installment plan, similar to paying for a car. They receive an initial payment, a secondary payment, and a final payment when the job is done. On the cost side, Oxford benefits. On the quality side, its patients benefit because they have information on their physicians for the first time. Oxford is the first HMO to issue "report cards" on its physicians. This is a controversial move that many physicians abhor, but Oxford officials say such information helps consumers make educated choices and will raise the overall level of quality.

A "report card" on an obstetrician, for example, includes the number of deliveries in a given period of time, C-section rate, and patient satisfaction scores. This way, patients can do their own analysis. Obviously, most women don't want a physician who cavalierly performs a higher percentage of C-sections than his peers. On the other hand, if the mother-to-be knows she's going to have a C-section, it might be best to have it done by a physician with plenty of experience in that area.

These types of statistics benefit Oxford and its patients in other ways. Physicians who score poorly will probably want to better their performance. Vicki Baldwin of Oxford also believes the system entices more physicians to be in the Oxford network. "This is a model for growth," she says. In addition, physicians who do perform will likely want to associate with and refer to better quality physicians as well. "This helps specialists find teams, which they don't do naturally," Baldwin says. "[They] won't want unpopular riders on their care team," she adds, noting that patient satisfaction figures will demonstrate popularity among enrollees.

The way Oxford is segmenting care into twelve specialty areas gives employers an opportunity to design their own benefit packages. For example, an employer could select specific patient care teams at specific prices that would enable them to hold down healthcare costs. "The specialist is the hub of the wheel because the specialist decides lab, radiology, physical therapy, home healthcare, hospital care, and consulting physician services," Baldwin notes.

In competitive markets like Philadelphia, Oxford's changes helped set it apart from more familiar plans such as Independence Blue Cross and U.S. Healthcare, by positioning Oxford as a customer-friendly HMO. And although most HMOs were known for their restrictions, the Oxford menu of services has innovative plans that cover alternative therapies such as acupuncture and massage therapy.

MANAGING CAPITAL

In terms of capital, publicly held HMOs such as Oxford need continuous infusions of capital to battle larger and larger competitors. Unfortunately, providing quality, cost-efficient care simply isn't enough. A case in point is Fallon Community Health Plan of Massachusetts.

At the same time it was selected as the best HMO in America by *U.S. News & World Report* in September 1996 and one of the four top HMOs in the country by *Newsweek,* the health plan was losing market share to better capitalized companies: Harvard Pilgrim Health Care, Tufts Health Plan, and HMO Blue, which is part of Blue Cross and Blue Shield of Massachusetts. Fallon had the state's lowest administrative expenses, 8.1 percent compared with 12.4 percent on average.[2] To compete, Fallon was moving into the Boston area, a huge market that it would have difficulty penetrating without spending millions of dollars on advertising and sales efforts.

HMO consolidators need capital for marketing and expansion, which fact prompts many of them to turn to Wall Street. Although the oldest HMOs are not-for-profit, it's rare now for a start-up HMO to be anything but for-profit. The capital needs are too great. What's more, the two biggest sources of capital for not-for-profit organizations, tax-exempt bonds and philanthropy, typically don't flow to not-for-profit HMOs. With limited exceptions, tax-exempt bonds must be used for capital projects, such as building hospitals, and few HMOs are into that. Philanthropy is problematic; how many Americans really want to put their HMO into their will? Very few, it seems, because HMOs are seen more as a commodity than a community service.

For most of our recent past, insurance companies were set up in the decentralized system that seems to work well for companies like Columbia/HCA, PhyCor, and Thermo Electron. In their case, the conglomerate was called Blue Cross and Blue Shield. The big difference was that the Blues were tax-exempt organizations, and in many communities they were regarded as the insurer of last resort. In other words, if no other insurance company would provide coverage, the Blues plan was obligated to do so. However, as the years passed, they became less of a community organization and more of a true business. On a federal level, they no longer received tax exemptions. Like other healthcare organizations, they had a need for capital. In their current configurations, they couldn't get it.

The Blues are now in a transitional phase in which five are for-profit companies or are trying to convert to for-profit. About thirty other Blues plans are considering converting to for-profit status, according to Consumers Union, which has gotten involved in these deals to protect consumer interests.

None of the conversions occurred without controversy. The most contentious was probably that of Blue Cross and Blue Shield of Ohio, which planned to distribute $15 million in compensation and severance packages to its top three executives as part of the deal.

One of the many myths of healthcare is that some HMOs are altruistic and others want to be profitable. They all try to be profitable. Even social HMOs, which one might argue are more oriented to community service, are moving to for-profit status. Known by the acronym SHMOs, they were authorized by Congress in 1982 to offer expanded benefits, such as homemaker services, transportation, and Meals on Wheels. Nine SHMOs have been approved by HCFA. Of those, two are for-profits and another is in the process of converting.

In terms of capital, consolidators also must be financially strong enough to withstand wide swings in contracting volumes of covered members. Perhaps the best example of that came in 1996 when the

American Association of Retired Persons decided to replace Prudential as the sole provider of its healthcare insurance product, a book of
business valued at $3.5 billion. Prudential had the exclusive contract
with AARP for what's called "Medigap" insurance, so named because
it fills in the coverage gap for what Medicare doesn't pay. Prudential
had been the exclusive insurer since 1981. Yet, with $40 billion in an-
nual revenues, the nation's largest mutual life and health insurance
firm didn't view the loss of the contract as a back-breaker. In fact, executives says the contract generated only $20 million in after-tax rev-
enues, a modest amount to Prudential's overall profits of $1 billion.

PUTTING IT ALL TOGETHER: MANAGING MANAGED CARE

Managed care has been able to put the skids on healthcare inflation
in a demonstrable way. Health-coverage premiums rose less than 1
percent in 1996, just a fraction of the increases that employers incurred year after year during the 1970s and 1980s. On the West Coast,
where managed care is most prevalent, healthcare premiums actually
dropped. That saved money for employers and also for employees.

Even so, there is no lack of criticism for HMOs wanting to cut services to boost profits. The consolidator's challenge is to show that
through management, it can improve quality. Less care often is better
care. Nearly 200,000 patients die each year from the care they receive
in hospitals and another 1.1 million are injured, according to a 1996
report, "Examining Errors in Health Care." About two-thirds of those
errors are preventable, the report says. In another study published in
1996, researchers spotted errors in the treatment of 45 percent of patients in the surgical units of a large teaching hospital. "The likelihood
of experiencing an adverse event increased about 6 percent for each
day of hospital stay," researchers said.[3] The study also noted that a majority of hospital errors probably go unreported. Obviously, there's a
lot of pressure not to report errors—not the least of which is being
caught up in a lawsuit in today's litigious society. "We should stop saying errors are rare and admit they're everywhere," James Conway, chief
operations officer of Boston's Dana-Farber Cancer Institute, told *Modern Healthcare* magazine.[4] Dana-Farber was caught in the cross-fire in
1995 when Betsy Lehman, medical reporter for the *Boston Globe*, died
from a chemotherapy overdose.

So, the verdict is fewer hospital days can mean fewer errors. But how low should HMOs go? The question is being asked in managed care circles, where the worry is that scrimping too much on care could mean lawsuits will ensue. Commercial HMOs in California say that they're managing care so well that hospital utilization is down to 140 days per 1,000 enrollees per year. Five years ago, the industry would have said that was not possible, even that it was criminal, to cut back services so severely. What is the right ratio? Wall Street and mutual fund portfolios compare the financial health of HMOs through medical loss ratios (the amount spent on medical services as a percent of revenues). Although the term may seem crass, the ratios enable investors to compare how efficiently various plans handle their expenses. For Oxford, its medical loss ratio is 80 percent, regarded as low in the HMO industry. HMOs paid out 89 cents in medical expenses per dollar of premium, up from 88 cents in 1995 and 86 cents in 1994, according to Weiss Ratings, a firm in Palm Beach Gardens, Florida, that rates the financial health of HMOs. The higher the amount paid in medical expenses, the lower the profit. The industry as a whole saw profits decline 60 percent in 1996, Weiss's public relations release reported, because competition meant HMOs couldn't raise rates.

Although consumers probably want to enroll only with financially healthy HMOS, they don't want one that crimps on medical services. "Medical loss ratio" doesn't sound like a consumer-friendly term. Couple that with anecdotal abuses by HMOs, and the sum is vitriolic rhetoric. Take the California battle in 1996 over Proposition 214, which would mandate more stringent regulation of HMOs. When the HMOs told consumers that such a law would cost "hundreds of millions in new taxes," they were assailed as a bunch of liars. "The HMOs are using a time-tested strategy: if all else fails, lie," declared Dr. John Roark at the time.[5] Roark was head of the California Physicians Alliance, whose supporters included the American Association of Retired Persons, Consumers Union, and the AFL-CIO.

Like consolidators on the provider side, HMOs must manage the public's perception of them as bureaucratic Big Brothers. If they can't, they become political fodder. Says GTE's Crowling: "They [HMOs] understand that employers are their customers. What they've forgotten is there are other powerful entities out there: politicians."

A host of new government regulations have burst out of state legislatures, mandating forty-eight-hour stays for maternity cases and abolishing "gag" clauses that restrict what physicians can say to HMO enrollees. Although government regulation has been a thorn in the HMO consolidators' collective side, it's also creating tremendous entrepreneurial opportunities. Two of the biggest government spending programs, Medicare and Medicaid, are privatizing their programs. Medicare spends 18 cents and Medicaid 14 cents of every healthcare dollar, according to government figures. Increasingly, those dollars are flowing to private HMOs.

THE BRASS RING IN MEDICARE

Government deregulation drastically altered the course of the airline, banking, and communications industries. It is about to do the same in healthcare through HMOs. As Congress starts to privatize Medicare and the states do the same with Medicaid, it's deregulating a $200 billion program. Medicare essentially is a type of monopoly because it has been the only administrator of healthcare services to persons over age sixty-five. They were required by law to pay into the system, and the system decided what was covered. Now, the monopoly is being deregulated and distributed to other private organizations. Although deregulation can be disruptive, it has brought big savings to other industries. Since 1978, when airline deregulation took effect, air fares adjusted for inflation have dropped by one-third. Also, long-distance rates have dropped by one-half since the break up of AT&T.[6] Deregulation could have the same effect on the Medicare program.

The momentum to spur more retirees into choosing HMOs has been building over the past five years. Currently, 13 percent of Medicare beneficiaries are in managed care, 87 percent in fee-for-service. California has the largest Medicare HMO presence, with 34 percent of beneficiaries enrolled. Congress has looked to Medicare HMOs to stem increases in expenses. From 1969 to 1993, the amount paid out in benefits for each Medicare recipient grew 10.9 percent annually, according to HHS. By today's standards, this seems rapid, but it actually was slower than the 12.5 percent annual growth rate in the private sector. Those were the days when insurers just kept passing on the increases.

However, the tables have turned. Private health insurance put the brakes on, and healthcare inflation hummed along at only a 3.5 percent annual rate compared to 9.7 percent for Medicare beneficiaries between 1993 and 1995. Without managed care, Medicare prices essentially went up three times higher.

Slowly at first, Medicare decided to try managed care. The federal Medicare program began paying a flat monthly fee for each Medicare enrollee. The payment represents 95 percent of the historical cost of serving Medicare beneficiaries in a particular county under the traditional Medicare fee-for-service system. It varies widely from state to state and even from county to county, which says a lot about how physician practice patterns can drive costs. Currently, at least half of the enrollees in Medicare HMOs must be non-Medicare beneficiaries, in other words commercial-type members. However, if Congress drops that restriction, as it is considering, more HMOs could qualify.

In fact, it's easy to see how Wall Street would back the cash flow going into an all-Medicare HMO. Medicare HMOs were so lucrative that some California physician groups mounted marketing campaigns to urge their elderly patients to sign up. Sending letters and staging raffles and senior dances, the managed care plans made Medicare HMOs sound like the best thing since, well, Medicare itself.

In addition, Congress is considering two other options that could encourage more beneficiaries to course through the HMOs' veins. One—negative premium HMOs—would allow HMOs to refund part of the premium back to the beneficiary. Currently, HMOs aren't allowed to do that, although they may add additional services, such as vision care or pharmaceuticals, thereby using up more of the premium dollar. The separate class of social HMOs, as we have seen, goes a step further. They enjoy special status with the HCFA and receive 100 percent of Medicare's costs per capita in a given market. In contrast, regular Medicare-risk HMOs receive 95 percent.

In the case of Medicare HMOs, the federal government created enormous opportunities for healthcare entrepreneurs because it priced the payments too high. The economics are really quite simple. The federal government now spends around $480 per month, or $5,360 per year, in healthcare on the average Medicare beneficiary. If an HMO can reduce the number of days the beneficiary is in the hospital, it can save sacks of cash. One day in the hospital costs an average of $1,000. Medicare beneficiaries spend twenty-four hundred days per thousand in the hospital each year. Reduce that by five hundred days, and you're talking about a $500,000 savings.

Critics charged that the HMOs were making money because they were attracting only the healthy seniors, but that wasn't necessarily so. "As time has passed, the early risk-contract HMO enrollees have aged and become sicker," says Jack Rodgers, who heads Price Waterhouse's

Health Policy Economics Group. However, seniors who joined Medicare HMOs tended to have a slightly different attribute, Rodgers's group found: they were poorer. This meant they were more sensitive to the cost of care. In addition, it meant that they had conditions such as diabetes and asthma. HMOs can be very effective at managing those conditions, compared to the cost of emergency room visits, for example.

Additionally, in 1997 Congress was considering setting a floor for HMO Medicare payments. Such a floor, say $350, would encourage these HMOs to go into higher-cost areas. For example, HMOs have shied from rural areas, where it may be more costly to deliver care and the number of elderly beneficiaries doesn't support the numbers that propel actuarial forecasts. Rural areas are home to a higher proportion of elderly than urban areas. As many as 55 percent of Medicare beneficiaries live in areas where there is now no HMO. In other words, they don't even have the option of trying a Medicare HMO.

The elderly join HMOs for many of the same reasons that younger people join them. The financial incentives drive them in, and the ease of use. If HMOs are generally accepted in a particular market, it's more likely that Medicare beneficiaries enroll in them because they ask friends and neighbors for recommendations. For example, 40 percent of Medicare beneficiaries in San Diego are in risk plans, a market that has heavy HMO penetration. Meanwhile, the percentage in New Jersey is 25 percent.

Medicare's dabbling into managed care is likely to cast a long shadow over the entire program. The agency is getting ready to take its expertise, such as it is, acquired in these Medicare HMO pilots and apply it to other areas, such as home healthcare, long-term care, and hospice care. Congress will continue fighting the funding battle over Medicare, and battles with HMO consolidators are likely to grow increasingly contentious. As President Clinton advocated shaving Medicare HMO rates by 5 percent, the HMO lobby armed itself, calling the move "penny wise, pound foolish."

This is especially true with Medicaid and Medicare HMOs and psychiatric programs. After a long and hard-fought battle, Oregon finally received a waiver from President Clinton to take more control of its own Medicaid program. That led to a parade of other states wanting to reengineer their own multibillion dollar Medicaid programs; the plans, largely, were to privatize as much as possible through HMOs. By 1997, fifteen states had federal waivers to go that route. Many more were considering it, a move that would dramatically alter the cash flow of a $150 billion Medicaid program.

RISK FOR RISK'S SAKE

Everyone wants to get into the HMOs' core business of managing risk. HMOs are starting to unload risk to other groups such as physicians, pharmaceutical companies, and hospitals. All are eager to profit from risk-contracting.

However, if an HMO begins to gradually unload its risk to other providers, such as hospitals and physicians, eventually it has no risk at all. Is it still an HMO then? No. It has become a claims processor, or even less than that: merely a sales and marketing machine designed to acquire and assimilate potential customers into a provider network. It won't take provider networks long to determine they don't need HMOs to do that for them.

Another scenario is that new entrants may compete with HMOs that have managed to slough off the risk to providers. Banks, for example, already process transactions with efficient systems. Consider the credit card: in exchange for a processing fee, they contract with consumers to pay for a service. They don't accept any risk, and banks may not need to in healthcare if the providers take on the risk themselves.

Consolidators see the HMO's role as that of trail-blazer, showing them how to manage risk through the use of capital and information. As the lines blur among consolidators, it becomes increasingly difficult to differentiate between HMOs and other managed care companies.

CHAPTER SEVEN

The Spreading Power
of Consolidation

N o person is an island in the competitive world of Med Inc. That's why consolidators will rule. Consolidators start with three or four of a kind, and before you know it they've got a couple dozen and then they're on their way to hundreds.

Some healthcare niches, such as home healthcare and nursing homes, have already gone through an early generation of roll-ups. They're dominated by for-profit firms such as Apria Healthcare and Beverly Enterprises that have access to capital markets and are developing integrated information systems. Because Medicaid and Medicare are the primary payers in those niches, there is little incentive to develop risk-sharing programs.

Consolidated delivery networks may be the only ones that can afford the integrated information systems needed to compete. Building an information infrastructure demands money, structure, and a strategic vision. On the vendor side, suppliers have found they needed to be one-stop shops for hospitals who wanted to buy a variety of equipment from a single vendor. A manufacturer couldn't do that if it operated only in a single niche. So companies like Hewlett-Packard, Marquette, GE, Nellcor, and Siemens began collecting other companies to fill holes in their product lines. The patient monitoring company SpaceLabs, for instance, wasn't satisfied being a dominant player in adult monitoring systems. It began acquiring other patient monitoring companies so that it could provide a family of monitors throughout the hospital, from the medical and surgical wings to obstetrics and neonatal.

It made sense in terms of communications as well. Divergent systems made by different manufacturers couldn't talk to each other very well. To do so, either they needed to adopt an "open architecture" that competitors could integrate with, or they needed to acquire similar companies and integrate the machines themselves.

The consolidation theory flowed all the way down the food chain. Durable medical equipment companies, which supply wheelchairs and beds, needed to grow to cover more territory for the managed care companies with which they signed contracts. Mom-and-pop independent medical equipment companies look like a dying breed.

Unlike those executives who moved from one physician consolidator to the next, some moved to other branches of the healthcare grapevine. Such was the case with David Colby, one of the early executives at Columbia/HCA Healthcare. Colby was Columbia's first CFO; in 1996, he was hired by American Medical Response, a highly successful roll-up of ambulance companies. American Medical was founded by Paul Verrochi, who was named 1995 entrepreneur of the year in *Inc.* magazine. Verrochi structured a company that would privatize many of the nation's ambulance companies. He brought in experts from Federal Express to design local systems that could dispatch ambulances more efficiently.

By 1996, American Medical Response was the largest U.S. operator of emergency and nonemergency healthcare transportation vehicles, with $725 million in revenues. Less than a year after Colby arrived, American Medical was snapped up by an even larger roll-up expert, Laidlaw of Burlington, Ontario. Once known as a trash hauler, the Canadian company got into the transportation business through the side door of waste disposal. It became the largest school bus operator in North America. Laidlaw purchased American Medical Response for a little over $1 billion.

It was a case of number two buying number one. The surviving company became the undisputed leader of ambulance consolidators, with 150 ambulance companies in thirty-four states; annual revenues topped $1.3 billion, giving Laidlaw 14 percent of the market. Actually, that 14 percent may be deceptive. The company may in fact control as much as

40 percent of the private ambulance market, since the market pie includes literally thousands of city and county emergency medical services (EMS) that aren't likely to convert to private ownership.

The business isn't just emergency work. Much of it is shuttling elderly patients from hospitals to nursing homes or vice versa. With the aging of America, Laidlaw sees its financial statement trending upward and onward. It doesn't hurt that profit margins in the medical transportation business average 12 percent, versus 8–9 percent in trash hauling.

In a further consolidation of the emergency medicine business, Laidlaw decided in 1997 to buy an emergency physicians' company in Dallas, EmCare. More than 90 percent of EmCare's $260 million annualized revenue is generated from managing emergency departments under 131 contracts in 162 hospitals. EmCare operates in twenty-one states and contracts with eighteen hundred physicians, who annually provide care for more than three million patients.

Like other medical consolidators, Laidlaw began building from one niche, ambulances, into a larger one, emergency medicine. The number two ambulance company, Rural/Metro, is aggressively doing its own roll-up shuffle and finding synergy with other roll-ups. In 1996, it forged a deal with National Health's Call Center Services to offer managed care customers the use of the call centers' information, technology, and software products.

As icing on the cake, Rural/Metro bought a 10 percent stake in National Enhancement, Phoenix, Arizona, for $2.5 million. It's a good match in which they combine "telephone triage"—definitely a nineties term—with the ambulance service to improve responsiveness. Need an ambulance? Maybe a nurse can simply talk the patient through a problem that a physician can handle tomorrow during office hours. This saves the managed care company a couple of hundred dollars in costs. Multiply by several thousand enrollees, and it adds up. In fact, Kaiser Permanente was one of the first HMOs to craft a deal with American Medical Response.

HEALTHSOUTH'S FOCUS
ON ONE SECTOR OF THE INDUSTRY

In the rehabilitation world, Richard Scrushy's HealthSouth Rehabilitation has grown twentyfold in three years. This Harley-Davidson-riding son of a nurse has combined the largest group of rehabilitation assets in this country and molded them into a prototypical consolidator. What's more, HealthSouth has been the gene pool for several other roll-ups, most prominently MedPartners, which has already eclipsed HealthSouth in size. Scrushy also started Capstone Capital, a real estate investment trust that buys healthcare properties. Scrushy, like other consolidators, has a golden touch. Capstone went public in 1996, when REITs were out of favor, but still managed to raise $98 million in its IPO.

Look anywhere in the rehabilitation industry, and Scrushy's footprints are there. As the company describes its history on its website: "Five men pooled their resources and formed a company that would restructure the rehabilitation industry in less than a decade." A respiratory therapist by training, Scrushy got his first taste of the hospital business working in cardiopulmonary services at Lifemark, a Houston hospital company whose stock rose from $3 a share to $46 when it was bought by American Medical International in the mid-1980s. Scrushy left with some colleagues to start HealthSouth in 1984. The company now operates more than one thousand inpatient and outpatient facilities; one in every four outpatient rehabilitation clinics in the country is operated by this Birmingham, Alabama, firm, according to analysts' estimates.

Rehabilitation professionals treat a wide range of patients, with spinal cord injuries, orthopedic problems, arthritis, or cancer. As Americans age, the incidence of these conditions increases. Because rehabilitation services aren't yet under Medicare's fixed pricing of diagnosis-related groups, they have been a lucrative area for providers. When hospital systems were feeling the pinch from the implementation of DRGs in the 1980s, rehabilitation was viewed as a pot of gold. According to federal estimates, the number of rehabilitation facilities grew 84 percent between 1985 and 1989, and the number of rehab units within hospitals grew 66 percent.

As an investment, HealthSouth has few peers; its credentials were underlined when the company's stock was added to the prestigious Standard and Poor's 500 Index in 1997. On the way to that mark, Scrushy added companies at a blistering pace in the mid-1990s. One of its most innovative projects was a San Antonio, Texas, medical facility that included a HealthSouth outpatient center and a Medical Care International surgery center. Medical Care, once the nation's largest surgery center chain, was subsequently bought out by Columbia. As a true consolidator, HealthSouth saw the synergy in surgery and rehabilitation, since one frequently follows the other.

It also began buying up surgery centers, most notably Surgical Care Affiliates, the second largest surgery chain. With that acquisition, HealthSouth became the nation's largest outpatient surgery chain, with 126 locations. The deal was one in a mix of $2.5 billion in acquisitions that Scrushy pulled off during 1995. In the same week that HealthSouth completed a $70 million deal to buy ReadiCare, an occupational health chain with thirty-seven centers, it announced a $270 million transaction with an imaging company. This deal was for Health Images, an Atlanta company that operates forty-nine imaging centers in the United States and six in the United Kingdom. At the same time, Scrushy announced plans to put imaging centers in three hundred cities in this country.

In 1997, the company agreed to buy Horizon/CMS Healthcare of Albuquerque, its largest competitor, for more than $1.6 billion. With the purchase, HealthSouth gained an additional 33 inpatient rehabilitation hospitals, 58 specialty hospitals and subacute units, and 282 outpatient rehabilitation centers.

Like many consolidators, Scrushy has been mindful of the government regulation side of healthcare. He's been a member of the certificate-of-need review board in his home state of Alabama, and is a confidant of Republican Speaker of the House Newt Gingrich. HealthSouth hasn't run into the for-profit/not-for-profit antagonism that Columbia encounters. Not-for-profit institutions aren't the lifeblood of rehabilitation, so they are not as threatened by the growth of HealthSouth (whose market capitalization tops $6 billion).

The company is an example of a corporate citizen that works hard in various charitable organizations, including United Cerebral Palsy and the Arthritis Foundation. Scrushy received the Arthritis Foundation's Humanitarian of the Year Award in 1994. Of course, that kind of visibility helps a company whose business is to rehabilitate patients.

ROLL-UPS THAT BENEFIT
FROM OTHERS' FAILURES

Although many entrepreneurs can make a success of leveraging economies of scale, healthcare has an added characteristic that makes roll-ups more appealing. In the restaurant business, for example, it's not a good strategy to expand by purchasing all of the failing restaurants around town. In fact, that would probably be a bad idea. But in healthcare, there's a significant undertow for bottom fishing. That's because it's usually cheaper to buy failing businesses that one believes will turn around than to start from scratch. It's the old "barriers to entry" argument.

Numerous examples abound, but perhaps the best is Vencor, a Louisville, Kentucky, firm started by a few former Humana executives. Humana had always been the area's premier healthcare corporation; it's also the state's second largest employer, whose headquarters, a huge pink palace, help define the Louisville skyline.

Although Humana had at one time tried to set a gold standard for healthcare delivery, its message got lost amid a power struggle between doctors, hospitals, and payers. Vencor's initial focus was clear. It targeted what might be considered a loophole in Medicare regulations. The federal program had a special payment provision for patients who were cared for in "long-term hospitals," wherein maladies often required being put on a ventilator. Because it took time and a great deal of therapy to wean patients off a ventilator, those patients needed a special payment mechanism. The restrictions on long-term hospitals were clear but, well, unclear. For one thing, the payment rate wasn't set as it was in other hospitals. Acute-care hospitals were under the onus of diagnosis-related groups when it came to payment; long-term hospitals weren't. However, there was a catch-22. Long-term hospitals couldn't collect their cost-based reimbursement until they were up and running for thirty days. For most, that would cause cash-flow problems. But not for a large corporation.

Vencor became that corporation and flourished by finding a singular niche. Although the hospitals didn't get paid for the first month, Vencor offset that with an admirable acquisition strategy. In an age of consolidation and overbuilding of hospitals, Vencor bought only hospitals on the verge of closing or those that had already shut their doors. Yet Vencor's executives leveraged that expertise into what is now one of the nation's largest long-term-care chains. It took a broader step into consolidating vertically and horizontally in late 1995, by buying Hillhaven, the nation's second largest nursing home company. The price of $1.9 billion was the highest ever paid for a long-term-care provider.

PRIVATIZATION OF
GOVERNMENT PROGRAMS

The government's privatization of healthcare services aids the growth of consolidation companies. Consolidation giants must learn early on how to work with the government, and if they can learn from that they get more government contracts. Both federal and state governments are increasingly contracting out to private enterprises for their health and welfare programs. They are less likely to contract with a fledgling local business than with a large one having an established track record in numerous locations.

Inmates don't have much choice in what they eat, so why should they enjoy choice in healthcare? This belief on the part of government has led to companies like America Service Group and Correctional Medical Systems, which outsource healthcare services to inmates. Outsourcing care to prisons and jails presents the same type of economies as in consolidating hospitals or physician practices. In fact, America Service's president and CEO is Scott Mercy, a former senior vice president with Columbia/HCA. In 1997, America Service joined Columbia's group purchasing program, allowing it to buy supplies at the same discounts that Columbia's hospitals receive.

As the government increasingly outsources to risk-bearing companies, correctional care is a natural step. Currently only about one-fourth of inmates receive healthcare services through private outsourcing contracts with providers, but that proportion is expected to increase at least as quickly as the inmate population is growing. The expanding prison system is ripe for efficient healthcare services; the U.S. inmate population doubled from the mid-1980s to the mid-1990s.

Healthcare services are provided to this group in the least cost-efficient, most fragmented way. But this is starting to change. It's an issue that cannot be cast aside. According to experts, some ten million inmates are released back into the community each year. Society would be better off if those providing healthcare services to inmates ensured that they leave healthy, that is, free of infectious diseases and chronic health problems.

Another example of a consolidator is National Mentor, which moves mentally retarded persons from nursing homes or institutions into private homes. National Mentor was a private company until it was bought by Magellan Health Services in 1995. Magellan is the former Charter Medical, an Atlanta corporation that went through some financially trying times in the early 1990s. The company and its competitors had built way too many private psychiatric hospitals in the 1980s. That and too much debt caused Charter to wind its way through a painful restructuring, which included a Chapter 11 bankruptcy reorganization. By 1996, Charter had transformed itself into a new company, Magellan, that was negotiating risk contracts from both private and public payers.

Magellan's woes in its former life stemmed largely from managed care's cutbacks in paying for inpatient psychiatric care. When private companies like Charter Medical, Comprehensive Care, and National Medical Enterprises (now Tenet Healthcare) built mental health hospitals, they relied on private-pay patients. For a while it was a great business, because private-pay always paid more than government sources like Medicare and Medicaid. Insurers asked few questions, and mental health benefits were plentiful.

Then the worm turned. There were too many hospitals and not enough patients, prompting some hospitals to pay physicians and referral sources "bounties" for admissions. Psych providers abused the golden goose, and the eggs stopped coming as managed care companies sprang up everywhere to slash inpatient admissions. At the height of the industry, around early 1990, Texas had about eighty psychiatric hospitals. In some locations within Houston, psych hospitals were built literally down the street from each other.

After cracking down on the industry's most obvious abuses, at least half of those facilities closed and many more continue to struggle with low occupancy. Disturbed adolescents and adults could be treated less expensively and more effectively out of the hospital, and what had been a normal thirty-day stay fell to an average of five days.

Having pared back drastically, the retooled companies like Magellan started focusing on government Medicaid and state contracts for psychiatric care. Magellan is now getting into juvenile justice, converting some of its empty psychiatric hospitals into treatment centers for young offenders. With its expertise in psychiatric care, the company can go to the heart of problems that plague sex offenders, a common problem among those housed in these buildings.

Magellan has strong support on Wall Street, attracting two of the Street's brand-name investors, the husband and wife team of Darla Moore and Richard Rainwater. Rainwater made multimillions on his Columbia/HCA bet, which only gilded his reputation even further. Rainwater and Moore bought a 12 percent interest in Magellan just after the company took a controlling interest in Green Spring Health Services. Although Charter Medical had tried to mount several bids to get into the Medicaid contracting business, that effort never jelled until it partnered with Green Spring, which had punctured its way in, giving Charter an easier route to those funds.

Other health related roll-ups are achieving similar economies of scale. For example, a Louisville organization called Res-Care started buying clinics and agencies that provide services to persons with disabilities and at-risk youth. This part of society, which most people would rather forget, benefits from the same economic laws as home health-care or hospital services. Res-Care buys group homes. Res-Care entered New Jersey when it was selected to help move individuals into community services as part of a downsizing of the largest state facility, in Princeton.

Another hospital CEO who moved into another type of roll-up is Gene Burleson, formerly of American Medical International, which is now part of Tenet Healthcare. Burleson joined GranCare, a long-term care company, and then segued to Vitalink, where he now serves as CEO. Vitalink merged in 1997 with TeamCare, a pharmacy subsidiary of GranCare, making it the second largest publicly traded institutional pharmacy company, with annual revenues of $420 million.

Home healthcare can fit into a number of roll-up strategies. For example, it works well with long-term and subacute care, both of which are out-of-hospital services. Integrated Health Services, one of the largest postacute care providers, bought a large Medicare home healthcare agency, First American Health Care, in 1996 for $154 million. Integrated took advantage of a bad situation; First American had been put on the block after its founders were convicted of Medicare fraud earlier in the year.

Capitation may encourage the development of single-niche roll-ups. HMOs in the purest sense do global capitation: they pay one flat amount for all healthcare services. However, many are becoming capitation specialists in which they provide medical surgical services but spin off laboratory or psychiatric services to other firms. In many cases, those companies are roll-ups.

What follows is a look at other provider roll-ups by segment.

Assisted Living

Consolidators zoned in on the need for "assisted living" facilities, which are housing communities that provide personal support services for the elderly. The facility's staff helps residents with bathing, dressing, or medication in a homelike setting that isn't as intensive as skilled nursing care.

Some assisted-living residences also provide services for individuals who are incontinent or have Alzheimer's disease or other forms of dementia. These centers provide more than the general room and board of a retirement center, but not the full-fledged care of a nursing home. This is another fragmented industry, although spending in it was estimated at $14 billion in 1997. This is a nascent sector of the long-term-care industry, and as such, it has huge capital needs. By mid-1997, eighteen assisted-living companies were publicly traded, and about a dozen more nursing home companies were expanding into this niche. It is largely a private-pay business, which operators like. However, in about twenty states, assisted-living care is subsidized by Medicaid, giving the consolidator a steady stream of capital. Where it's not subsidized, developers depend on middle-to-upper-income residents who can pay for the services out of their own savings or income.

These companies depend on the laws of supply and demand. The aging of America is creating burgeoning needs for housing, personal care services, and medical services. The age group seventy-five and older is one of the fastest growing segments of the population; according to the Census Bureau, it's expected to increase from 13.2 million in 1990 to 16.6 million in the year 2000, a 26 percent increase. Those in the eighty-five-and-over age group are growing at an even faster rate. That fraternity is expected to expand from 3.1 million in 1990 to 4.3 million in 2000, a 39 percent spurt.

In spite of the demand, most states don't have enough nursing homes because of certificate-of-need regulations. Those laws mandate that new nursing homes go through a state approval process. Nursing homes average 95 percent occupancy, and hundreds of them maintain long waiting lists. In most states, operators can build assisted-living facilities without state approval.

One assisted-living roll-up emanated from another roll-up. Vencor helped start Atria, and Vencor's chairman doubles as Atria's chairman. Both are based in Louisville.

Dentists

You can apply to dentists all of the factors pushing physicians into PPMs. But the fragmentation is even greater. Of the approximately 140,000 dentists in the United States, only 12 percent are in practices with more than two dentists, according to the American Dental Association.

Consolidators include Orthodontic Centers of America, Gentle Dental, Apple Orthodontix, and American Dental Partners. Dental services are a growing business, generating $46.5 billion in 1995. That's expected to nearly double to $83.3 billion by 2005, according to Price

Waterhouse estimates, for an annual growth rate of 6 percent. Consolidation among payers is likely to prod dentists into larger systems. Currently, more than twenty million Americans are covered by prepaid dental plans, and that number is increasing by more than 20 percent a year, according to the National Association of Dental Plans. Employers are more likely to contract with a prepaid dental plan— also called a dental maintenance organization (DMO)—because it gives them a cap on dental expenditures.

The largest, Delta Dental Plans Association, which covers twenty-eight million individuals, is a fairly loose association of plans. More organized and aggressive consolidators, such as United Dental Care, are making acquisitions and expanding their dental networks. Consolidation here moves dentists into the information age. They're still laggards, processing just 10 percent of their claims electronically.

Home Healthcare

Many home healthcare services are already provided through some kind of roll-up. Mom-and-pop home healthcare agencies may always have a place in the industry, but consolidators entered the race in the 1980s and bought groups or opened their own storefront agencies. Nursing is the biggest component of home healthcare, generating an estimated $20 billion annually. The largest company, Apria Health Group, was formed through the merger of two home healthcare companies, Abbey Healthcare Group and Homedco Group in 1995. Another company, American HomePatient in Nashville, targets small to medium-sized markets. During 1996, it acquired thirty-three companies with eighty-eight centers and raised $67 million in a secondary stock offering.

One of the backbones of this industry, the Visiting Nurse Associations, has gone through its own wrenching changes. VNAs are among the oldest home healthcare providers in the United States, and the only large entity composed of not-for-profit agencies. Although they operate in nearly every large metropolitan market, until about five years ago they didn't work together to leverage efficiencies or bid aggressively for managed care contracts. As a result, many of them sold or signed affiliation agreements with local hospital systems. Of 151 VNAs surveyed in 1996 by the Visiting Nurse Association of America, 72, or nearly one-half, had entered an affiliation, merger, or acquisition agreement with another group. "If they don't line up with a larger system in the community, then they'll be cut out of referrals," said Lorrie Briggs, the association's membership director.[1]

Many are better off being part of a hospital where the continuum of care eases patient anxiety. Hospital-based home healthcare has been a financial win for many hospitals because of the way Medicare reimburses them. Hospitals get paid on a cost-based reimbursement for home care services, and on a fixed payment for inpatient services. With a home healthcare division, hospitals could shift some of their costs—administration, information systems, etc.—to the home healthcare agency and get at least partial reimbursement for it.

Because only about three cents of every dollar spent on healthcare goes for home healthcare, this industry has not received as much attention from information companies as hospitals have, since the latter have more capital to spend. But the potential is great. If Federal Express can equip its drivers with palm-sized computers for processing information, so can consolidators equip home healthcare nurses.

The growth of this industry has attracted the attention of Congress. In 1987, Medicare spent $1.9 billion on home care. By 1995, this had grown to $14.5 billion annually as technology and payment pressures pushed patients out of the hospital faster. Although more care may move to the home, patients are likely to have a bigger hand in the care.

Hospice

One of the more interesting roll-ups is Vitas, a hospice care company. Hospice care has grown in popularity and benefits from a Medicare funding mechanism that allows physicians to put terminally ill patients in hospice. The number of patients receiving hospice care doubled to 300,000 between 1985 and 1994, according to Medicare officials.

In talking about how healthcare has changed from being a community service to a commodity, it's interesting to consider hospice care. If any care is viewed as a community service, it would be hospice, and yet corporate principles are alive and well in this segment. However, end-of-life expenditures are a frequent topic of debate on healthcare costs. Medicare spends 28 percent of its budget on patients who are in their last year of life. But "efforts to ration end-of-life care in the name of cost containment run up against our relative inability to identify who really is at the end of their life," commented Bruce Vladek of the Health Care Financing Administration.[2] HCFA, which operates the Medicare program, knows a bit about the costs of dying patients; the program pays for care associated with 65 percent of all deaths in the United States.

Nursing Homes

The demographics of this industry are compelling, but it has never generated the profits of hospital or physician care because of the lack of strong government funding. Only eight cents of every dollar spent on healthcare goes for nursing home care. Medicaid is the biggest payer of nursing home care, and the per diems don't make for lucrative profit margins, even in a roll-up situation.

About 75 percent of all nursing homes are owned by for-profit chains, compared to only 15 percent of hospitals. This $80 billion industry boasts high occupancy rates, usually in the 90 percent range, compared to 50–60 percent in hospitals. That could increase, which would prompt the need for well-capitalized chains that can build new facilities. This is problematic in states where certificate-of-need laws restrict nursing home construction.

Even so, by the year 2030, nearly 20 percent of Americans will be over age sixty-five, according to federal estimates. That's up from about 12 percent today. The burst in demand coupled with the need for more intensive medical services is bound to boost the call for nursing homes as well as assisted-living centers.

For a number of years, Beverly Enterprises has been the nation's largest nursing home chain, with more than six hundred facilities and more than $3 billion in annual revenues. At one time, Hospital Corporation of America owned an interest in the Fort Smith, Arkansas, chain as it was expanding rapidly in the 1980s. However, the 1990s were a decade of some retrenchment for Beverly, which has diversified into other long-term-care services such as hospice and assisted living.

On the long-term-care front, the fastest growing company has been Integrated Health Services of Owings Mills, Maryland. Integrated bills itself as "America's leader in postacute care." Its services encompass subacute care, home healthcare, inpatient and outpatient rehabilitation, respiratory therapy, hospice care, diagnostic services, and skilled nursing services. With more than one thousand locations in forty states, the company's network includes 180 nursing homes and other medical facilities, 145 subacute care units within facilities, 600 home health service locations, and nearly 300 other locations providing rehabilitation, respiratory, and mobile radiology services. The company has been an extremely acquisitive consolidator. In 1997, it expanded through acquisitions of Community Care of America, which operated fifty-four nursing facilities mostly located in rural communities, for $94 million, and one of the largest home healthcare companies, RoTech Medical, for approximately $915 million.

Workers' Compensation

A $60 billion dollar industry by most analysts' estimates, workers' compensation services have all the ingredients to make it ripe for consolidation. Consolidators can bring economies to a business that is known for its wasteful spending. In terms of government regulation, it's a quagmire, but a national consolidator has a better chance to get a handle on it. Each state has different payment mechanisms and regulations for workers' comp. The federal government requires employers to provide medical care for work-related injuries at no cost to the employee. Many large employers self-insure, which makes them anxious to outsource this business to an expert consolidator.

Because the employee has no out-of-pocket costs, there is little incentive to use fewer services. In fact, some studies have shown a large percentage of medically unnecessary services in this area, prompted either by disgruntled employees or profiteering providers. Enter the consolidators, eager to manage the available information and risk. One of the largest companies in this niche is a PPM firm introduced briefly in Chapter Two, OccuSystems, which merged with CRA Managed Care. Together they formed Concentra, which represents another broad consolidation that combines the provider and insurer sides of the industry. As was mentioned in Chapter Three, the Dallas firm was started by a veteran in the consolidation industry, John Carlyle, formerly of Medical Care International, the nation's largest chain of surgery centers.

These types of consolidations pave the way for other, broader applications. If Concentra can make it work within the niche of workers' comp, then larger managed care and provider companies may be able to make it work as well.

CHAPTER EIGHT

Faster, Cheaper, and Smarter

I n a concrete-boxed business park situated just under the flight path into Dallas/Fort Worth International Airport, a small healthcare company is trying to change the way medicine is practiced. Four seminar planners work in small cubicles along the back windows of the cramped corporate offices, calling surgeons throughout the country. They're scheduling seminars to teach surgeons how to transfer their surgical skills from a hospital operating suite to the comfort (and, incidentally, lower-cost setting) of their own offices.

"We start with one market as a beta site, from which we develop a 'cookie-cutter' model that can be duplicated in other markets," Angela Juengerman, marketing director of Medical Alliance, explains about the seminars. Surgeons pay Medical Alliance between $395 and $995 for one of more than two dozen Saturday conferences, each of which teaches them a specific surgical procedure. The key is this: the surgeons already are experts in their trade.

Medical Alliance teaches them everything they need to know about transferring their well-honed and precise skills from a high-cost setting to a low-cost one without compromising quality. The change in setting diverts millions of dollars that now flow from one provider segment to another. A hospital's loss may be an insurance company's gain.

Healthcare consolidators know that healthcare is a cash-rich business that goes through funding peaks and valleys. Profits are in the timing. The faster a provider can adapt to a new cost-effective technology, the richer it becomes. It's a race against time—before reimbursement catches up. When the federal government is doing the reimbursement, it's not much of a contest because the bureaucracy churns at such a slow rate. Taking advantage of this disparity in pricing especially benefits large, consolidated players. They can adjust and disseminate new technology much more quickly than small providers who aren't part of a system.

Who will profit in this race? It varies, depending on which organization has the biggest lock on the technology. Nearly all of the capital equipment manufacturers are making devices that are smarter, smaller, and cheaper than yesterday's counterparts. This evolution plays into the hands of providers, recouping savings far quicker than the payers adjust their payment levels. Today's reimbursement is always based in some form on yesterday's costs.

The repercussions affect two ubiquitous themes in healthcare: money and quality of care. Medical Alliance, which has been acquiring other third-party providers, provides a list of about thirty procedures that can safely be done in a physician's office. Knowing that much of healthcare reimbursement is "venue-based," meaning that insurers pay $3,500 for a minimally invasive procedure done in the hospital while in a physician's office the same procedure will cost them less than $1,000, consolidators understand that where there's disparity, there's opportunity for profit.

As discussed in Chapter One, the successful consolidators are the ones that excel at managing capital, information, risk, and government regulation. Glomming onto highly profitable high-tech procedures is a hallmark of these companies, on both the provider and the vendor sides. Although government regulation is a negative factor to most consolidators, it is their friend when it comes to reimbursement. The government is slow to adapt to lower cost structures, which gives consolidators an opportunity to leverage capital and information for higher profits.

This pliability in pricing makes healthcare unique in the U.S. economy. Buyers may haggle over the price of a Chrysler minivan as they shop from one car dealer to the next, but rarely are the price swings as wide as in healthcare. Again, these differences create enormous opportunities for healthcare entrepreneurs, or "entrepreneurial therapy managers," as some describe them. As technology advances and consolidators learn from the market, the disparity grows wider. That's because the dimension of time enters the equation. Unlike consumers who compare the price of a minivan from dealer to dealer, the payers in healthcare rarely shop for the best "real-time" prices. And if the cost of a particular procedure drops, providers aren't likely to advertise that fact. They'll likely collect the profits.

THE $30 BILLION MARKET
FOR HEART SURGERY

In Nashville, large maroon and white billboards blast the news: "New Heart Surgery. Faster Recovery. Less Risk. Less Cost." Beneath that is the name Columbia Centennial Hospital and the 800 number of Columbia/HCA Healthcare. The message is blunt and prompts consumers to make the connection themselves: faster recovery, less risk, less cost—what more do I want from medicine?

It's no accident that a consolidator like Columbia leaped at new technologies that would bring money to the bottom line. The most dramatic and profitable could be the MIDCAB, another healthcare acronym, this one standing for minimally invasive direct coronary artery bypass. Columbia teamed with CardioThoracic Systems, a Cupertino, California, company that has developed tools to do the "beating heart" bypass surgery. Officials say it could replace the current bypass surgery now being done 600,000 times a year. It also may replace many of the 350,000 angioplasties done annually. In angioplasty, a physician inserts a balloon and inflates it to open up clogged arteries; it is a less invasive technique than bypass surgery. The problem is, 40 percent of them fail in the first six months.

Yet surgeons and patients often opt for the less-invasive angioplasty before going to bypass surgery. Here's why. Current bypass surgery involves cutting through the breast bone (a sternotomy), cracking the rib cage, and stopping the heart. The patient is kept alive through the use of a heart/lung machine. Now, instead of the fifteen-inch incision in traditional bypass surgery, MIDCAB surgeons make a two- to three-inch incision between two of the ribs just below the patient's nipple. Then the physician works in that small space, taking a nearby artery and grafting it onto the heart, which remains beating throughout the procedure, independently of any machine. This cuts down on time harvesting an artery from a leg, a process that CardioThoracic's president Richard Ferrari says can take as much as an hour. Operating room time, which costs about $60 a minute, is shaved to twenty minutes.

Ferrari also foresees a large number of patients over the next few years not requiring the heart/lung machine. MIDCAB patients don't need it. He notes that 70 percent of the complications in open heart surgery, such as strokes, bleeding, and inflammation, arise from the need to use that piece of equipment. Many MIDCAB patients are not even sent to the cardiac care unit, or the intensive care unit, which saves even more money. In fact, the patient is usually discharged in forty-eight hours and back to work in two weeks, versus a one-week hospital stay and nine to twelve weeks off work in the case of traditional surgery.

The financial bottom line was detailed for us by a surgeon from Lenox Hill Hospital in New York. Medicare now pays the hospital a global fee, which includes both the hospital and physician payments, of about $33,000 for bypass surgery. In contrast, private insurers reimburse at about $38,000, and managed care payers pay a lower amount, about $18,000. The MIDCAB costs between $8,000 and $10,000, giving providers a very high profit margin that likely will stay that way for some time. Why? Because the Society of Thoracic Surgeons has stated that a MIDCAB bypass is still a bypass and requires as much skill or more to perform the new operation. If Medicare does review reimbursement, it will not be for a few years. In the meantime, large systems that train their physicians in MIDCAB and market it to patients profit nicely.

CardioThoracic got a break, enabling it to hit the market quickly. The FDA exempted the first three tools of the MIDCAB kit—the Access Platform, the Stabilizer, and the Lima Loop—from required filing of a 510(k) in May 1996, which gave them a quick entry to the U.S. market.

Columbia could recoup as much as $20,000 per procedure when the difference in costs is weighed. Surgeons at Columbia's Medical City Dallas Hospital, its largest in the Dallas/Fort Worth area, and Centennial Hospital, its largest in Nashville, were among the first to perform the procedure. CardioThoracic also agreed to customize its training program to teach cardiac surgeons at Columbia's ninety-five cardiac surgery centers, and to track outcomes and cost-efficiency data on their patients with a clinical patient registry.

What CardioThoracic and other players are aiming for is the 13.5 million Americans who suffer from coronary artery disease and problems with current treatments. In addition to being expensive, cardiac surgery is invasive. Angioplasty is relatively noninvasive, but its efficacy is limited because the veins frequently clog up again, an occurrence called restenosis.

The business scenario strikes a familiar theme: a high-volume procedure commercialized by an aggressive publicly held company. It sounds like what happened in the 1980s when United States Surgical Corporation quickly began training surgeons to remove the gallbladder through laparoscopic surgery. No longer were patients having their bellies cut open; they could now go home with two small Band-aids.

When U.S. Surgical came out with the tools that enable surgeons to do gallbladder surgery through two tiny incisions, it profited. Now the world's largest manufacturer and marketer of surgical staplers, it established the standard of care for minimally invasive surgery. The company has had periods of wild profitability; in 1996 it cranked up gross margins of nearly 60 percent. It expedited the advent of computer-assisted surgery, which healthcare organizations are beginning to demand because it is more cost-effective and delivers better long-term results.

In fact, the MIDCAB could be even more lucrative than the switch in laparoscopic surgery. The earlier type of surgery was typically done on a younger population, non-Medicare patients. It was reimbursed by private payers, which are far more likely to cut reimbursement quickly if costs drop. CardioThoracic developed a program, called the Comprehensive Optimal Revascularization (COR), to educate surgeons on the technique. Of the seven COR institutes now set up, two are in Columbia/ HCA Healthcare hospitals. So the MIDCAB is being pushed by Cardio-Thoracic to gain rapid commercialization, and by Columbia as well.

The MIDCAB isn't the only emerging alternative to bypass surgery. CardioGenesis, a Sunnyvale, California, firm, is putting its R&D dollars into percutaneous myocardial revascularization, called PMR. This procedure uses a catheter-based percutaneous laser system, which is used in a cath lab while the patient is still conscious. This in turn may compete with another emerging heart procedure, called transmyocardial revascularization. TMR also can be performed on a beating heart using a special laser device to create pathways within the heart muscle. The laser bores between fifteen and thirty holes in the oxygen-deprived regions of the heart muscle.

Thirty-five years after the first laser was discovered, its versatility is finally coming home to heart patients. In TMR, it zaps the heart every three minutes, causing a tiny geyser of blood to erupt, a process that actually strengthens the heart by creating more routes for blood to flow. PLS Systems of Milford, Massachusetts, is one of the biggest vendors in this niche. Again, the financial incentives are strong. The surgery takes about one-third the time of traditional bypass, and the total cost is $11,000–$15,000 per procedure, well below the average reimbursement of about $18,000 to $40,000.

Because many of these procedures will be reimbursed by Medicare, the profit margin could be a bonanza for physicians and hospitals. One option is being sold by Heartport, Redwood City, California, which developed the tools for what's called PortAccess. This system uses a set of specialized catheters that give a surgeon access and visualization of the heart through "ports," or small incisions in the patient's chest. Heartport executives describe it as "bloodless surgery" that's more like angioplasty or a cardiac cath procedure. Because this surgery is fairly complex and many heart surgeons aren't familiar with minimally invasive surgery techniques, Heartport set up large training centers in the United States and Sweden.

Regardless of whether cardiac patients go with the "beating heart," TMR, PMR, or "port" surgery, it's clear that one of the consolidators' biggest revenue generators is undergoing substantial change. Consolidators will affect changes in heart surgery, by latching on to one or all of the minimally invasive techniques. What's more, they'll likely negotiate competitive prices with the vendors, ensuring that costs don't get out of control. That was one of the problems when gallbladder surgery became less invasive. Payers complained it wasn't any cheaper. Even though the procedure sliced the length of the hospital stay, the expensive tools drove the cost back up.

The lightning speed with which consolidators adopted procedures like the MIDCAB demonstrates how large organizations can integrate cost-effective procedures into their organizations. Now that the emphasis is on controlling costs instead of prices, these technologies make their way to market much faster. This is exciting, considering what's on the horizon. Artificial bones, skin, organs, and blood are all on the cusp of reality. In tandem with minimally invasive and computer-assisted surgery, the way patients are repaired in the future is about to be revolutionized.

OUTSMARTING THE FEDS

In the late 1980s, some ophthalmologists started becoming millionaires. Why? Healthcare's biggest payers, which are the federal and state governments, couldn't adjust their payment methods nearly as quickly as the market adapted. Using laser surgery, eye surgeons suddenly were performing a cataract procedure in ten minutes. It was common for them to do dozens a day, at $2,500 a pop. However, Medicare was still reimbursing these surgeons as if it took a couple of hours to do the procedure and the patient were staying a week in the hospital. The federal agency couldn't adjust payment as quickly as the technology took hold. In the meantime, profits flowed. The only question was which ophthalmologists could attract the most patients; some scrambled to entice patients with limousine rides back and forth to the patient's home.

Even though more than one-third of a hospital's revenues come from the burgeoning field of outpatient care, Medicare bureaucrats have spent the past decade trying to move away from cost-based reimbursement, which rewards them for spending more. Methodologies for figuring out a more efficient way to pay providers have come and gone with virtually no progress. It is also to the providers' advantage that at the federal level one hand doesn't know what the other is doing. The FDA, which approves money-saving technologies such as lasers or minimally invasive clamps for sale in the United States, is far removed from the Health Care Financing Administration, which sets payment. If the FDA clears the way to market a device that cuts the cost of providing a specific treatment, HCFA doesn't subsequently adjust payment for that treatment throughout its DRG payment system.

In most free markets, technological improvements that cut costs usually yield price fallout. It, in turn, typically increases volume. For example, falling chip prices affected the price of personal computers. When fax technology became cheaper, prices fell, and soon nearly everyone had them. But it doesn't work that way in healthcare because Medicare needs at least two years to change the reimbursement for a DRG.

We are poised for an era of breakthrough technology that will be developed and marketed by the best-funded companies in history. After years of decrying the slow pace of medical device approvals, the dam seems to have broken. The FDA, which cleared forty-five hundred devices in fiscal 1996, eliminated its backlog of 510(k) devices under review for more than ninety days. It reviewed them in an average of one hundred days, twenty-seven days faster than in the previous year. The 510(k) process applies to already-approved devices that are being reviewed for use in a new procedure and treatment. In terms of new technology, device makers must receive a premarket approval. This still takes more than a year for the FDA to review. However, the time dropped during 1996 from an average of 606 days to 568.

Observers credit both the FDA and manufacturers for turning the tide. Amid pressure from Congress, the FDA began to look at its approval process. Sales in the medical device industry were flattening in the mid-1990s, and politicians knew this could be bad because these companies provided thousands of high-paying manufacturing jobs.

MANAGERS OF CONSOLIDATED MANUFACTURERS

Successful device manufacturers realize that the regulatory hurdles of this business revolve around the FDA. In a consolidating industry, the companies can afford to spend less on marketing against a dozen competitors and more on how to get the product to market. Many of these companies are actively working with the FDA to submit clinical data in a format that reviewers prefer, thus expediting the process. Not only did the FDA institute its own changes, but vendors became more proficient at maneuvering through the FDA hoops and hurdles. Large consolidated companies can dedicate legal and regulatory staffs to FDA matters, something a small company would struggle to do.

FDA staffers are under pressure to approve new, break-through devices that improve patient care. Now, economists and political pundits are predicting dire times ahead because of forecast cuts in Medicare. Yet providers can adjust their costs downward much faster than HCFA can similarly adjust its payments. From the time that a change is even suggested, it must go through HCFA bureaucrats, be published in the *Federal Register,* go through a comment period, and be considered even further. Even after going through all those steps, some reimbursement changes are never made. This time lag could become more important in a consolidating medical device industry. Weaker sisters will fall out as only a handful of medical device companies grow stronger.

From a quality standpoint, this is good. It means that instead of spending money on marketing to distinguish themselves from the dozen or so other players making Holter monitors, manufacturers focus their capital on research and development. Most of the giant steps in capital equipment technology came before the explosion of me-too manufacturers in the 1980s.

Medical suppliers are mirroring the consolidation of the provider side. As hospital systems enlarge, they tend to trim their list of suppliers. By funneling volume to just one or two vendors in a particular product niche, hospital systems—or the group purchasing organizations that negotiated for them—learned that they could get better pricing. This helped the larger players, which could trade equipment at discounts for purchasing volume. It also created larger companies that established a franchise. In retail, they call large chains "category killers." Companies like Medtronic, Boston Scientific, and U.S. Surgical established franchises in their niche, expanding through acquisition and gaining name recognition and trust among their customers.

In 1995 alone, Boston Scientific bought an angioplasty company (SciMed), a catheter maker (Heart Technology), and an intravascular ultrasound firm (CVIS), all of which reaffirmed its commitment to the field of heart surgery. Medtronic cemented its reputation with pacemakers. Then, when it entered the stent business, long-time customers were already comfortable with the company. It was like learning a new technology from a trusted friend.

THE THERMO MODEL

"You don't have to worry about the banking, the legal problems," says Hal Kirshner, president and CEO of Trex Medical. Meeting with a group of clinical and industry analysts in Dallas, Kirshner is proud of the accomplishments his company has made in digital imaging and its latest product enhancements. Holding a slide projector remote control, he switches it from hand to hand, enthusiastically telling the Thermo story, how it has $2 billion cash, and what that kind of financial stability has done for Trex.

Trex is a consolidator, having rolled up four companies that make X-ray machines, mammography equipment, and cath labs. More importantly, Trex is a consolidator within a consolidator. Its majority owner is Thermo Electron, which we also met in Chapter Two along with Trex and Kirshner. An ardent salesman, Kirshner distributes a video about Trex that features a Star Wars theme, telling customers that the company is "the best of the best."

More manufacturers are likely to follow the consolidation example of Thermo Electron, which set up its own research and development organization in Waltham, Massachusetts, for a family of technology companies. A billowing cloud on the consolidators' horizon, Thermo developed a template for success that allows it to manage the four critical factors we have repeatedly mentioned: capital, information, risk, and government regulation.

With $2 billion in cash and a proven record for taking companies public, Thermo can access capital and manage it aggressively. Thermo buys technology companies with a singular strategy: acquire money-losing or marginally profitable enterprises, and feed them with capital and expertise. Then, spin them out as publicly held companies while retaining a substantial stake whose value is buoyed by the public offering. Thermo has $2 billion in annual revenues, formidable indeed. Yet, its true size is much larger. This is because it holds controlling interests in twenty publicly traded companies. All of them were at one time part of Thermo Electron but were groomed and pushed out of the nest to soar on their own—six in 1996 alone.

Thermo Electron represents just one version of a consolidation strategy to own equity interests in a family of companies. In other versions, it's manifested by a web of joint ventures between doctors and hospitals, hospitals and vendors, vendors and research institutions, research institutions and doctors, and back again and through. One Thermo spin-out is ThermoCardio, which makes the only FDA-approved left ventricle assist device. The implantable device takes over pumping of the heart, enabling a patient to stay alive while awaiting a heart transplant. In two countries, England and Sweden, it is being used as a permanent heart device, so patients don't need a transplant. Thermo hopes the FDA will do the same in the United States. Actually, Thermo started funding an effort to develop an artificial heart way back in 1966. The company invested in nearly twenty years of development before gaining approval to sell it, and only recently has it been able to capitalize on the potential commercially.

Consolidators can make that kind of long-term commitment to develop breakthrough products. Thermo can also offer its managers the financial incentives to excel. "We are an entrepreneurial company, and we encourage all of our scientists and managers to move on to as many areas as they can. As a matter of fact, we end up spinning out the companies whenever we develop a new market, and we give participation to the managers and the scientists of their own company. We give them options in their own company," said Thermo's CFO John Hatsopoulos.[1] Those types of perks—stock options, 401(K) plans—help Thermo companies, and other publicly held consolidators, lure talent. If a manager or scientist with Hewlett-Packard is reluctant to leave because of its strong retirement or investment plan, the Thermo company can offer similar incentives. It works both ways, though; the incentives can be golden handcuffs that prevent a drain of talented workers.

In terms of government regulation, Thermo knows the ins and outs of dealing with the FDA. However, it also is particularly astute at drawing government grants to help fund its research and development costs. The company spends 7–10 percent of its sales on R&D, and about one-half of that flows in from government or other outside grants. The power in Thermo stems from the strong financial advantages of a big company.

The spin-out is freed from many administrative hassles, yet its managers are offered stock options as an incentive to grow the business. Thermo operates with "none of the handicaps of the big company, and the advantages of the big company. We provide, for a 1 percent fee, all of the services, all of the overhead services that the company needs to operate; and all they have to worry, basically, is about making and selling their own product," notes Hatsopoulos. "So we have the advantages of the small without the disadvantages of a small company."[2]

Another Thermo manager describes it as having a "rich uncle." This gives companies the confidence to take risks. Some small-company entrepreneurs know that they might be just one lawsuit away from extinction. Thanks to rich Uncle Thermo, companies can take on more risk. Most small companies try to keep at least two months of cash on hand. With Thermo as majority owner, the subsidiaries don't need to keep any cash on hand; they can invest it in other products or ventures.

In terms of information, Thermo shows how a collection of technology companies can learn from each other. Its companies develop everything from bomb detection devices, used in about seventy airports throughout the world, to lasers that remove unwanted hair. Thermo's R&D subsidiary, ThermoTrex, was started by scientists who worked on President Reagan's Star Wars system. Through the resources of Thermo, Trex took one of its product companies, Lorad, from less than 10 percent market share in 1990 to 35 percent in 1996, Kirshner says. As the imaging industry moves away from film to digital images, Trex is developing the equipment to handle that transition as well.

Often healthcare is slow to adopt the technology used in other industries. For example, fiber-optic scopes were used to examine the insides of airplanes in the 1950s. They arrived in medicine twenty years later, and it took another fifteen years before they revolutionized the field of surgery with a whole host of laparoscopic procedures.

For example, SpaceLabs Medical, one of the leading patient monitoring companies, grew out of NASA's work in monitoring the vital signs of astronauts. Some three thousand hospitals now have Space-Labs equipment in their facilities. Consolidators learn from the companies they acquire and leverage that into faster, cheaper, and smarter machines.

SMARTER MACHINES
AND LOWER-SKILLED WORKERS

Refinement of machines benefits providers not only in less expensive equipment but also in labor savings. More healthcare tasks are transitioning from higher-paid professionals to lower-paid technicians. For example, 95 percent of radiologic procedures don't need to be done by a radiologist. So maintains Jonathan Lehman, president and chief operating officer for InPhact.

InPhact was founded by Dr. Jeffrey A. Landman, a Nashville radiologist who owns one of the busiest imaging centers in town. At his center, radiologic technicians run the MRI, CT, ultrasound, and X-ray machines, and a physician views the "films," which really aren't films at all but digital images.

Landman founded InPhact, which provides outsourced radiologic services to other hospitals where a radiologist isn't on staff or is a "circuit rider" that comes around once or twice a week. By contracting with InPhact, the company slices one-third off the cost of those radiologic procedures. For example, the cost to create and store a typical radiology image is $14, according to InPhact figures. The biggest expense is the film itself, which costs about $6, followed by film storage, which is another $3.25 for each procedure. The remainder of the cost includes paper, chemistry, processing, and amortization of the camera itself. In contrast, with digital equipment used by InPhact, the same procedure costs $9.56, of which the biggest cost is $8 for digital capture and storage. Most of the cost is to amortize the digital capture device itself. "After that, your costs just drop off a cliff," Lehman noted.

Advanced Technology Laboratories, one of the leading developers of ultrasound machines, is developing an ultrasound machine that is so simple a hospital technician can learn to use it in one hour. The technician running scans on this machine doesn't need to be nearly as highly skilled as in the past; this translates into cheaper labor costs.

Manufacturers are developing many such products that take less time to learn. When Hewlett-Packard developed a new mammography machine, its developers realized that sonographers don't have time for long training sessions. So, the $110,000 machine comes with a Discman and training CD that operators can listen to at their leisure. HP executives also realized that hospitals and clinics see a lot of turnover in sonographers. New technicians can simply listen to the training disk and be up to speed in a few hours. What's more, the machine includes a modem port so that HP can send upgrades remotely when they're needed.

Smarter machines that do much of the thinking themselves are the future of medical care. Consider a new Pap smear technology made by Medlab Clinical Testing of Wilmington, Delaware. It uses artificial intelligence to find potentially cancerous cells that a cytologist might have missed. Computer-aided diagnostic devices are making a clinical technician's job easier and faster. Consolidators staff their operations with individuals whose skill mix matches the tasks at hand. Axing staff just for the sake of lowering costs doesn't work. In fact, a study by consultant E. C. Murphy of Amherst, New York, found that indiscriminate staffing cuts produce bad outcomes. The study looked at results from three thousand hospitals between 1993 and 1995 and found that hospitals cutting staff by 4 percent were 200 percent more likely to experience significant increase in mortality.

Despite the replacement of workers with smarter machines, employment in healthcare is not expected to slow; in fact, it is forecast to become one of the highest areas of growth. Why? With the aging of America, medical services continue to generate strong demand. In addition, Americans will not be demanding less from their healthcare providers as they age; they'll demand more. Healthcare services, business services, and social services—all areas that arguably overlap the medical industry—are expected to account for nearly one of every two jobs added to the economy between 1994 and 2005, the federal government reports. Nine of the ten fastest-growing industries in job growth are in one of those three segments, according to the Bureau of Labor Statistics' news release. As the baby boomers age, the need for healthcare services is expected to mushroom. For that reason, the single fastest growing industry will be health services, the federal agency reports. This segment will grow an astounding 84 percent in the decade from 1994 to 2005.

The top occupations? The government says they are personal and home care aides, followed by home health aides. Also in the top ten, amid a host of computer-related positions, will be physical therapists, occupational therapy assistants, and physical therapy assistants. Interestingly, these are all high-touch positions. Despite the move to high-tech, the need for high-touch remains a constant in healthcare.

It's interesting to note the government's projection about home care workers. Obviously, technology drives that movement. Medical equipment that's easy to use, portable, and inexpensive enables more patients to be taken care of at home. But the government, in the form of Medicare and Medicaid, may actually fight this movement by making home healthcare a service that is not cost-effective for providers. How can that be so? If the government's level of reimbursement remains low for home healthcare, providers may be unable to justify sending a patient home. Undoubtedly, some segments of home healthcare make it more expensive than care provided in a hospital setting. In a hospital, a nurse can efficiently visit dozens of patients. At home, it takes many hours longer to do the same.

This is where managed care may rationalize payment in a way the government has never been able to do. Medicare has been reluctant to pay for new technologies in the home because the agency believes it only increases the overall cost of the program. It can't rationalize any savings. For example, keeping a patient healthy at home is less expensive than having her in and out of the hospital. A one-week stay in a hospital may equal an entire year's salary for a home care aide.

This type of savings can be rationalized by risk-taking payers that look at the entire continuum of care. They're most interested in getting patients into the lowest-cost setting. Wherever that happens, technology follows.

In terms of actual jobs, the government also believes that registered nursing will have one of the largest growth spurts. Although the rate of growth will lag behind other occupations, the sheer number of nurses is expected to increase by nearly one-half million in the period between 1994 and 2005. The growth rate itself will be a rather modest 25 percent. But the government may be wrong here. The past rate of growth has been breathtaking, but hospitals are more likely to hire professionals with less training than they are registered nurses. However, the rate could increase greatly if nurses become physician extenders, prescribing medications and treating patients.

This would also coincide with another projection by the U.S. Labor Department. The workers of the future are more likely to receive short-term on-the-job training, rather than long-term or moderate-term. Clearly, tomorrow's healthcare workers will be trained quickly on technology that is fast and easy to use. The counterbalance to this is that as nurses lose their jobs to lower-paid professionals, unions will gain a foothold. That's already starting in California, where nurses are unionized at Kaiser Permanente and the Mercy Healthcare Sacrament System. The Service Employees International Union has identified healthcare as its biggest potential growth area for the future.

Just like any other workers, healthcare professionals are sure to fight back when technology and consolidation affect their income. As procedures become easier to do or more computerized, more nonphysicians try to step in. An example of this encroachment is already taking place in photorefractive keratectomy, a laser surgery on the eyes. Known as PRK, this surgery was approved in 1995 by the FDA to correct myopia, or near-sightedness. But qualifications for performing surgery are a matter of state law. In early 1997, both New Mexico and Idaho rebuffed attempts by optometrists to be permitted to perform PRK. Nonphysicians argue that computers are enabling them to perform the kinds of tasks that only surgeons could perform in the past. Surgeons are masters of touch, but through lasers and computerized programming fewer variables are left to the surgeon's individual skill. Optometrists claim that they can read the computerized programming as well as more highly compensated ophthalmologists. Of course, ophthalmologists are appalled at such a suggestion. It's not hard to imagine teenagers learning computer-assisted surgery on a CD-ROM and becoming experts at it before they even enter medical school.

FINDING THE RIGHT FINANCIAL INCENTIVES

In a consolidated healthcare environment, the financial incentives are shared more widely. Instead of a zero-sum game in which one group's profit robs another's, consolidators look for win-win scenarios. As healthcare becomes a more convergent industry, it manages the costs in a more convergent manner as well. Instead of trying to reinvent the wheel time after time, consolidators acquire the research they need by purchasing competitors or complementary technologies. This shortens the development cycle and gives providers more time to outrun reimbursement.

Since Medicare and Medicaid are moving toward contracting out to HMOs, the time equation narrows as more savvy buyers know and understand the costs involved in providing a service. This is why consolidators will find the right incentives among payers, providers, and suppliers. For example, to return to the vignette that opened this chapter, Medical Alliance was started by a former medical laser salesman, Paul Herchman. He saw the opportunities that lasers and other microendoscopy technology brought to the industry but was frustrated because the financial incentives didn't encourage providers to be efficient. It was 1987, shortly after Medicare established its prospective pricing systems, and Herchman wasn't having much luck selling capital equipment to hospitals. Although many hospitals were on their way to making record profits under the new DRG system, they didn't know it at the time. So great was their fear that they'd lose money under DRGs that they stopped spending money on new equipment. Doctors didn't want to buy these newfangled surgical tools either. Why? No one would reimburse them for buying a $60,000 laser or other new technology.

The dilemma is exactly why healthcare economics is so mixed up. Time after time, no incentive exists to save money. Even though procedures could be done less expensively in a physician's office, there was no incentive to do so. The hospital didn't want to lose a steady revenue stream. The physician would be paid the same regardless of where the procedure was done, so why should she spend her money on a new technology? The insurance company would have an incentive, but why go through all the hassle when the costs could simply be passed on to the employer or beneficiary?

Managed care coupled with entrepreneurial zeal made Herchman's dream possible. He's still involved in medical technology, but now he buys them and contracts with physicians to use them. Then he bills the insurance company or the patient.

It's been slow going. Sitting in the tapestry chairs of his spacious office, Herchman describes how it took six long years to get a contract with Blue Cross and Blue Shield of Texas, the state's largest health insurer with more than 1.2 million covered lives. Actually, Herchman said it took the company an average of four years to get each of its

Blue Cross contracts, but now that Medical Alliance has contracts with some 125 managed care organizations, the bandwagon is rolling. Since moving to new offices in the business park, the company has doubled its staff and is cramped for room.

With managed care on its side, the company has the physicians by their wallets. For example, Medical Alliance has a contract with a managed care plan in St. Louis. If a plan enrollee walks into his St. Louis physician's office and the physician recommends a certain procedure on Medical Alliance's list, the insurer tells the doctor that he can perform the procedure, but it has to be done in his own office and the doctor must use Medical Alliances equipment. Medical Alliance comes into the doctor's office, sets up the needed equipment, and lets the doctor get to work.

In most cases, the physician receives the same fee from the managed care organization that he would receive for performing the same procedure in a hospital or outpatient surgery center, or in some cases an extra $100 to $150 as an incentive to do it in the office. The old conventional wisdom: consolidators outrun technology to grab lucrative profits from uninformed payers. The new conventional wisdom: consolidators share risk with payers to take advantage of new technology in ways that benefit patients and payers alike.

CHAPTER NINE

Investing in Structural Technological Leaps

New Jersey patient pauses at a framed window box, the only opening between the crowded waiting room and the inner sanctum of the physician's office. She hands the clerk something that looks like a credit card, bearing the name of her insurer, Prudential HealthCare. The clerk swipes the card through a small point-of-sale terminal.

The terminal looks like those boxes in thousand of grocery stores, card shops, and clothing boutiques where clerks or consumers swipe through credit cards. Technology is finally knocking on healthcare's door. By making as few as five or six keystrokes, the physician's office clerk completes one of eight different transactions, ranging from approval for a particular procedure to referral to a specialist.

Rather than waiting for hours or days for a confirmation from the insurance company, the transaction is completed in fifteen seconds. "They don't have to call; they don't have to fax," says Deborah Hammond, Prudential's vice president of medical management systems support. "It's the same speed as the ATM." The process not only saves grief for the provider, the patient, and the insurer, but it saves money as well.

Prudential, one of the nation's largest health insurers, figures it costs 25–50 cents per transaction in this system compared with between $3–$12 under the paper system. Multiply that by the thousands of transactions processed, and the savings are startling. "The system more than paid for itself in the first year," Hammond says.

Systems of this type represent the first line of data gathering and electronic transactions as large healthcare consolidators flex their financial muscle. Prudential is spending about $500 million a year on information technology as it races ahead in a business fixed on squeezing out cost without sacrificing quality. These systems may seem like mere conveniences, but the savings are real. One of the biggest problems with managed care companies is maintaining a handle on the amount of healthcare services provided for which claims have yet to be submitted ("incurred but not reported," in accounting terms). Many hospitals, physicians, and other providers often don't immediately notify the health plan when they have provided services to a plan member for which they expect to be reimbursed. The time lag between providing the service and notifying the health plan becomes problematic. Not only does a health plan not realize its true costs, but the gap can throw off forecasting in pricing plans and projecting earnings to Wall Street.

Real-time transactions occur in numerous industries, and healthcare is the next frontier. Prudential wanted to automate this process so badly that it paid for the terminals and computer software itself. The project started with thirty-nine hundred physicians in twenty-two hundred offices in New Jersey, New York, Connecticut, Delaware, and Pennsylvania. "They loved it," Hammond said about the reaction. One big benefit: it's not exclusively a Prudential system. Physicians can use the terminal for other payers, and even for VISA and MasterCard charges from patients.

The insurer, which spends about 5 percent of revenues on information systems, is so pleased that it plans to expand the program to twenty-seven markets by 1999. And executives hope to add other transactions to the process. "Eventually, we want to do online claims adjudication," Hammond says. Claims are still processed at the end of the day in what is described as "batch" processing. But that too will end soon. With refinements, the system will improve to give providers even more information. "What the physicians have told us is they want to be paid, and they want to know how much they'll be paid," says Hammond.

UP THE ORGANIZATION
AND START ANEW

Healthcare information systems are going through a metamorphosis. Yesterday's systems just won't cut it. "Some of the big players are dealing with legacy systems that don't process managed care claims very well," says Price Waterhouse's Annie Scibienski. Legacy systems are old computer systems that don't communicate with each other. "But the old HMO systems don't do a good job with claims logic because the model was, if the doctor approved it, we have to pay for it. What if the diagnosis doesn't match the treatment? A lot of big plans have been struggling to finds systems that allow them to do both."

First, consolidators need to change the way they collect data, an effort that companies like Prudential are already funding. Next, they need to change the way they store, or warehouse, it. Today's consolidators want information on practice patterns, quality, and cost. Finally, they must develop systems to analyze it for the good of patients and profits.

Health plans will be able to take terabytes—trillions of bytes of data—and formulate what-if scenarios. What if I capitate the cardiologists, but pay the primary care physicians fee-for-service? What if I switch from brand-name to generic? What if this patient is taken off a ventilator sooner? These are scenarios that healthcare consolidators can answer by taking information they're already collecting.

Employers don't want to micromanage the quality initiatives of physicians or hospitals. They do want to scrutinize and interact with their intermediaries in health insurance. They want "report cards" on the cost and quality of the care provided through those intermediaries. The health plans, in turn, want to measure the providers with which they contract.

Entering the information age and keeping up with technological progress is an expensive ride. You can see how huge the potential is when you consider what healthcare organizations can expand upon from other industries. The technology that monitors whether shoplifters have taken merchandise from the store will someday be able to track and tabulate what supplies are taken into each patient's hospital room.

Buying these expensive systems helps drive small organizations to consolidators. Healthcare organizations need capital, and consolidators have a greater opportunity to borrow and raise capital through financial markets. But that's what vexes not-for-profit hospitals and

HMOs. They can't access the financial markets to raise capital. Why do they need capital? Not to build more expensive hospitals, but to purchase information and telecommunications systems.

MOVING AWAY FROM PAPER

Despite an abundance of data, the healthcare industry is statistically poor. It's drowning in data that are unusable because they are on paper or have been gathered incorrectly. The amount of claims processing on paper is not as large as it used to be, but it's still overwhelming. In 1995, 56 percent of the 3.7 billion healthcare claims filed were processed electronically, up from 36 percent in 1992.[1] Pharmacy claims led the pack, with an 83 percent electronic rate, followed by claims for hospitals with 82 percent and, a distant third, physicians with 35 percent.[2] The dental industry is still farther behind on the technology curve. Only 10 percent of all dental claims are processed electronically, according to the 1997 *Health Data Directory*. However, that's up from 8 percent in 1995, according to that source.

Processing claims is only one facet that needs to be computerized, however. In other ways, the health system is even further behind. Fewer than 5 percent of all physicians have computer-based patient records in their clinics, according to industry estimates. Although payers want to help physicians automate, it can be problematic. Physicians don't want ten different computers in their offices any more than they want thirty different administration manuals on their shelves.

The beauty of the Prudential system is that it's an "all-payer" system that allows physicians to communicate with other insurers, such as Blue Cross plans or other HMOs. Hospital automation is also clunky, but implementation of computer-based patient records in hospitals is advancing a bit more quickly. In fact, as more providers and insurers keep records on doctors' treatments, it behooves physicians to track, or at least have access to, the same information. Between 1996 and 1998, HMOs plan to spend 22 percent of information systems budgets on clinical analysis, according to InterStudy, an HMO research and consulting firm in Bloomington, Minnesota, up from 15 percent in 1995.

As consolidators grow, they must latch onto technology and invest the needed funds to make it happen. The move to Electronic Data Interchange, or EDI, spurs provider consolidation because of an increased demand for outcomes information. Only in consolidated networks with central information processing systems can the purchasers of healthcare make apples-to-apples comparisons.

The Health Insurance Portability and Accountability Act, passed by Congress in 1996, demands that providers be able to conduct business in the EDI mode by early 2001. By early 1998, the federal government is required to have rules in place for this exchange. If the government actually carries out that mandate, it will be a kick in the pants to consolidators.

Although financial services firms spend 7–8 percent of revenues on information technology, healthcare organizations only spend 2–3 percent on average. For example, Columbia/HCA Healthcare talks about spending $500 million on information technology; that's just 2.5 percent of revenues.

Good intentions are the hallmark of healthcare systems and information technology. A 1997 survey by the Healthcare Information Management Systems Society (known as HIMSS) reported that one in five respondents intended to increase their information technology spending by 50 percent or more. Fifteen percent said they expected their information technology staffs would increase by more than 25 percent in 1997. Interestingly, one-fourth of the group (which includes some nine thousand individual members) identified the physicians' offices as the place most in need of computer technology.

Because the industry has a history of raising prices before cutting costs, it lags in computerization. Now that consolidated providers can no longer raise prices, the emphasis on cost-efficiency is imperative. They can't analyze what they can't measure, and they can't measure the daily flood of information without computerization. Consolidators are demanding information to measure their networks, and they're looking to information technology vendors that have honed their craft in other segments of American business.

Healthcare systems and vendors want to be able to integrate data throughout their companies, whether they be regional or national. The development of intranets enables them to do so. For more on the use of Internet and intranet technology, see Chapter Twelve.

Even though hospitals and physicians were worried about the move to Medicare's DRG system in the 1980s, information companies were developing the technology for real-time systems that electronically capture and transmit information. Banks, going through their own consolidation process, plunged in, but healthcare systems held back, unwilling to invest in a future they regarded as uncertain. Now, healthcare can benefit from the banks' learning curve.

The point-of-sale system used by Prudential is made by Envoy, a Nashville company that was formed in 1981 to serve financial services companies but switched horses in 1995. It decided to focus on the next unconquered territory of healthcare, selling its financial services part of the business to First Data Corp. Envoy's transaction network includes some 188,000 physicians, 44,000 pharmacies, 30,000 dentists, 3,700 hospitals, and 600 payers, including 46 Blue Cross Blue Shield Plans, 50 Medicare plans, and 25 Medicaid plans.

AUTOMATING THE CLAIMS PROCESS

In football, the basics are blocking and tackling. In baseball, they're hitting, fielding, and pitching. In the hospital business, it's billing and collecting.

Why can't hospitals and physicians get this right? Is there anything that causes more general dissatisfaction with the healthcare system? Taking ninety days to pay a healthcare bill is common and considered nothing to worry about. In fact, the standard of long payment times is so ingrained that it makes organizations reluctant to embrace technology. Some payers are reluctant to do electronic funds transfer because they benefit from the "float," the days between when the claim is made and when they pay for it. If they get the bill on a Monday and don't pay it for two weeks, they collect the interest on the money they hold for two weeks. "This is one of those things that make me shake my head and say, 'Do the electronic funds transfer in two weeks,'" says Price Waterhouse's Scibienski.

Consolidators know, however, that transactions in healthcare will mirror banking and retailing, being done on real-time basis. In 1997, HCFA began the process of selecting vendors to begin implementing the Medicare Transaction System, a consolidated, standardized network for processing Medicare transactions. The government has been using nine different systems, one for each of the intermediaries that process those payments. Processing claims is a labor-intensive business that goes through several steps:

- Data entry of patient and treatment or procedure
- Eligibility verification (is patient a member of this plan?)
- Repricing (payer determines reimbursement rate)
- Determination of whether the treatment or procedure is authorized under the member's plan
- Determination of whether the treatment or procedure is medically necessary

It can take six to twelve weeks to process a paper claim, compared with one or two weeks for an electronic one. Eventually, real-time claims adjudication will make such time spans seem unreasonable.

Manual entry of claims information is not only time consuming but can be error-intensive. Paper claims have two to three times more errors than those submitted electronically, experts say. This also has implications in fraud investigation. An investigator may be more suspicious in areas where human intervention could illegally increase reimbursement.

STORING THE DATA

An increasing number of companies see a need for data warehousing, in which the vast sums of data they're collecting can be analyzed across multiple dimensions. For example, if a consolidated hospital system wants to know the cost and profit levels for coronary artery bypass, it asks for several layers of information. It wants to know the cost and profit by region, facility, individual physician, anesthesiologist, equipment use, rehabilitation method, and nursing station. Each variable carries a particular insight that can help in managing the process of care for that bypass.

A health plan may want the same information for contracting purposes. So might the patient or a patient advocacy group. All of the data is available somewhere. The question is gathering them from a host of proprietary databases. Just getting all the data into some form of "data warehouse" is a huge effort that demands thousands of hours of detail work. One problem is that so many of the same treatments and procedures are called by different names. Diabetes is just one example, with symptoms, diagnoses, and treatments going by dozens of different names.

The pharmacy industry has solved this problem, which is one reason why that segment is more electronically driven. In the 1970s, the national group developed a coding system to identify pharmaceuticals. The sticking point was that the federal government was getting ready to issue a nationwide contract for pharmaceuticals. It never happened, but the end result was beneficial. Each pharmaceutical now has a nine-digit code, or eleven digits if special packaging is involved.

According to the *Health Data Directory,* approximately 80 percent of the 1.3 billion third-party pharmacy claims processed in 1995 and 83 percent of the 1.4 billion claims in 1996 were processed electronically. The publication believes that only a small percentage of nonclaim pharmacy transactions, such as delivery of prescriptions by the physician to the pharmacist or formulary inquiries to pharmacy benefit managers, are delivered electronically through real-time online systems. In fact, pharmacy patient data can be a backdoor to building an information warehouse for consolidators creating information banks. When MedPartners acquired Caremark, it procured Caremark's pharmacy data because Caremark was administering a pharmacy benefit program.

The benchmarks for this industry have been subjective because no repository of clinical information exists. So much of the clinical data are claims data, which show what was done and what the diagnosis was. However, they tell very little about outcomes.

The new systems that are being installed with physicians and hospitals consume data at the "point of care." It's scary to think of the huge files of data stored in manila folders in the thousands and thousand of physician offices and hospitals throughout the country. Right now, those data are going nowhere. They're sitting in those file folders, maybe looked at by one physician or one nurse every now and then. As the industry consolidates, it becomes much more interested in sharing data through partnerships because no one has all the data. The physician companies have one source of data, the hospitals another, and the vendors still others.

The first change is that data must be gathered differently. Instead of gathering them on the back end, when the claim is filed, they need to be gathered at the front end and all along the way—gathered, that is, at each point of care. Then systems can compile a kind of just-in-time patient record and risk assessment card. Next, the data need to be automated and standardized. Finally, the data must be secure enough that providers feel safe in sharing them.

Once this happens, the sharing will move at lightning speed. The technology is already there to do so. Witness the deal between IBM, Sun Microsystems, Netscape, and Oracle to develop smart cards that allow a user to tap into a company's network from a personal computer via the Internet.

Managing information is the precursor to managing risk. Data can reveal business opportunities. For example, Franklin Health manages care for corporations, concentrating only on the sickest 1 percent of the U.S. population. Franklin officials figure these "complex care" patients, with diagnoses that range from AIDS to liver disease, account for about 30 percent of all healthcare expenditures. That adds up to nearly $300 billion. Franklin, which claims to have the largest database of complex care patients in the country, teamed up with HCIA, which collates and analyzes financial data from Medicare cost reports on all of the nation's hospitals, to develop an information system to measure the financial and clinical impact of intensive, team-supported, patient-centered decision making in these complex cases. In a test run in which Franklin compared a year of its experience in managing these patients against HCIA's universe of data, the latter company figures that Franklin could save $20,000 per case.

Even the smallest details in healthcare can come down to putting the proper information systems and financial incentives in place. A New Jersey company, Datascope, decided to start a registry for its balloon pumps to collect information on how they were used and how patient outcomes were affected. Balloon pumps essentially keep a heart beating, supporting the patient until surgery is under way or until the heart can start beating on its own. Datascope owns 80 percent of the balloon-pump market. To ensure quality, its pumps go through one thousand hours of testing before they're even shipped to hospitals. Still, competitors were slashing prices, and threatening to steal market share.

Using a Lotus Notes platform, Datascope designed a way for practitioners to tell Datascope about its pumps, gathering precise information about how they're used and how long, and how satisfied physicians are with them. Datascope asked hospital workers to fill out a simple ten-minute questionnaire. But ten minutes may be more time than a harried hospital worker will choose to free up. So, Datascope pays $10 for each completed survey. Responses pour in. The market research is that valuable to Datascope, because it delivers clinical information that the company can use in a competitive market.

TREATING HEALTHCARE BILLS
LIKE OTHER BILLS

Joe Hodge, a Nashville businessman who spent most of his career in information systems at Hospital Corporation of America (HCA), was devastated when his daughter was diagnosed with a malignant brain tumor. But like so many who work in healthcare, Hodge learned from the experience and came away with a business idea.

He was frustrated with the red tape and complex billing systems involved that complicated everything. "Why can the credit card industry [process transactions] so much more efficiently?" asks Hodge, who devised information systems for HCA in the 1970s and 1980s. He identifies the answer: "Technology, very highly automated payment, and consolidation."

Hodge is combining those three elements into his company, IPN Network, which is buying receivables and business office companies to offer a consolidated billing service. A seventeen-year veteran of HCA, Hodge proposes a system of billing called "one family, one statement," in which local hospitals, physician offices, clinics, and home healthcare agencies all funnel their billing into one system. From that system, a monthly bill—much like a credit card bill—goes out.

Such a system takes enormous coordination, but it's not impossible. After all, a family gets a MasterCard bill that includes charges from such diverse businesses as Chili's, Blockbuster, Fina, and Barnes and Noble. Yet healthcare providers aren't used to working together to share financial information. In the secretive world of medical services pricing, this would amount to sharing proprietary information. Suppose a family gets a bill that includes multiple procedures or treatments from different providers. They could do something they can't today: make price comparisons. An MRI costs $1,000 here and $800 there. An office visit costs $25 at this doctor, $80 at that one. Clearly, the effects could reverberate throughout a community. Competition in healthcare would assume a whole new paradigm.

One could argue that managed care does this now because an individual pays a monthly premium of, say, $200 and all healthcare costs are covered. Right? Wrong. Usually, there are copays, carve-outs, and items that aren't covered. In addition, many patients are in managed care plans that are simply discounting systems. Also, most of the elderly are still in the regular Medicare system, rather than Medicare HMOs. For them, the paperwork associated with their medical services is a nightmare.

It's easy to see that the price competition inherent in a one family, one statement system coupled with the cost savings associated with administration could slash healthcare costs. "The idea makes infinite sense," Hodge says. "There's so much money spent just moving paper around. If you could cut just half of the amount spent on administration . . . and that's doable. When you take all the little cuts from the premium dollar, administration payment can cost between 20 percent and 25 percent. We wouldn't contribute to United Way if it spent as much on administration. We'd say 'I want more money going toward the healthcare itself.'"

In fact, when Hodge talks about the high administration costs associated with healthcare, he notes those costs are much higher on the private payer side. That's because most Medicare and Medicaid payment is electronically filed and paid. That cuts down on administration. Why this hasn't happened already says a lot about the political realities of the healthcare industry. Hodge speaks of IPN as being a "politically neutral" third party, what he calls a shared service organization, that could facilitate this process. Some providers want to issue their own bills on their own stationery. They sense a loss of control if they turn over the billing process to someone else.

NEXT, CLINICAL DATA

The drive to managed care demands that consolidators not be left out of any segment of the information system loop. For example, the National Committee for Quality Assurance, which accredits HMOs, began demanding that plans provide one hundred different standardized performance measures in what's called the Health Plan Employer Data and Information Set, or HEDIS 3.0. The most efficient way to gather that data, of course, is electronically.

Nearly 90 percent of HMOs voluntarily report HEDIS and similar data to employers, according to InterStudy, an HMO think tank. Until 1997, they only had to report on sixty items, details that ranged from immunization rates to financial figures. However, in 1997, they raised the bar, asking for more than one hundred data elements from each HMO.

Managing information is a crucial competency for managed care plans, but the industry is wasting time compiling separate proprietary systems that don't allow comparisons. Most of those systems were designed to process claims or bills; they simply can't perform sophisticated quality improvement and performance measurements. If they can't do those, they certainly can't share information so that payers can make comparisons.

Drawing from a group of one hundred experts representing information systems specialists and vendors, the national committee established a comprehensive set of data elements and standardization across all patient settings for content and medical coding. Last year, the committee marketed the Quality Compass, a CD-ROM crammed full of statistics from 250 health plans, or about one-half of all the health plans that could report such detailed information. The disk contained an analysis of the HEDIS data, and employers who bought it could build their own reports cards. It sold for $3,200, a pittance to self-insured corporations that could view quality indicators for the first time.

NCQA only sold about 250 of the CD-ROMs, a disappointment considering that this kind of comparison had never been done before. James Tierney, the committee's assistant vice president for information products, said the data may have been too unwieldy for some buyers. It presented information on 250 plans, rated on sixty to sixty-five different measures. In addition, some of the measures may have had as many as fifty data elements each. Future annual releases of the data would include more summaries, so readers can easily discern what the information meant.

The data may be of most interest to the small to medium-sized employer that doesn't have access to this type of information. Large corporations can fairly easily receive such data from the HMOs with which they contract. And if they're considering adding new HMOs to their benefit mix, they can get it from them as well. The large multi-billion-dollar employers have the clout to demand that information for free—and even more detailed information—in a due diligence negotiation with an employer. Small employers and consumers do not.

NCQA's Tierney also pointed out that the data were useful to some of the HMOs and health plans themselves, many of which were used to comparing financial data, patient days per thousand, and quality indicators such as immunization and cholesterol screening rates, access to services, and average length of maternity stay. "Some payers use HEDIS data to negotiate with health plans," he said, noting that they tied financial incentives to meeting specific quality indicators.

In 1997, the committee went one step further, providing health plans with a roadmap of how their information management systems need to evolve to create an "information framework" for reporting standardized data. Although the committee is not a governmental entity, this may be the framework needed to set the standards the industry needs. Such a body might provide oversight to the health plan market, just as the Securities and Exchange Commission does for the publicly traded securities market. The SEC doesn't control prices or service offerings, but it does ensure a level playing field on which investors can judge stocks.

However, NCQA notes that providers must start building computerized patient records, which is far from a reality in many provider settings. To fund the effort, the committee suggests a "cooperative investment initiative involving health plans and the federal government." This really is the question. Where will the money come from to buy these systems? Healthcare providers lag far behind other industries in the amount they spend on information systems. The biggest health-care spenders have been hospitals, with physicians and other clinicians falling even farther behind.

When it comes to a decision to buy new capital equipment or a new information system, the capital equipment often wins out because physicians are pushing for it. Some states still have certificate-of-need laws that require state approval before hospitals make large capital investments, information systems being among them. Anecdotal evidence shows that some hospitals have circumvented these laws by breaking up multimillion-dollar purchases into smaller purchases to get under a state-mandated cap. However, many hospitals haven't wanted to hassle with doing that.

USING TECHNOLOGY TO CONNECT PATIENT TO PROVIDER

A woman calls a toll-free number and tells a nurse about her toddler's fever. This nurse, though, doesn't work for the woman's physicians. She's part of "demand management," a system implemented by a growing number of HMOs.

The king of the hill in this business is Access Health, also known by the moniker "Ask-a-Nurse." Access runs call centers for hospitals and health plans, providing information "on demand." Healthcare call centers are probably the ATMs of the 1990s for consolidated health-care providers, giving them instant access to healthcare information that they're entitled to. If you think of a healthcare insurance policy as a bank account, the account holder historically has had a difficult time getting a "balance" on his account.

Through a healthcare call center, a policy holder can get information about coverage as well as some treatment. The centers perform a type of telephone triage, as we called it earlier. Access Health attempts to do what is frequently missing from the managed healthcare equation: manage consumer demand. (Some attempts to do this through the Internet are discussed in Chapter Twelve.) So much is being done to manage the physician and the hospital, yet no healthcare organization can truly manage risk without managing the patient's behavior as well. Humana, the Louisville HMO with 4.8 million members, offers a similar service called HumanaFirst. A registered nurse answers twenty-four hours a day whenever a member calls the toll-free number. The service is free to members.

Rather than attempt to do this themselves, many health plans have turned to Access. The company has grown from 200,000 members in 1994 to more than ten million by the end of 1996. Enrollees use a program called Personal Health Advisor. They dial a toll-free number and talk to a registered nurse. The nurse advises the patient on how to receive treatment, whether through a physician, hospital, home care agency, or even self-care. Although most of Access' members are covered through their insurance, the company also sells directly to individuals for a monthly fee of between $4.95 and $6.95 per family.

Healthcare call centers will increasingly interface with Internet strategies. Much of the information supplied by call centers is available on the Web. However, just as bank customers still want to see a teller rather than an ATM, so some patients want to talk to a "real" customer service agent.

CONSOLIDATOR TO THE CONSOLIDATORS

Solving the information technology needs of healthcare is a beast unto itself and, not surprisingly, going through its own consolidation. Just as there are too many medical vendors, it's easy for anybody who knows about computers to put up a shingle as a healthcare systems firm. Some fifteen hundred companies sell healthcare information technology systems, according to BTAlex. Brown, an investment banking firm.

This industry, which has been flush with public-offering capital, is growing through acquisitions as well. Still, consolidators can take advantage of the competition. They can demand a payback, and some vendors are responding by providing money-back guarantees if the provider network does not recoup its entire investment within the first year.

Information systems vendors estimate that the market for their products in the hospital setting alone is about $6 billion a year.[3] Price Waterhouse estimates that the healthcare information technology industry generates $11 billion annually and will grow to more than $20 billion by the year 2000. Like other consolidators, healthcare information companies have tapped Wall Street for expansion capital. Envoy, which is Prudential's partner in information systems development, raised $83 million in its IPO and spent some $100 million in acquisitions in 1996. Its biggest purchase was National Electronic Information, one of the nation's largest clearinghouses of batch claims for commercial payers.

This industry is building its own consolidators. They include software vendors, such as HBO & Company, database companies such as HCIA, and outsourcing companies such as Medaphis. Although this initially was a cottage industry, big corporations are encroaching, notably EDS, Dun and Bradstreet, and the regional Bell operating companies. That league of players is obviously attracted to an industry with equally big players. In the past, national corporations often overlooked the healthcare industry as one of small businesses. They didn't want to put the time and energy into pursuing small-potato clients. Now, that's changing with the emergence of large healthcare providers such as Columbia/HCA, MedPartners, and HealthSouth Rehabilitation. This also drives small providers into larger systems, where they can tap the leading edge of technology.

Consolidation of physician practices gives vendors bigger targets for sales calls. Frost and Sullivan reported that physician practices plan to increase their information systems expenditures by 16 percent a year, from $2 billion in 1995 to $5.6 billion in 2001. Virtually all providers, not-for-profit ones included, will join integrated delivery networks, which are more likely to have adequate pooled capital to spend on information technology. By some estimates, the thousands of healthcare providers will combine into 500–750 integrated delivery networks. When these well-capitalized systems put out bids for information technology systems, they'll look to big players like Hewlett-Packard, EDS, and HBO & Company.

ENCROACHING TECHNOLOGY AFFECTS SUPPLY AND DEMAND

Dr. Theresa Tilton, a Nashville radiologist, sits in front of two oversized computer screens, "paging" through black and white images of a patient's spine. The images are digital X-rays sent from a rural center via telephone lines to Tilton's office. A self-described "computer illiterate" until two months ago, she now is a pro at using the computer to read radiology images.

Now, the jeans-clad physician with neatly trimmed salt-and-pepper hair is a whiz, using the computer's mouse to zoom in on certain areas, making an analysis, and dictating notes. This technology has increased her productivity at least twofold, she claims. "Instead of hanging up all the X-ray films, we can see them all here," she says, motioning to the dozen rectangular images filling the two computer screens. "And we can infinitely magnify them," she remarks while looking deeper and deeper into a scan of a patient's arm. "I've found things I would never have found, and I've been looking at X-rays for twenty years."

InPhact demonstrates that information systems that share data in broad geographic areas bring savings beyond the obvious levels of claims processing and electronic funds transfer. "The average radiologist reads between 12,000 and 15,000 cases a year," said Jonathan Lehman, its president and COO. "We think we can increase radiology productivity by a factor of two or three."

The company was founded by a radiologist who simply decided to start a billing company. It subsequently blossomed into a teleradiology and outsourcing company that snagged a key contract with Arcon Healthcare, a chain of rural health centers based in Nashville.

In a room down the hall from Tilton, two other workstations are centered in cubicles where radiologists read patient cases. It is a vision of the future when radiologists are almost like air traffic controllers, looking at digitally transmitted images in darkened rooms. This is the future, but it's a future that needs far fewer radiologists than the twenty-nine thousand now practicing. Technology will drive down the costs of radiology procedures, and the need for radiologists. It also is likely to drive radiologists into larger groups that can bargain on their behalf, groups like unions or the physician practice management companies discussed in Chapter Three.

IT'S A SMALL WORLD

The multicolored file folders that fill a physician's office could choke any organization. Yet, information isn't enough to change health delivery patterns. The information must have force. Consolidators can't analyze what they can't measure, and they can't measure the daily flood of information without computerization.

Consolidators are demanding information to measure their networks and they're looking to information technology vendors that have honed their craft in other segments of American business.

Healthcare systems and vendors want to be able to integrate data throughout their companies, whether they be regional or national.

The development of intranets will enable them to do it. For more on the use of Internet and intranet technology, see Chapter Twelve.

The Internet also might be able to better rationalize services in a misshapen distribution system. Urban areas overflow with physicians, particularly specialists, while rural areas go wanting. Through the Internet and its ability to send digital images, rural patients can receive the diagnostic expertise of top-flight specialists in urban areas. If a rural physician detects a problem that requires follow-up treatment, a patient might typically have to take off work for a day to travel to a specialist. Some rural hospitals have programs in which specialists rotate through once a week. In that case, the patient might wait for the rotation.

Either way, telemedicine offers a better option. It allows specialists to stay in the urban areas they (presumably) enjoy living and working in but provide needed services to a rural area. Perhaps we'll see joint ventures between hospitals and Kinko's, which provides teleconferencing capabilities.

Dr. Edward Jonas Domanskis, a plastic surgeon in Newport Beach, California, put up a website that allows him to view patients who are interested in plastic surgery. These patients can be anywhere; they just need a PC and an attached video camera, which can be purchased for a couple hundred dollars now. He charges $250 for a thirty-minute consultation.

CHAPTER TEN

Overstepping
Old Boundaries
in Marketing

B y now it's a familiar litany to managed care plans: employers want high-quality services and low per-member costs, with annual cost savings guaranteed. To stay competitive, plans must look for innovative ways to reduce costs without sacrificing quality. Balancing the cost-quality equation requires them to rethink how they are structured to deliver services, whether it is more economical to "make or buy" (outsource) certain services, and whether they're allocating scarce resources to obtain the best results for the populations they serve.

Changes in the marketplace create new opportunities for companies that are watchful enough to spot them and flexible enough to take advantage of them. In this chapter, we see examples of manufacturing companies that, in exploring strategies for providing health plans with lower-cost alternatives, have found themselves crossing the line to become providers of services.

Prescription drug benefits are a difficult area for health plans to manage, in part because of the growing number of medications available. Managing such costs requires skillful manipulation of the levers that drive it: drug costs, prescription dispensing costs, claims processing costs, and the volume of prescriptions written. The challenge is to control costs without affecting the quality of care.

Recognizing this need, companies began popping up here and there, offering to manage health plans' and self-insured employers' pharmaceutical benefit costs on a subcontract or carve-out basis for a per-member, per-month amount. These self-appointed watchdogs, called pharmacy benefit managers (or PBMs), signed contracts with self-insured employers and other payers to manage costs by buying drugs in bulk for volume discounts and altering physicians' prescription-writing patterns. PBMs also could reduce costs by streamlining claims processing and lowering dispensing charges through techniques such as mail-order delivery of prescriptions. These last two approaches have the added benefit of helping the health plan improve customer service. It's no wonder that PBMs became big business; one leading company, Express Scripts, has grown to providing services for more than ten million individuals in the United States and Canada.

PBMs weren't popular with everyone, though. In some cases, the PBM managed so aggressively that its managers called pharmacists or physicians directly to talk about generic or therapeutic substitution. These are sensitive subjects for physicians, who don't want a managed care company telling them what to prescribe. Generic substitutions aren't nearly as combative a subject as therapeutic substitutions, however. In the latter cases, a different kind of drug entirely is suggested to treat an illness or condition.

As PBMs grew, they began to consolidate into larger and larger companies. As the big PBMs grew even larger, they demanded bigger and bigger discounts from the drug makers. Drug company margins eroded as pricing pressures escalated. Another wave of consolidation began when pharmaceutical companies saw a way to get back in the driver's seat: they could buy the PBMs. Merck, Eli Lilly, and SmithKline Beecham, all drug giants, each acquired a PBM at a huge price.

If the company managing the "drug cost" element of the benefit equation is also the manufacturer of many of those drugs, the manager has access to many drugs at manufacturer's cost. Serving in this dual role of manufacturer and manager eliminates one layer of pricing markups. Therefore, the PBM strategy allowed drug companies to regain some control over the distribution channels for their products, as well as offering managed care plans an attractively priced product that would cap their pharmaceutical benefit costs.

Some cynics may say this is akin to having the foxes watch the henhouse. Pharmaceutical makers deciding what drugs are most cost-effective? Of course, their own patented drugs are the best, right? However, as GTE's managed care negotiator, George Crowling, said, "The alternative is too unmentionable to contemplate." If an employer doesn't contract with a PBM, at least for the indemnity side of the business, "the only alternative is to pay the full-boat idiot price."

Drug company executives would argue that the situation puts their knowledge of drugs into action and gives them the opportunity to lower costs. Indeed, through PBMs, pharmaceutical companies could contract with payers, which provides them with access to data about sales and practice patterns involving their competitors' drugs as well. In risk contracting, information is power. To further widen their influence, some drug makers began considering other aspects of medical management. After all, drugs make up only 10 percent of America's healthcare bills.

A case in point is Schering-Plough, one of the nation's largest drug companies, with $5.7 billion in 1996 revenues. Schering-Plough is probably best known for its consumer products, such as Dr. Scholl's foot care and Coppertone sun care lotion. Its predominant source of revenue is from manufacturing prescription drugs like Claritin, a nonsedating antihistamine, and Proventil, the nation's largest-selling inhaler for asthma patients. Proventil is packaged in an L-shaped plastic canister that allows a patient to easily palm it while depressing a cylinder that delivers a tiny puff of albuterol. The albuterol, which is inhaled, triggers the lungs to open their air passages. Schering-Plough spends more than three-fourths of a billion dollars annually on research and development of drugs like Proventil. "We think that with today's products, no one should be dying of asthma," says Gary Binder, senior director of health management operations at Schering-Plough. Yet "the statistics showed that asthma morbidity and mortality are increasing."

Executives decided to find out why. "It was almost a byproduct because we were doing the research anyway," Binder says. Schering-Plough already had a huge repository of data from doing the research and clinical trials for its respiratory drugs. Researchers looked at guidelines for diagnosing and treating asthma issued by the National Institutes of Health. "Although the guidelines were widely accepted, they were vague in some areas," Binder recalls. So Schering-Plough formed an independent subsidiary, Integrated Therapeutics Group (ITG), to put together an asthma program, researching how asthma was diagnosed and what drugs were prescribed, and then outlining recommended action plans to implement the specific guidelines. They also would identify when physicians were and weren't being consistent with the guidelines.

They found that some physicians were prescribing albuterol inhalers, but there didn't seem to be treatment of the underlying cause of the asthma with an anti-inflammatory drug. Many patients shouldn't average more than one albuterol inhaler a month, but ITG found cases in which patients had received as many as five a month, Binder said.

The information collected through this research presented Schering-Plough with a dilemma. ITG realized that the lessons learned in conducting this research helped identify best-practices information regarding the treatment of persons suffering from asthma. If those best practices could be implemented with an asthmatic population and monitored for compliance, the patients' asthma could be controlled better. ITG researchers also knew that better management of the disease would cut drastically into hospitalizations. For example, asthma is responsible for 17 percent of children's visits to the emergency room, according to the National Institutes of Health. Consequently, ITG recognized that its best-practices plan presented opportunities for dramatic cost reductions in the treatment of asthmatics. In addition, ITG's sophisticated research database provided valuable information as to which patients were more likely to develop asthma problems, enabling providers and health plans to intervene preventively. This would directly cut down on healthcare dollars spent and improve patient care.

But the information forced Schering-Plough to make some tough management decisions. If the ITG asthma management protocols really were effective, it could change the use of asthma medications and reduce Proventil prescriptions, which in turn would reduce the drug company's revenues. In the end, about the potential revenue loss, Binder says, "realistically you have to do what's best for the patient."

The natural markets for the service were health plans and provider networks. ITG knew that it would be a tough sell; HMOs and networks might also perceive it merely as a marketing ploy for Schering-Plough to sell more of its product. To get its first customers for the asthma management program, the company agreed to be compensated only by a percentage of any savings generated. In the end, Schering-Plough was able to win over reluctant providers and health plans, and the opposite turned out to be true. Although Binder won't release specific figures, the asthma program was so successful that ITG later expanded into other areas in which Schering-Plough has clinical expertise: cardiovascular, oncology, and antiviral.

What's more, some networks are asking them to look into areas in which Schering-Plough doesn't even market drugs. They like the management aspect so well, they want the company to take over elsewhere.

Consolidators have descended on market segments such as the $7.4 billion end-stage renal disease (ESRD). Wall Street likes this business because the need for it is increasing; the number of patients needing dialysis increases about 9 percent annually. Also, there is one large payer source: Medicare pays for nearly 85 percent of ESRD care. It is the only chronic care that Medicare pays for, and it would be extremely unlikely that Medicare would pull the plug on funding, since it's a life or death situation. Because Medicare pays for nearly all dialysis services on a flat-fee basis, higher profits are available to companies that know how to manage costs without sacrificing quality.

One way to reduce costs is to manage the business better. That has been Baxter International's focus with regard to Renal Management Strategies, a company it formed in late 1996. Baxter is one of the nation's largest diversified medical supply companies. The company partners with nephrologists to better manage ESRD patients, whose care averages a whopping $62,000 per patient per year.

What Baxter proposes to managed care companies is to carve out the care of these high-cost patients and turn it over to them. A single HMO "doesn't have enough of these patients to go and learn how to manage them," says Brant Kanak, vice president of marketing and business development for the new company. Renal Management Strategies can lower costs by "keeping these patients healthier and getting them the right care at the right time," he adds.

Another major player in the ESRD market is Fresenius Medical, a kidney dialysis machine manufacturer. Fresenius bought one of the nation's largest chains of dialysis centers, National Medical Care, in 1996. In a merger valued at $4.4 billion, Fresenius bought the business from W. R. Grace, a huge chemical conglomerate that drifted into the healthcare business and managed to amass this chain of centers that provide life-giving dialysis to clinic-based ESRD patients. The acquisition made German-owned Fresenius the world's largest clinic-based dialysis company. Serving in the dual role of equipment manufacturer and service provider eliminates one layer of pricing markups, hence slimming the cost structure and maximizing the profits.

PITFALLS AWAIT

When manufacturers become providers, this raises questions about conflict of interest. Is the company just trying to sell more product, or is it really interested in improving patients' health status? From a business standpoint, other problems arise. Soon, a consolidator may be competing with its own customers.

History has shown that this strategy can be fraught with pitfalls. Take Baxter's foray into the home healthcare services business in the 1980s, for example. Baxter formed Caremark International (at one time, the nation's largest home infusion therapy firm) when that therapy was just starting to take off. As Baxter's home care business thrived, hospitals began to chafe. Most had set up their own home care businesses in an effort to hold the line on eroding revenue bases. Now they found they were buying millions of dollars of supplies from a company that was trying to take market share away in other areas. Did this mean they were indirectly subsidizing their home care competitor?

What do these companies have in common? All have recognized and capitalized on the market's need to optimize resource distribution and conservation, and to develop high-quality, cost-effective treatments. However, the industry is still learning by doing, and what appears to works best in theory may not work best in practice.

For example, carve-out strategies aren't always successful with health benefits managers or health plans. In fact, some health plans that previously carved out certain benefits (for example, mental health and substance abuse) and contracted them to vendors outside their medical-surgical network have taken these services back, in what may be referred to as "carve-ins." They now believe that carve-out approaches interrupt the continuity of care. Frequently, patients do not present with a single disease but often at least two. It's one thing to carve out mental health treatment, but what happens if the patient is also diabetic? Will the medical network and the mental health vendor interface as they should?

CHAPTER ELEVEN

Becoming the Brand
That Customers Love

H ealthcare marketing is now a sophisticated science for consolidators, which are testing the waters of market research and advertising. The old wisdom is that in healthcare, successful marketing is directed at physicians, who make purchasing decisions for the patient. The new conventional wisdom: consolidators strive to endear themselves to their ultimate audience, the consumer.

However, taking products directly to the consumer market has a price. It's called advertising. Consolidators spend more on advertising and branding as they promote a unified image. These are relatively uncharted waters for healthcare companies. Although there are obvious exceptions, advertising traditionally has been viewed as borderline taboo by most providers. Most advertising has been done by systems that simply want to inspire consumer confidence in their institutions and their physicians. For example, Johns Hopkins, the venerable Baltimore medical institution, developed an ad that features eleven heart doctors and healthcare workers dressed in white lab coats. "At Hopkins, these are just the people who specialize in the left ventricle," it tells consumers.

The huge consolidators—companies that are operating these health-care systems in markets from coast to coast—want more. They want their brand names to be as recognizable to consumers making health care choices as are Delta, United, American, and TWA to consumers making travel plans. To do so, companies like Columbia/HCA and HealthSouth spend massive amounts on advertising and branding to get the message across.

Branding is a way of conveying and building on customers' trust. "Even with the proliferation of managed care, healthcare providers need to remember that patients do have a choice," says Janet Howe, president of Howe Associates, a healthcare marketing and communications firm in Dallas. "However, providers need to shift from authoritarian positions to ones in which they recognize that their patients are better informed than ever, thanks to the Internet and electronic media focusing on healthcare."

In the years ahead, consumers will have more and more healthcare information—and propaganda—thrown at them. Furthermore, consumers won't be making à la carte selections of physicians and health-care facilities from an unlimited menu. Instead, they'll select a healthcare system to provide all of their medical needs, from hospitalization to home health to nursing home care. This will be confusing.

To help diminish the confusion and make choices easier, consolidators are striving to develop brand loyalty through marketing. For example, HealthSouth, the nation's largest rehabilitation provider, has branded its name on numerous places and efforts. It created a catalog of branded merchandise and has discussed releasing "Health-South" athletic shoes and nutrition drinks. The company's website includes articles from HealthSouth's *Sports Medicine Update* magazine, to which consumers can subscribe for $18 a year. In 1996, construction began on the Richard M. Scrushy/HealthSouth Sports Medicine Center at the Colorado Springs Olympic Complex, where future Olympic hopefuls will train. Scrushy, HealthSouth's president and CEO, also has developed a traveling interactive and educational road show that's really more like a circus. With athletes like Bo Jackson, Michael Jordan, and Kristi Yamaguchi, HealthSouth teaches kids about how to manage their lifestyles and their healthcare on and off the playing field. HealthSouth's Sports Medicine Council, made up of top athletes and physicians and surgeons, is an outgrowth of that road show.

If it is successful, a branding campaign has an important byproduct: it appeals to Wall Street. Branding makes a company more recognizable to shareholders, delivering a higher trading multiple. Although much of the stock market's rise has been driven by savvy money managers, a segment still relies on the average Joe, who doesn't want to buy stock in a company he's never heard of.

However, branding can be problematic. Although Americans cling to brand names for athletic shoes or cake mixes, they may not be steered to healthcare by the same nose ring.

In mid-1997, Columbia/HCA Healthcare's two top executives were forced to resign, and the company's vice chairman and largest single shareholder, Thomas Frist, Jr., stepped in to lead the company. Now, Frist was no stranger to healthcare, having founded Hospital Corporation of America. He knew the peculiarities of the industry. Healthcare is regarded as something of a public trust. We don't own our local hospitals, but we don't exactly view them in the same way as the local car dealer, either. Most Americans don't regard hospitals as a corporate entity.

One of Frist's first orders of business was to axe the branding campaign. No longer would Columbia be marketed as a healthcare brand. The company would take a kinder, gentler approach to business. No energy would be spent broadcasting to the world the merits of Columbia's hospitals, physicians, and other healthcare services. Columbia had been the most aggressive healthcare company in building name-brand recognition, spending nearly $200 million on advertising in 1995 and 1996, keeping the company name and the ubiquitous "1-800-Columbia" in consumers' faces. It spent 58 percent more in 1996 on a per-hospital basis than the average community hospital.[1] A significant portion, $50 million, was spent on a branding campaign of television ads that employed humor to get across points such as the fact that a consumer can receive treatment in a Columbia facility virtually wherever in the country she may happen to be. Indeed, it was the 800 number that seemed to be at the core of Columbia's marketing strategy.

WHO OR WHAT IS 1-800-COLUMBIA?

It's the spring of 1996 and calls are funneling into a national telecommunications center housed in a converted Wal-Mart in a Fort Worth suburb. Similar to the dozens of telephone centers that have cropped up across the nation's landscape, this one has trained its operators well in the etiquette of customer service.

The center is crammed with soft-sided cubicles furnished with ergonomically correct desks and chairs. Installed in the cubes are friendly telephone operators, some of whom are bilingual. This is not a hotel chain, nor a magazine subscription house. The employer of these headset-clad operators is a healthcare company. Nobody's taking credit card numbers and expiration dates. Even so, the calls represent the potential for millions of dollars. The callers are individuals who have dialed 1-800-Columbia looking for a hospital, a physician, or just medical information.

Unlike the rushed greeting given by many a hospital or physicians office receptionist, an operator here is friendly, taking time to answer questions about Columbia's growing network of providers. Operators can provide referrals and even schedule appointments in the caller's local area.

GETTING THE WORD OUT

Consumers no longer have to wait until they're sitting in their physician's office to find out about the newest advancements in medical science; now they can call Columbia twenty-four hours a day. In Rick Scott's vision, consumers started to rely on consolidators like Columbia for more medical information than what they got from their own doctors. That information is passed along to consumers through the Internet. Columbia interwove its marketing strategy with its massive investment in Internet technology (which is discussed in Chapter Twelve). Its investment in and presence on the Internet is so great that it requires an entire department—a seven-person website team headed by a director of interactive marketing—whose sole function is to make the company's presence seem even larger than it is. By the end of 1997, all 340 Columbia hospitals were expected to have websites launched. They provide information about the local facility and also link into the huge corporate website in Nashville. Through the Internet, almost any information about Columbia is available at the touch of a button.

Other consolidators see patient education as an important aspect of their websites. After all, empowering patients to make decisions about their care can save providers money and time.

How far is information from the temptation to self-diagnose one's own maladies? That's a question for consolidators to answer. For example, through an affiliation with the American Diabetes Association, Columbia's website offers a self-test that Net surfers can use to determine whether they might be at risk for diabetes. After the surfer fills out a series of questions, the website processes the responses and gives the individual a score. If it's within a predetermined range, the test-taker is prompted to call or visit his physician for follow-up. The test is available to Net browsers twenty-four hours a day and is completely impersonal. What could be easier?

And if you don't have a physician? No problem. The website visitor can fill out another form, which is immediately e-mailed to the 1-800-COLUMBIA call center. There, operators either call or e-mail the patient back with a physician referral. They also can schedule an appointment, if the patient wants.

Columbia also has used the Internet to tap into Americans' desire to talk to a physician without feeling rushed or boxed in by a set agenda. Even more important, the web's anonymous nature provides a venue for consumers to get answers to potentially embarrassing personal questions that they are reluctant to ask their physicians face-to-face. Consequently, Columbia partnered with America Online a couple of years ago to sponsor physician chats between AOL users and Columbia physicians. In 1996, these chats involved more than 200,000 AOL users.

With the AOL chats, the website, and its other marketing programs to consumers, Columbia is building a foundation. It establishes a comfort level with the billion-dollar corporation. This takes time to build, but once it exists, consumers may rely on consolidators like Columbia as their primary source of medical information.

CAN IT SUCCEED?

If there were any doubts about whether the branding concept can work in healthcare for a nationwide consolidator like Columbia, they were erased one night at the telecommunications center. A call came in from the White House. Columbia's chairman and CEO, Rick Scott, was scheduled to meet with President Clinton the next day. White House aides needed more information about Scott.

Like a good soldier, the call center manager beeped the boss, Lindy B. Richardson, senior vice president of marketing and public affairs.

"Why did you call the 800 number?" Richardson queried the White House deputy assistant for economic policy, Gene Sperling, the next day. After all, Scott's office and home are in Nashville.

"We've seen your ads," he explained simply.

It's a new world, with a healthcare provider whose commercialized national exposure is recognized even in the White House.

CHAPTER TWELVE

The Internet

The Consolidator's Best Tool

W hat cyclosporine did for organ transplants, what the heart-lung machine did for cardiac bypass surgery, that's what the Internet does for healthcare information. It changes everything.

Healthcare consolidators love it and will exploit it to the extreme. The whole information paradigm is changing, making an Internet strategy as essential to a consolidator as a telephone system. The Internet is the consolidators' giant electronic file cabinet. It's also a way for consolidators to take a chain of disparate network systems and make them communicate with each other. Without communication, the operations won't function effectively.

Many healthcare providers are reluctant to shed those expensive information technology systems they have now, even though their boxes can't communicate with anyone outside their own organizations. Some view that as an advantage; it protects patient confidentiality. But this antiquated mind-set changes as healthcare organizations learn to use data encryption and other new security devices.

Through the Internet, consolidators can move from the business of consolidating to the business of operating. They can manage information through the Net, which gives them the means to manage risk and capital, and understand government regulations. Although it might be fun to download video clips from recent movies or peruse an entire month's worth of Dilbert comic strips, the Internet's true value is in putting previously inaccessible information within reach. This phenomenon is particularly dramatic in all aspects of healthcare. Meaningful medical quality and pricing data have been inaccessible to consumers, and even to practitioners. The industry operated for centuries in a vacuum where such information was unavailable, scattered, or unintelligible to even sophisticated users.

Use of the Internet is inevitably entwined in all aspects of patient care. Imagine Courtney Consumer, who buys a home pregnancy test and receives a positive result. Courtney needs to schedule an appointment with an obstetrician, so she goes to the computer and dials into the Internet, typing in her health plan's website address. There, she peruses a list of obstetricians. If she doesn't speak English, the website has other language versions and displays only those physicians who are fluent in her language.

Courtney views data on each physician's credentials as well as general information about location and office hours. If she clicks on a physician's photo, she can view a video in which the obstetrician talks about his theories on childbirth. Next, she views quality indicators about how many babies each of these doctors delivered this year, how many were by C-section, and how many patients experienced complications. She clicks another icon and watches another video of selected obstetricians performing C-sections or vaginal deliveries. How do they work under pressure?

Once she's selected a physician, Courtney schedules an appointment online and fills out the needed registration. Most of her medical records are already online, so she merely needs to update them. Next, she goes to that physician's webpage and downloads nutritional information. She selects the closest pharmacy so that the physician can electronically send a prescription of prenatal vitamins. Having chosen an obstetrician, she's able to access information, including quality indicators, about the hospital where that doctor practices. She also signs up for Lamaze, first aid, and sibling classes online and orders a subscription to the hospital's monthly newsletter for women. Of course, it's delivered through e-mail.

Finally, Courtney receives a tabulation of how much the whole birth process will cost, from prenatal visits to delivery. If there are co-pays, she inputs her credit card account number. Meanwhile, the physician's office staff records the appointment and checks her eligibility status and any recent hospitalizations or physician visits. Staff workers also determine how much the physician will collect from the health plan and what services won't be covered.

When it's time for the baby to arrive, Courtney's friends and relatives automatically receive a message on their desktop screen saver. They simply dial into the hospital's website, type in an access code, and learn the laboring mother's progress. "It's a girl!" flashes on the screen when the baby arrives, accompanied by a photo or video of the birth. Through an advertisement on the site, friends order a potted plant or a bouquet of balloons sent to the room.

At her bedside, the TV is connected to an Internet site where she gets information about the baby's vital statistics. She sends e-mail about the birth to friends and watches videos about nursing and bathing the baby. The same information is available to her at home as well.

Back home, through the Internet Courtney joins a chat group with other new mothers. The interactive calendar on her computer flashes to remind her of well-baby visits, monthly breast exams, and check-ups. When she's ready to go back to work, she searches the online want ads.

MANAGING INFORMATION WITH IMAGINATION

This scenario blends truth and fiction. Some of these transactions and processes are available today. Others won't be here for ten years or more. So far, no one has been able to pull this whole scenario together. When someone does, will it work? Yes, it will work very well, for the patients and for the consolidators with Internet access.

With the Internet as their tableau, consolidators can operate their businesses and let their imaginations run wild on how best to manage information. Networking has been a disaster among healthcare facilities, which rarely could get all of their information systems to talk to each other. Through the Internet, consolidators can begin considering applications that failed in other information technology frameworks. Finally, healthcare businesses have a standard language with which to communicate.

The Internet enables large healthcare companies to accelerate decision making through decentralized organizations. Through an extranet or an intranet, a consolidator can communicate with hundreds or thousands of decentralized, geographically dispersed organizations.

To succeed, consolidators have to develop and constantly retool an Internet strategy. Healthcare organizations are just starting to tap the Internet's potential. According the 1997 HIMSS/Hewlett-Packard Leadership Survey, 87 percent of healthcare organizations are using the Internet for electronic mail and 66 percent are using it for research. Yet only 35 percent are using it to post healthcare information for consumers, and just 11 percent conduct electronic commerce with groups other than payers. Five percent are using it to access patient record information, and 4 percent for insurance reimbursement processing.

Establishing a vibrant, dynamic presence on the Internet's World Wide Web will be part of the cost of doing business. Initially, it won't save money or even generate revenues. However, over time Internet gateways and intranets will cut the costs of communicating and transacting business.

Successful healthcare companies must manage information efficiently, and the Internet gives them the framework to do so. Currently, some managed care plans are already using the Internet to enroll members or have them sign up for wellness programs. Others allow members to change their physician or find a specialist through a website. Still others use it to communicate a healthy feeling about their organizations. The Hall of Health, cosponsored by Children's Hospital of Oakland and Alta Bates Medical Center in that same city, is a community health education museum and science center dedicated to promoting wellness and individual responsibility for health. Consolidators can use the Internet as their information disseminator, transaction machine, and marketing mouthpiece.

HEALTHIER PATIENTS
THROUGH INFORMATION

There is nothing that Americans consume about which they know as little regarding price or quality as healthcare. This improves via the Internet, a real-time disseminator of all types of data. "We have long since passed the day when you could simply pat a patient's knee and say, 'There, there, little lady. You just sit back and don't worry about a thing,'" says Ann James, the healthcare attorney in Nashville whom we met in Chapter Three.

In the past, patients came into a doctor's office with a problem and they wanted answers. Now, patients come in with a problem and they already know some of the answers. The balance of power has just shifted. Historically, physicians' authority was rooted in their vast, proprietary knowledge. Through the Internet, patients have access to much of that know-how. Physicians are still a necessary part of the equation. But now, their role is to help patients interpret the information, arrive at treatment decisions, and implement them.

Not all physicians will welcome the well-informed patient. Remember the physicians who worked with the Odone family, whose quest was turned into the movie *Lorenzo's Oil*. After being told their son's plight was hopeless, the parents spent years searching through hundreds of medical references before finding a treatment for Lorenzo, who had the deadly disorder adrenoleukodystrophy, or ALD. Even though the existence of websites and search engines would have made the family's research much easier, an even more formidable effort was to convince recalcitrant doctors to change their way of thinking.

Healthcare companies empowering their patients need to be aware that empowered patients may be increasingly impatient patients. As they become adept at gathering information quickly and cheaply, they'll expect it. In Bill Gates's book *The Road Ahead*, the nation's richest CEO discusses the imminent information revolution brought by personal computers and the Internet:

> Information that today is difficult to retrieve will be easy to find:
>
> > Is your bus running on time?
> >
> > Are there any accidents right now on the route you usually take to the office?
> >
> > Does anyone want to trade his or her Thursday theater tickets for your Wednesday tickets?[1]

Gates mentions fifteen questions in that passage, only one of which concerns medical services: "What are the symptoms of a heart attack?" Just a year after his book was released, dozens of websites were already serving up the symptoms of a heart attack. They ranged from midsized local hospitals to megaorganizations like the American Heart Association (www.amhrt.org) and the Pharmaceutical Research and Manufacturers of America (www.phrma.org). But those are just the first baby steps of useful healthcare information. The quantum leap comes in giving the heart attack victim or family member the information directly that they need to take action. Which hospital boasts the best survival rate for bypass surgery? Which physician is the most skilled at this procedure? What is the average recovery time for her patients? How much will it cost? Does the patient's health plan cover all or most of the cost? Now, that's useful information. No, it's not available yet, but soon.

In 1996, the American Medical Association transferred its biographic information on 650,000 physicians to the Internet, giving consumers a one-stop shopping reference that had been nonexistent. Consumers can "shop" for a physician, searching by name, specialty, or zip code. This type of use for the Internet is incredibly cost-effective. It cost the AMA about $250,000 to develop the website (www.ama-assn.org), just a fraction of what it would have cost to print and distribute directories with such information to consumers.[2] The AMA's website also features a reference library, another superb use of the Internet because it enables users to wade through vast galleys of data and find what they really need.

In 1997, the AMA went one step further, licensing its information to another organization, Medi-Net. For a small fee, the Carlsbad, California, firm supplies a report that includes a physician's education, American Board of Medical Specialty certifications, licensure data, residency training, and any sanctions or disciplinary actions taken against them by any state medical board. Medi-Net charges $15 for the first report, $5 for the next five. In addition to the AMA's database, Medi-Net (www.askmedi.com) draws from disciplinary data from the FDA, the Drug Enforcement Administration, HHS, and state medical and osteopathic boards.

Patients can also check a doctor's board certification status or seek out a certified specialist in their area on the American Board of Medical Specialties' website, www.certifieddoctor.org. This organization also offers a toll-free number that provides verification and lists of board-certified physicians in each community. But isn't it much easier to point and click? This is a wonderful example of how the Internet makes information that previously was nearly inaccessible available at the touch of a button. Who would have the time and patience to call fifty state boards for information on physicians they were using?

It's almost ironic that the federal government, which is notoriously difficult to wrest information from, may be the most prolific deliverer of useful health information. Both the National Institutes on Health (www.nih.gov) and the National Library of Medicine (www.nlm.nih.gov) have sites that are rich in information. Through its website (www.fda.gov), the FDA gives women the names and addresses of mammography centers that it endorses through certification. Type in the first three numbers of a zip code, and at the touch of the button, you can select from dozens of approved sites. The FDA site goes one step further, referring women to the National Cancer Institute's Mammography Information Service at 1-800-4-CANCER, where an "information specialist" answers cancer-related questions and makes referrals for free or low-cost mammography exams.

Another example is prescription information, a critical service since so many Americans misuse the drugs they are prescribed to take. By the year 2000, 75 percent of Americans must receive comprehensive and understandable information in writing from their pharmacists about adverse drug interactions. By 2006, at least 95 percent must receive the same according to a 1996 Congressional mandate. If pharmacists aren't meeting those goals, the government says it may step in and impose mandatory prescription labeling. Details are available from the health and human services department at the website:

http://www.os.dhhs.gov/news/press/1997pres/970114.html

Estimates are that it will cost manufacturers $14 million annually to prepare the information and pharmacists $107 million to provide it. How much easier it is to put that data up on a website. The cost is minimal, especially when compared with how much drug manufacturers spend on marketing information and advertising to sell such drugs as Tagamet and Premarin.

Once a consumer selects a physician to visit, he can be armed with the knowledge to ask good questions. Search engines like Yahoo, Excite, or Alta Vista make the search for information simple. Individuals can just type in a disease, and a whole host of websites appear. Newsgroups, for example alt.support.arthritis, are a good source of suitable information. In addition, patient support groups are publishing web pages at a rapid pace. For example, the Sapient Health Network posts websites for patients with prostate and breast cancer. They include an online library that draws from books, newsletters, Medline, and links to other organizations and cancer treatment centers. It also publishes the latest news, bulletin boards, and chat areas. Occasionally, the company hosts an open house to welcome visitors to the site. One that focused on breast cancer included online discussions with breast cancer survivors, physicians, and Pam Goddard, campaign coordinator for the National Breast Cancer coalition's signature drive. Goddard is trying to gather 2.6 million signatures from women living with breast cancer to convince Congress to appropriate $2.6 billion in research funding between now and the year 2000.

Consolidators likely will roll-up websites as well, making themselves one-stop services for consumer health information. Mediconsult, a Boston company, claims 180,000 patient visits a month to its patient education site (www.mediconsult.com) through agreements with patient support organizations. Among its partnering organizations are the Brain Tumor Society, American Liver Foundation, National Stroke Association, Mended Hearts, and the National Stroke Association. Mediconsult calls its site a virtual medical clinic for patients with chronic conditions, diseases that they must learn to live with for their entire lives. Not only does the site feature online discussion areas and videotapes and books on specific disease groups, but it offers the latest peer-reviewed medical information. The next step may be for physician consolidators to link with these sites or create them for their own physicians and patient populations.

Until now, this broad array of patient health information was rarely available to patients unless their physicians went the extra mile to keep them continuously informed. Mediconsult describes itself as "the medical web destination patients use most." Traffic on the site is meticulously measured. Consolidators can do the same, counting visits to the site as they would visits to an outpatient clinic. It all integrates with a consolidator's desire to measure first, then analyze.

Medifor and SoftWatch deliver patient-specific educational materials in the form of personal medical web pages with embedded links to other sources of medical information. SoftWatch sells a medical diary as well as records management software that allows a patient to manage his drugs, vital signs, diet, and medical appointments. Plus, the patient can communicate with his doctor, nurse, or other provider via the Internet. An Israeli company, SoftWatch has already latched onto the need for providers and patients to meet in cyberspace.

THE NEW MEDIA
COMPETES FOR READERS

This information machine is so vast that few have time to surf endlessly. For example, the number of web-based services for physicians is literally exploding. Indeed, many corporations are jockeying to be the medical supersites and online libraries that physicians log on and subscribe to. The web is an ideal environment in which to share, catalog, and sort through reams of timely medical data.

As all good webmasters know, the big money isn't in getting subscribers for the website; it's in garnering sponsorships and advertisements. The rule of thumb in the publishing business is that subscriptions only pay for circulation expenses; advertising carries the rest of the expense load. Medical supersites vying for physicians want to lure in the pharmaceutical dollars that will fund their efforts into eternity. Among the entrants are Medscape (www.medscape.com), which boasts more than 100,000 physician subscribers and sponsors online programs that carry continuing medical education (CME) credits. Another contender is Healthgate (www.healthgate.com), which markets to consumers as well. Others are the Doctor's Guide to the Internet and the Physician's Guide. In some cases, the physician and hospital companies provide access to their own physicians through password access within the website.

With estimates of huge financial potential, healthcare sites are attracting institutions steeped in money and power. For example, in 1996 Harcourt Brace, Wolters Kluwer NV, and Times Mirror got together and formed MD Consult LLC, an online information service for physicians. For consolidators, making it work means making the best use of available information and generating revenues.

One appealing aspect of the web is its anonymity. It can be a repository of answers to medical questions that patients find difficult to ask. How often are patients reticent to ask their doctors sensitive, but potentially embarrassing, questions? Go Ask Alice, a website maintained by Columbia University, lists more than one thousand questions available on women's issues; the Centers for Disease Control and Prevention offer information on numerous diseases, particularly ones related to sexual functions.

Drug manufacturers, such as SmithKline Beecham, also see the benefit. The Testosterone Source (www.testosteronesource.com) was launched in 1997 by the manufacturer as the first website devoted exclusively to helping men, women, and physicians understand the impact of testosterone levels on the libido of midlife men. "Unfortunately, the embarrassment men feel initiating a conversation with their physician regarding sexual concerns in general prevents them from seeking the appropriate medical treatment, and instead drives many men to use medically unproven remedies," said Dr. Adrian Dobs, associate professor of medicine in the Department of Endocrinology and Metabolism at Johns Hopkins University, in a news release announcing the site. "The anonymous nature of the Internet provides a venue for men to gain answers to their questions, without compromising their privacy."

SEPARATING SUBSTANCE FROM FLUFF

Hiring "information specialists" is a requirement to compete in the new healthcare economy, and those healthcare corporations with the most informed, most user-friendly specialists will succeed. Consumers have to depend on a handful of such specialists to wade through the avalanche of information headed their way. To go back to Gates's example of heart attack symptoms, many of the websites offering that information are using it to sell a product or service. Patients may not want to wade through hundreds of sales pitches to find the information they need. For instance, Card Guard, an Israeli company, talks about heart attack systems while pitching its telemedicine product, which allows people at risk for heart attacks to transmit a picture of their heart beat directly to a cardiologist.

Cardiac Alert, a company backed by venture capital funding, expects its service to reduce the delay before coronary heart disease is treated, minimizing irreversible damage to heart muscle. Subscribers first have a cardiovascular examination, during which a baseline is recorded and held in a computer file. If subscribers subsequently feel what they suspect are the symptoms of a heart attack, they can record their heart beat and transmit it to the monitoring station for comparison with the baseline electrocardiogram.

The implications of this technology are vast. Quicker intervention is bound to save lives, but there also may be malpractice implications if something goes wrong in the transmission. It also brings up questions about who is manning the monitoring station: the cardiologist or a technician?

Also providing information on the symptoms of a heart attack are companies selling videos, physicians who have developed their own home pages, and hospital groups such as UCSD Healthcare, an alliance of university-based and community-based physician groups and hospitals in San Diego County. In its website, UCSD Healthcare (www.health.ucsd.edu) claims it provides the widest possible range of healthcare services, including primary care, subspecialty care, and access to the latest treatment advances.

HeartPartners (www.virginia.edu/percent7Eheart/HeartPartners/media.htm), a joint effort of the American Heart Association, Martha Jefferson Hospital, and the University of Virginia Medical Center, relates stories about what it's like to have a heart attack. The project aims to decrease the delay time patients experience once they're having signs and symptoms of a heart attack, with stories like this:

> Fred was certain it was the barbecue he'd had for lunch. The indigestion lasted through the afternoon and into the night. His wife urged him to call the doctor, but Fred insisted he'd be fine. When he finally did see his doctor the next morning, tests indicated he was in trouble.
>
> He was whisked to the hospital. Only then did he begin to experience the crushing chest pain usually associated with a heart attack. Within minutes, Fred received powerful drugs that can minimize damage to the heart if they are used right away.
>
> Trust your heart. Use your head. If you or someone close to you experiences the signs or symptoms of a heart attack—pressure or pain in the chest, arm, shoulder, or jaw; sweating; faintness; shortness of breath; or nausea—don't delay. Call 911 or go immediately to the nearest emergency room.

If consumers don't want to launch their own search for information about heart attacks, they can use a web agent. This type of software program goes out on the web, making its own searches, snagging data, and notifying users when an update is available. Such agents work much more extensively than the first generation of search engines. They're real-time reading services, becoming more valuable as the amount of data on the web grows exponentially. Currently there are twenty million websites, and by 1997 the number of medical websites alone was growing at a rate of 10 percent a month.

Web agents become important to those who use the Internet on a daily basis. As the Internet grows more pervasive within the workplace through intranets, workers are apt to use them for both professional and personal needs. Agents speed up and ease doing both. "Push" technology, such as PointCast, will do the same. Through artificial intelligence embedded in these systems, individuals are constantly bombarded with the information that they want, or that their employer wants them to have. This information appears without prompting by the user; in programs such as PointCast, it appears as a screen-saver.

Several websites pop up to deliver "personalized" healthcare information. Electronic information publisher Creative Multimedia operates the Health Explorer website (www.healthexplorer.com) to assist consumers with health questions. Billed as the "first stop to exploring health information on the Internet," Health Explorer taps into more than three thousand consumer health Internet sites. Creative Multimedia's credentials in the healthcare information world include the medical reference CD-ROM *The Family Doctor,* introduced in 1991, and *Dr. Ruth's Encyclopedia of Sex*—both of which, by the way, are sold through the website, thereby creating a revenue source for access to all that free information.

Obviously, this is the key. So much information is free via the web that getting consumers or even businesses to pay for anything may be a stretch. Savvy searchers of the web know that it's foolish to pay when so much information is free for the taking, and downloading. But web agents are valuable to those who are overwhelmed with data. One such is Citizen 1 Software (www.citizen1.com), which is marketed as a tool for businesses users and allows them to specifically find information about the pharmaceutical, medical device, and diagnostics industries. If you search for information on diabetes, for example, you may draw up tens of thousands of references through a standard search engine. A web agent such as Citizen 1 helps distinguish what's in those references that is worthwhile.

Data isn't lacking on the web. But the *right* information can be elusive.

SO MUCH FOR DATA, WHERE'S THE MEAT?

Oxford Health Plan broke new ground in providing the most controversial data via Internet when it began to provide quality of care information about physician groups in 1997. "We said to ourselves, 'Wouldn't it be wonderful if patients could choose who would deliver their care and if providers were rewarded for customer choices rather than for fragment treatment?'" says Vicki Baldwin of Oxford Health Plan, an East Coast HMO. This would be a healthcare system that was held accountable.

Patient education is great; about this, everyone agrees. Yet there are two aspects; one is not controversial, and the other is very much so.

Nobody minds giving patients information about physicians: name, address, phone number, board certification. But giving them information on quality indicators, as Oxford is doing, represents the other side of the coin, and one that is much more valuable.

Ironically, Cheerios provides consumers with more information about its nutritional content than physicians give with a blood pressure medicine. Baldwin says what Oxford is doing is simply keeping up with the times: "We've never seen patients more informed." If other HMOs and provider networks follow the lead of Oxford, quality information will be at the click of a button on the Internet.

In August 1996, the National Committee for Quality Assurance, which accredits health plans, released its $3,200 Quality Compass CD-ROM comparing 250 health plans on more than sixty different measures (see Chapter Nine). The data gathered were exhaustive and represented a true breakthrough in providing valuable healthcare information. However, most consumers didn't see it, unless they happened to read *U.S. News & World Report,* which summarized the results. About 250 employers and health plans bought the CD-ROM, and some plans used the ratings they garnered in their marketing.

Yet James Tierney, the committee's assistant vice president of information products, said the initial release represents just a first step. Eventually, consumers will be able to access the information themselves. "The Internet is a great vehicle for disseminating this information," Tierney says. "Software is being developed that allows consumers to enter the criteria that are important to them when selecting a health plan." In other words, a couple who want to have a baby would select a plan that rates high in obstetrics and pediatricians. A diabetic would select one that ranks highest in treating that type of chronic care. "The information is out there already," Tierney says, noting that it's just a matter of gathering it and implementing the software needed to access it in a personalized fashion. The committee already provides some summarized information on its website (www.ncqa.org).

THAT ELUSIVE BIT OF DATA: PRICE

The next frontier is price information. One of the most innovative healthcare information companies also helps sell used cars to consumers. How big a leap will it be to do the same with healthcare services?

In January 1997, this company, Reynolds and Reynolds, made a deal with the mother of all information companies, Microsoft, to launch the world's largest used car database. Reynolds, of Dayton, Ohio, had already agreed to partner with Microsoft on CarPoint, its online new-car buying service (http://carpoint.msn.com). Launched in July 1996, CarPoint received nearly four million visits within its first year. With the newer agreement, CarPoint shoppers will be able to choose among both new and used cars. Retailers who want to participate in CarPoint must complete an Internet sales certification program.

Unlike the situation in the auto industry, prices in healthcare usually revolve around what Medicare pays for a procedure or treatment. Expenses rise to meet that reimbursement level, often shadowing the true costs involved. This is frequently the case when price controls exist. Medicare rates have been the precursor to Medicaid rates and many insurance formulas, particularly prior to managed care. Managed care has set its own pricing scheme. Rather than charging what the market will bear, providers spent what Medicare would pay, and the repercussions flowed from that. A recent example involved bone densitometers, which are used to measure osteoporosis, particularly in elderly women. In late 1996, the HCFA, which determines Medicare payment, slashed the reimbursement level for peripheral bone densitometers but left alone the reimbursement for (radial) bone densitometers, which measure the strength of weight-bearing bones. When that happened, Norland Medical Systems, the largest maker of peripheral densitometers, responded in the only way it could. It slashed prices. A peripheral scan, previously reimbursed at $120, now would be reimbursed at just $40 by Medicare. Norland reasoned that its system had to cost less or no one would use it. In fact, prices dropped so low that a pharmacy chain, CVS, started offering peripheral scans for $29, making it easy for women to pay out of their own pocket.

So, one month Medicare was paying $120 for a scan, while consumers were paying only $29 the next month. Where is the logic here?

This type of pricing logic, or lack of same, isn't obvious to consumers. Most patients never know how much their insurance companies are paying for their treatments. Trying to find information about quality or cost of doctor services or hospital days has been like wading through molasses. For decades, pricing information about healthcare providers wasn't even formally collected. Then, even when it was collected—on paper, of course—only a select group of professionals could get their hands on it. Infrequently, but with great fanfare, it was released. Then, as was the case with some employer coalitions, it was branded as skewed and misleading by many hospitals. The great debate was charges versus amount collected: "Yes, this may be our hospital's charges, but we don't collect that much because of charity care and other factors," hospital CEOs said. For years, insurance companies shielded consumers from the cost or price while providers shielded them from information about quality. This provided equal protection for all involved—all but the consumers who were paying the bills.

Price is a totally unknown concept in healthcare, but it's becoming more important than ever. What is the basis for negotiation in most managed care contracts? Price. The entire healthcare system is becoming very price sensitive, and a primary reason is that it is one of the few known variables that payers can negotiate. What does it cost for a vaginal delivery? Payers can get a price from one hospital, and then another, and compare the two.

Occasionally, individuals ask hospitals to divulge prices, and sometimes they receive the information. Sometimes not. Yet they never know whether the "list" price is cheaper or more expensive than what everyone else is paying. Mike Jones might pay $1,200 to a hospital for an MRI scan, while the local HMO is only paying $350. With the Internet, more providers will post prices. If consolidators see this as an advantage, they'll set the trend.

However, before consumers are convinced to take the lower priced MRI scan, they must believe that they're getting the same quality. Is the quality of the MRI scan the same regardless of its cost? Truly, consumers don't know. That's where the consolidators have to deliver outcomes data to be paired with price. Then they can hook consumers, who want value in their medical care as well as their cars.

Interestingly, hospitals have been more than willing to give discounts, a characteristic that gave rise to the preferred provider organizations of the 1980s and early 1990s. Almost anyone who set up a PPO that would bring patients to a hospital was offered a discount. The concept benefited only one party: the PPO administrator who was taking a cut of the action. But through the Internet, information about pricing will slowly become available.

STREAMLINING OPERATIONS

The Internet enables consolidators to communicate with each other and their patients in ways and at speeds that previously were unimaginable. Hospitals and other providers are also using the Internet and their own intranets to compete smarter and communicate better to cut costs. For example, in Dallas, Baylor Health Care System contracted with a California firm, Action Technologies, and Netscape to develop an intranet-based application that enables the system's eight hospitals to accelerate their review of contracts with pharmaceutical suppliers. By shortening the time previously required to have each of the eight hospitals review these contracts, Baylor could lock in volume discounts faster. This is expected to save Baylor $120,000 in its first year of application. "In the highly competitive healthcare market, we will differentiate ourselves by our connection to customers, physicians, and community via our Internet and intranet applications," says Bob Pickton, Baylor's senior vice president and chief information officer for BHCS.

Through intranet applications, the time required to make complex decisions is slashed. In the past, the process of contract negotiation on pharmaceuticals could take up to six months as executives met monthly to assess, discuss, and take action on the individual contracts. Through the intranet process, agreements are finalized in one or two meetings, Baylor officials say. Each negotiated contract can save the system about $3,000 per month, or up to $36,000 annually. Baylor negotiates about twenty contracts each year, so it adds up to real savings.

The Internet can be a funnel for all types of computers. "The web is our salvation," said Dr. Clement J. McDonald, codirector of the Regenstrief Institute in Indianapolis, at a meeting of the American Medical Informatics Association. "Finally, we have a way to unify our incompatible, diverse, and geographically far-flung clinical information systems."[3]

By the 1990s, most hospitals had computers, but they amounted to a tower of "babble." There were twenty or more disparate information banks that kept data on medical records, pharmaceuticals, patient care, ancillary services, billings, collections, admissions, outpatient departments, and on and on. In the future, large systems will use private, in-house intranets that accept widely established protocols, allowing communication between diverse computing platforms. Hospital systems, physicians, and vendors can exchange a variety of information, whether it be lab results or reimbursement.

Most healthcare companies initially used the Internet for marketing purposes. But increasingly, it is becoming a means of commerce and information transactions. Physicians will begin using payer websites to check the status of claims, insurance eligibility, and benefits of patients covered. They'll accept patient referrals and precertification transactions over the Internet.

To see how health plans can interact with enrollees, visit the Healtheon website (www.healtheon.com). Founded by Netscape's founder and chairman, Jim Clark, Healtheon plans to use the Internet to reduce the administrative costs of managing and distributing benefits information. Most employers distribute that type of information on paper, using phonebook-sized directories of doctors and pamphlets on what's covered and what's not.

Clark, who was the Internet's first billionaire thanks to his 28 percent stake in Netscape, represents a new class of executives who are looking at healthcare from a completely different perspective. A former associate professor of computer science at Stanford University, Clark founded Silicon Graphics in the early 1980s, took it public, and then left in 1994 to start Netscape.

Through Healtheon, he believes that big savings can come by cutting administrative costs and integrating with employers' payroll and human resource systems. With that capability, a benefits manager can keep track of the company's spending from her desktop computer at work or at home. The implications of this are huge because small employers would be offered many of the benefits that are enjoyed only by large corporations. In addition, a substantial cut in overhead spending means that employers won't see their healthcare costs climbing. They'll get less pressure to make the cuts that cascade down to hospitals and physicians. It puts more money in the system that previously was spent shuffling paper. Healtheon has already signed deals with Blue Shield of California and Rocky Mountain Health Care to pass data back and forth.

Claims processing will be a natural for the Internet. In fact, it could do much to remedy the black hole of record keeping. At least that's the conclusion of some twelve hundred healthcare technology managers surveyed in early 1997 by HIMSS and Hewlett-Packard. One-quarter of the survey respondents believe that access to medical records via the Internet will be common within five years. In fact, IDX Systems, a Boston firm, has codeveloped a product with Microsoft that allows physicians to access patients' medical records on the Internet. Currently, medical records can only be accessed from linked computers. Through the product, called OutReach, physicians can type in a password and access the information, which is encrypted for security purposes. IDX officials said the systems will cost $5,000 to $10,000 per physician.

The system could have another advantage. Patients would be able to view their own medical records from home, another quantum leap in their level of access.

INDUSTRY'S LARGEST
CONSOLIDATOR ON THE NET

Through the use of the Internet and an intranet, Columbia has become an information company as much as a healthcare services company. Investing $500 million a year on information systems, the company recruits physicians and employees, sends clinical and financial information, and buys equipment electronically.

More than fifteen thousand Columbia employees are able to program in HTML, the language of the Internet. In a fourth floor office crammed with software and manuals, J. Tod Fetherling, director of interactive marketing for Columbia/HCA, heads a website team.

Almost any information about Columbia is available at the touch of a button. Want to put on a health fair? A marketing director in a Columbia hospital in California can call up a list of health fairs scheduled throughout the system. Want to open a chest pain center? The services provided by each Columbia hospital are on a searchable database, enabling other hospital managers to communicate with those experienced in this type of project. "We had 150 notebooks of information system applications, and we put it all online so people can just point and click," Fetherling said. "That's saved a lot of money because the applications are searchable and people can just read or print the selections they need."

On Columbia's intranet, called Koala, more than ten thousand users in Columbia hospitals and offices throughout the world communicate with each other and share best processes on a real-time basis. In the past, hospital administrators typically had to call each other or wait until annual get-togethers to share stories about ways to save money or deal with technology issues, improving patient care, or physician dilemmas. Now, they share it all online.

"One of our huge priorities this year is patient satisfaction," Fetherling relates. Gallup, the opinion research guru, conducts all of Columbia's patient satisfaction surveys, calling 125,000 patients each quarter. Until 1997, those surveys were delivered each quarter to hospital CEOs.

The surveys show how the CEO's hospital is being graded by patients and also measures that level of satisfaction with other Columbia hospitals in the network. Patient satisfaction is an integral part of how Columbia measures quality. Obviously, a hospital can deliver the best patient care on earth, but that won't mean much if the patient doesn't feel good about the experience. Part of quality patient care comes in the low-tech qualities of efficiency, kindness, understanding of patient needs, cleanliness, and good food.

Now, the patients' satisfaction reports are online for CEOs to read. Every time Gallup completes a patient survey, it updates the information in the database. That's something Gallup hadn't done with a client before Columbia. "We push the vendors a lot," Fetherling comments. It is just one example of the gorge of information available to Columbia hospital CEOs. They also can buy equipment from each other via the intranet through a program called CEQUIP. Each day, hundreds of pieces of surplus medical equipment are listed on the CEQUIP page of Columbia's intranet. The list is searchable, so if a hospital is looking for a CO_2 laser, it can call up just those listings. "Cine film processor, $9,000." A price and contact name is listed. Sometimes, no price is listed if a hospital has already depreciated the piece of equipment and is willing to pass it along free to another facility. "We've traded entire laundry facilities," Fetherling says proudly about CEQUIP's ability to fulfill the equipment needs of various hospitals.

The equipment stays on CEQUIP internally for thirty days. Then it's advertised outside Columbia on the Internet for another ninety days. After four months, if the equipment has already been depreciated on Columbia's balance sheet it can be donated to one of four not-for-profit relief organizations. Those groups distribute the equipment internationally to needy hospitals and clinics. How did Columbia hospitals exchange equipment before this? "We faxed lists back and forth," Fetherling explains. The Columbia intranet is also connected to twenty vendor intranets so that Columbia employees can tap into information about products they use in the hospital.

The bottom line to all this is cost savings through time and paperwork. Fetherling couldn't put an amount on the savings but said he's starting to gather that information. For example, it typically costs $15,000 to $20,000 to recruit a physician. Through the website, it costs $50.

Columbia grew through acquisition, which meant that it quickly ended up with a storehouse of different computers. Connecting them would have been an executive's nightmare, albeit a consultant's lucrative dream assignment. However, all of those computers can communicate through Columbia's intranet, Koala.

LIVING LARGE THROUGH
HEALTHCARE BRANDED WEBSITES

Anyone can publish on the Internet; this means the quality of the information can range from bogus to valid. Virtually anyone can publish on the World Wide Web, too; either they learn HTML or they simply buy a software program like Microsoft's Front Page or Publisher. So how is a consumer to tell the difference between a website that sells quackery and one that delivers sound advice from credentialed professionals?

Branding. Consumers buy from the names they trust. Consolidators that establish brand names draw business. That's why consolidators should jealously guard their reputations on the Internet. Although pundits discount the value of branding in healthcare, it may be the only thing that distinguishes one player from another on the web.

One of the most active branders in healthcare is Columbia, which interweaves that marketing strategy with its Internet strategy. Becoming a brand name through the Internet helped Columbia overcome something it always lacked: a pedigree. Because Columbia is an investor-owned system, it could never have the pedigree that's so valued in hospitals. The Mayos, the Massachusetts Generals, the Ochsners, and the Methodists of the world were steeped in tradition and loyal followers and philanthropists.

Two other large medical corporations, MedPartners and Health-South Rehabilitation, also are sophisticated users of the Internet. Med-Partners' website looks like nothing that Americans are used to seeing from their medical establishment. For one thing, the site practically invites the media to call and interview their doctors. Anyone who's ever been a journalist knows that getting a hold of doctors is nearly impossible. They rarely call you back, and only then when some hospital flack hounds them into doing so.

The MedPartners website (www.medpartners.com) has a separate page called Media Resources that features a small drawing that looks like a remote radio station with the call letters WMDM. (MDM is MedPartners' stock ticker symbol.) Even more incredible, the page features in large italic letters this quote: "People who are funny and smart and return phone calls get much better press than people who are just funny and smart." The quote is attributed to Howard Simons of the *Washington Post.* The web page goes on to tell journalists that Med-Partners wants to "make your life as a journalist a little easier." Reporters can simply click on "Physician Resources" to get a list of medical experts that are—get this—willing to be quoted. Or the site can provide story ideas and a list of corporate spokespersons that can be contacted by phone or e-mail.

This openness to the press from a physician group is startling, to say the least. However, MedPartners is raising the bar in openness to the press, and other physician companies may be forced to follow. Although the AMA site lists physicians, MedPartners, too, showcases its physicians through its own locator search engine.

HealthSouth's site (www.healthsouth.com) includes articles from the company's *Sports Medicine Update* magazine (subscribable online). Elsewhere in the website technology race, California's Kaiser Permanente, an HMO with five million members, relaunched its website in 1997 (www.kaiperm.org). The site now includes a health tip of the day, employment opportunities, and a quarterly webzine called *Partners in Health.* Members may also sign up for prenatal classes, request membership cards, inquire about benefits information, or chat with healthcare professionals.

LINKS AND SECURITY

There are two other essential issues in making an Internet strategy work for consolidators: linking and security.

Consolidation is all the rage in healthcare, and consolidators are hot on partnerships. On the Internet, it's easy to partner with someone; just set up a link to their website. Links may be advertisements, or simply free references to useful medical information organizations, noncompetitors, or industry journals. These types of links can drive revenue to the site. For example, Amazon Books, a vast virtual bookstore on the Internet, invites healthcare organizations to set up their own virtual bookstores. You get physicians or patients to review books, and then link to Amazon books (www.amazonbooks.com). If the visitor to the site actually orders a book from Amazon, the referring website gets an 8 percent commission.

Finally, healthcare websites and security are inseparable. People who are worried about giving their credit card numbers to websites are probably downright paranoid about seeing their medical records.

However, that's where things are headed. The levels of security will be different for patients, physicians, hospitals, employers, and managed care companies. Yet information from all those groups is essential to building the ultimate destination: healthcare information that can be measured and used.

Interestingly, healthcare technology managers believe the biggest threat to security may be from people within their own organizations. The 1997 Healthcare Information and Management Systems Society identified "curiosity seekers" within their own firewall as the biggest threat to security.

Another level of security exists in publishing on the web itself. The webmaster may be so desperate for good content that he throws anything fresh and new on the site. Healthcare organizations need to build an approval process for content on their website. Just as the editorial content of newspapers or magazines goes through a series of editors, so must healthcare businesses do the same. Essentially, a website puts them in the publishing business. The organization will want to develop rules about what gets published and what doesn't, and they need to follow them meticulously. Most of the healthcare providers using technology realize that it is a means to an end. The end is to make it work: providing better patient care, producing profits, and growing.

Although the web may be a great equalizer in terms of accessing information, it is the consolidators that are best positioned to finance a dynamic presence there. A website designed to handle online commerce costs about $1 million in its first year. However, simply launching a website isn't nearly as costly. Fetherling estimates that Columbia's cost no more than $100,000 in its first year.

Through it all, fixating on the goal rather than the wizardry is what makes the wheels go round. Savvy consolidators know that they must manage information within their organizations and with various constituencies, such as patients, physicians, hospitals, employers, and insurers. In the future, they'll figure out how to best use an intranet and the Internet to accomplish their organization's goals as they work to get beyond the consolidation stage and on to managing them.

CHAPTER THIRTEEN

No Turning Back

An industry that once was distended like an over-fertilized vine, tangling up patients and providers alike, is developing a new hybrid of managed care consolidators. They are the Med Inc. companies of the future. We're in the first generation of consolidation, in which these companies struggle to manage capital, information, risk, and government regulation.

Consolidators are just starting to push the envelope in healthcare. Another decade of experience will take these first-generation consolidators into true operation of huge, national networks. In the second generation of consolidation, which is a decade or more away, the healthcare consolidators will see even more merger activity and rationalization of cost structures.

Ironically, all of the acquisitions and roll-ups designed to bring efficiency to this business will probably end up costing more in the short term. Business processes and information systems must be reconfigured for efficient handling of the needs of larger and larger, diverse organizations. Healthcare has been an industry that rewarded inefficiency. The financial incentives were to perform more procedures, file more paperwork, prescribe more drugs, and build more hospitals. This is changing, as tomorrow's consolidators challenge each other to become more efficient and drive costs lower. "There are greater efficiencies through more businesslike attitudes to address the whole continuum of care," says Daniel O'Connell of United Technologies in Hartford.

As corporate director of employee benefits and human resource systems, O'Connell negotiates with the health plans for United Technologies' seventy thousand domestic employees. He talks about a local hospital that was failing and was briefly resuscitated by state officials before it finally closed. "It's a big waste, especially if those services can be provided elsewhere," he said. "There are a lot of those institutions around." O'Connell's comments are somewhat predictable. Fairly or not, hospitals stand as the most visible signs of waste in the healthcare system. Huge multistoried institutions, stuffed with well-paid employees and expensive equipment, they stand as a superfluous symbol of medicine in many communities. They are the twenty-four-hour medical convenience stores that society demands and for which it pays a high price. America has twice as many hospitals and physicians as it needs.

Efforts to rein in hospital overcapacity will be a bellwether for payers and providers. "We could end up with a half-dozen or fewer health systems in the United States," adds O'Connell. "That would mean employers as large as us wouldn't have the bargaining leverage we have now. However, it could be a positive if these systems are agile, nimble competitors."

Size didn't help the dinosaurs, and it won't help healthcare consolidators either unless they can use it to operate efficiently. If size works against efficiency, these consolidators will go the way of Tyrannosaurus Rex. However, the ability to drum out excess through consolidation will make this industry attractive to investors into the new millennium as the nation's healthcare bill passes the trillion-dollar mark.

Other industries go through cycles, but the demand for healthcare continues to swell. The great unknown for consolidators today and in the future lies in the personalities behind them. Where would Columbia be without Rick Scott, HealthSouth without Richard Scrushy, MedPartners with Larry House? Yet Scott was forced out at Columbia, the largest healthcare consolidator, and others were left to scrutinize which of his strategies worked and which didn't. The "new" Columbia under Thomas Frist, Jr., unraveled some of the consolidation efforts that Scott had undertaken, such as buying home healthcare agencies. One of Frist's first decisions was to sell the home care business because of possible Medicare problems. Can consolidators like Rick Scott learn from their mistakes? If not, other hard-charging entrepreneurs surely will.

IS WHAT'S GOOD FOR CONSOLIDATORS GOOD FOR AMERICA?

This book dissects the medical business thirteen years after Dr. Stanley Wohl wrote what was then considered a groundbreaking text, *The Medical Industrial Complex.* His book discussed all that was bad about mixing business and medicine: "Medicine concerns the inalienable right of each individual to enjoy the healthiest, most disease-free body that state-of-the-art knowledge allows."[1] The belief is widely held. Many say that healthcare is a right that should not be abridged for anyone.

That notion in the 1980s contributed to the highest healthcare inflation rate in history. In the decade after Wohl's book was published, healthcare posted double-digit inflation rates that finally slowed only in 1994. Indeed, any predilection to rein in spending was often systematically attacked as an attempt—horrors!—to ration care. Still, sometimes less care is better care.

It's worth noting that the profit-seeking organizations of corporate medicine that Wohl and other critics attacked were not the only ones running up the bills. Not-for-profits controlled nearly 90 percent of the nation's hospitals, which is where most of the healthcare was being delivered during that decade. The gluttony of the nation's healthcare providers is evidenced today by an oversupply of hospitals and physicians maintaining the intention of doing everything for the patient regardless of the price. The U.S. healthcare system also became characterized by a maldistribution of healthcare dollars. Those who can pay are showered with services without limits, and those who can't pay are sentenced to bureaucratic systems where care is rationed. Such a system can only continue if there's an endless stream of money. But corporate America said no, we're tired of these double-digit premium increases.

It's worth noting, however, that without the excesses of the past, this new era of consolidation would not be possible. Reluctance to cap healthcare costs created an oversupply of doctors, hospitals, and medical product vendors. Now, as Congress faces a nearly bankrupt Medicare Trust Fund, who are these senators and congressmen turning to? Congress is turning to the corporations of Wohl's so-called Medical Industrial Complex. Yes, they're contracting with HMOs and other managed care companies that have incorporated business practices to slow the private rate of healthcare inflation.

Those moves are good for the elderly and good for the Medicare budget. Medicare beneficiaries enrolled in HMOs receive a fuller range of services for less money than the average fee-for-service beneficiary, according to a Price Waterhouse study. In addition, the case management approach of HMOs allows them to provide this range of services at lower costs than comparable fee-for-service providers. "Even though the risk contracting program may have cost Medicare more in its early days, the maturation of the Medicare HMO market has created small but significant changes in the mix of HMO enrollees," said Jack Rodgers of the Price Waterhouse Health Policy Economics Group in Washington. "The result is a distribution of enrollees between HMO and fee-for-service programs that allows HMOs to earn a reasonable profit while still providing Medicare with the 5 percent savings it has sought."

But government speaks from both sides of its mouth. On the one hand, it's turning Medicare and Medicaid over to managed care. On the other, it's shackling managed care with more and more restrictions on how to deliver that care. "They're pushing us back to where we were before," says Arthur Ryan, chairman and CEO of Prudential. "We're no longer dealing with 14–15 percent inflation rates. You can't have both."

NEW STANDARDS IN MANAGED CARE

Consolidators must lead the industry into new territory and develop new measures of efficiency in cost and quality. It's interesting to consider a much-publicized study in the *New England Journal of Medicine* in 1997 about hospital administrative costs. It proclaimed that investor-owned hospitals have significantly higher administrative costs than not-for-profit hospitals, as if that were a watershed for efficiency. "We found that for-profit hospitals spend 23 percent more on administration than do comparable private not-for-profit hospitals and 3 percent more than public institutions," said the authors, Dr. Steffie Woolhandler and Dr. David U. Himmelstein.[2]

Both the American Hospital Association, which represents the hospital industry at large, and the Federation of American Health Systems, which represents investor-owned hospitals, questioned the findings. In fact, news accounts went on to quote Donald A. Young, executive director of the Prospective Payment Assessment Commission, which advises Congress on Medicare rates, as saying, "I don't find anything inherently wrong with administrative costs if an organization is efficient. Some of the best corporations in America also have high administrative costs. That, in part, is why they are good businesses. You need good administrators to manage a large, complex organization."[3]

This pretty much describes today's and tomorrow's healthcare consolidators: large, complex organizations, indeed. Healthcare consolidators may in fact end up spending more on managing the business. The ones mentioned in this book all look toward better management of diseases as the biggest potential for profit. The more efficient these consolidators are, the better for everyone. America faces the largest healthcare bills in history as baby boomers reach middle age and, eventually, retirement. This nation can't afford an inefficient, fragmented healthcare system. As healthcare organizations become more efficient, the price of healthcare should hold level or decrease. Those that can't hold the price level lose contracts and profits.

First of all, the variance in pricing narrows as prices are published and shared with a broader community of payers, including consumers. Most payers haven't been aware of these variances, but that's changing. Just days after President Clinton ruptured his hamstring muscle in March 1997, one organization published a news release on the Internet telling everyone that treating the malady would be cheaper if Clinton went home to Little Rock. Medirisk, in Atlanta, reported that it would cost a managed care provider in Little Rock $1,039 to do so, while a private-pay surgeon in New York City would charge $2,775. Companies like Medirisk that help payers negotiate with managed care companies are in demand in the search for the ideal blend of low costs and high quality.

Second, the savings that can be achieved through outcomes measurements, administrative streamlining, and patient education are enormous. If any of those possibilities, which we have discussed in earlier chapters, become reality, then the industry becomes far different than it is today. Consolidators have the best chance to make these things happen. However, Med Inc. companies will be scrutinized, torn asunder, put back together, valued, vilified, invested in, and organized over and over again. More healthcare businesses of all stripes will be asked to take on financial risk, and that means having the capital resources to do so and the informational resources to manage it.

For healthcare businesses, the financial risk is bigger than ever before because the pot of money is getting shifted around with unprecedented accountability. Venture capital companies are placing their risk capital with healthcare companies that may be asked to take on risk from payers. Payers are risking the capital they received from employers or employees. And on and on.

But spreading the risk means spreading culpability. Consider the case of Schering-Plough, discussed in Chapter Ten. For a long time, the company was simply in the business of selling inhalers for asthmatics. Once Schering entered the business of risk sharing, managers there made the company a more responsible healthcare organization. They started developing programs to manage the best plan of care for the patient instead of just figuring out how to sell more products. Isn't that what patients want from their healthcare companies?

Healthcare consolidators worry more about costs as they become, or partner with other, managed care companies. In the past, manufacturers rarely worried about what it cost to make a new device. Instead, they focused on getting to the market quickly, and more quickly than competitors. Tomorrow's consolidators consider cost in every step of development:

- Will this device be cost effective?

- Will payers pay for it?

- If my company were paying the bills, would we approve its use for patients?

Management gurus consistently preach the message that if businesses take care of their customers, the profits will simultaneously flow from that prioritization. The same is true for successful consolidators.

BAXTER'S EXAMPLE TO CONSOLIDATORS

Consolidation fever cannot continue unfettered. Eventually, growth slows as prime acquisition targets are snapped up. Vernon Loucks, chairman of Baxter International, has advice for tomorrow's consolidators: focus. "There's a lot of reasons to consolidate entities, but when you do that, you find that not everything you acquire fits," he says.

Loucks has the battle scars of a consolidator that's bulked up, slimmed down, and is now acquiring (but only in specific niches). At one time, Baxter was not only one of the world's largest medical supply companies but also operating growing networks of physicians and home healthcare agencies. Going in too many directions can deter growth in the new technologies that matter, Loucks says. When Baxter was selling everything from surgical gloves to sophisticated cardiovascular products, it found that declining profits in the commodity lines were robbing cash to fund research and development. "We started blowing our budgets," Loucks reflects. The new Baxter concentrates on what Loucks describes as high-margin, high-growth businesses in biotechnology, cardiovascular, intravenous therapy, and renal care. "In 70 percent of our products, we're the clear number one in the world," Loucks says.

Leveraging from a position of strength allows Baxter to take financial risks, such as a $100 million plant being built in Switzerland to produce a blood substitute called HemAssist. Baxter has spent thirty years on developing this substitute. Loucks also points out that this industry demands rapid technological advances, which historically have come from small companies. Eventually, these smaller entrepreneurial companies are absorbed into larger ones, but in an industry that consumes 14 percent of the gross national product, there's always going to be a way to do things smarter and cheaper. "There's no such thing as perfect flypaper," Loucks adds. "Nobody has a monopoly on good ideas. This whole cycle of renewal that's going on defies any conclusion of where it's going to end up."

PRIVATE REFORM

This industry has proven that it can improve upon itself without government's heavy hand. Ironically, it was just such a fear that led to the massive restructuring and consolidation. Although some still want to dynamite the underpinnings of the nation's healthcare structure, even more do not. That was glaringly apparent in the response to President Clinton's attempt in 1994 to reform the system. In the wake of the failed Clinton healthcare plan, healthcare inflation dissipated and the industry restructured.

The evolution of healthcare consolidation only comes from within; its pace is what the market can bear. Government, however, does more than stand on the sidelines. It polices this business more than ever before. The stakes are high.

Wrongdoing in healthcare is nearly always entwined with government. On the clinical side, patients may die if providers mess up. On the financial side, taxes finance so much of healthcare that mismanagement can lead to charges of fraud. Not coincidentally, the Justice Department is dramatically increasing its pursuit of fraud in healthcare. Healthcare is the number one target now that the defense industry has slipped in the importance of government suppliers.

One-half of all government whistle-blower cases now involve healthcare, said Debra Cohn, special counsel to the Deputy Attorney General.[4] It's a lucrative area for the government, bearing fruit of $700 million in the past three years. The feds also have new ammunition, thanks to the Kassebaum-Kennedy health insurance reform law, which was enacted in 1996 and makes healthcare fraud a separate federal crime.

There's a huge lack of culpability in healthcare. Everyone gets frustrated sooner or later with the finger-pointing of America's healthcare system. It's the hospital's fault, the insurer's fault, the physician's fault, the patient's fault. It's always somebody else's fault. Americans and their providers need to own up to their own responsibilities and culpability in this system. Perhaps the healthcare consolidators will do that, or provide the leadership to do so.

A TALLY SHEET FOR CONSOLIDATORS

Consolidators carry the momentum of the market today. They're more likely to attract capital, which can pay for the information systems to manage risk contracts for large populations. If automation brings the savings that experts predict, it can lower costs for everyone.

Employers and HMOs will start moving blocks of insured patients to managed care consolidators, whether they be hospital systems, HMOs, physician companies, or medical supply vendors. The lines among these managed care companies are blurring. They're merging vertically, horizontally, and virtually. Successful consolidators demonstrate the quality and cost efficiency of their services. The Internet brings promises of cost efficiency and access to information. However, it's not a universal solution. The Internet won't be accessible to low-income and elderly groups, which means many of the Medicare and Medicaid patient groups will be left out. Those groups offer the greatest potential for savings through risk contracting, but gathering and managing information on them may be more difficult.

The danger in getting big comes from outside influences. One is government regulation. As the consolidator grows, it's more likely to lose track of what its managers are doing. In the quest to maximize profits, a manager could overstep ethical bounds, financial standards, or even the law.

The residue of consolidation will be broken healthcare businesses that are too inefficient to compete. Yet they are still community employers and may entreat governments to prop them up in the name of jobs. On a related note, consolidators attract more union activity. The California Nurses Association, a politically active group of forty-five thousand members, already has zeroed in on Columbia as an enemy. The group also tried to stop the merger of two not-for-profit hospitals, University of California San Francisco Medical Center and Stanford Health Services. Obviously, the group worries about job security in any such merger. In addition, physicians themselves are starting to consider unionization. About 10 percent of physicians are currently in unions, and for some this type of bargaining unit represents a significant alternative to PPM companies. Some physician unions are even talking about starting their own managed care plans.

What if unions start to gain enough power to fell the healthcare consolidators? What if Medicare goes bankrupt or raises the eligibility age to eighty-five? What if biotechnology companies develop ways to keep people alive until they're 150 years old? This industry can't be contained by a handful of consolidators. Its future rests within the fabric of society and government.

HEALTHCARE'S HORIZON

Those leading healthcare consolidation have a golden opportunity: moving this industry from scapegoat to hero. Corporate America, for example, casts a jaundiced eye toward the industry. This was documented in a late 1996 survey, sponsored by Siegel and Gale, a marketing communications firm, and Roper Starch Worldwide, a market research and opinion research firm, which polled about 350 business executives. The researchers found that U.S. executives neither admire nor trust the industry, placing it second to last among twenty-five industries. As almost a slap in the face, executives placed the healthcare industry above only the tobacco industry in terms of trustworthiness. This certainly doesn't speak well, considering the volume of litigation aimed at that latter industry and its attempt to cover up research about cancer.

A specific complaint is that executives saw a difference between an essential "standard of care" and the care they received. In addition, only one-third of the executives polled said they understood their health insurance coverage. Many didn't understand such staple health-care acronyms as COBRA and POS (point of service).

"The healthcare sector must restore its lost credibility, by creating clear, effective forms of communication that facilitate a dialogue between provider and patient. Only then can a true partnership among companies, the industry, and government be formed," said Alan Siegel, chairman and CEO of Siegel and Gale, in releasing the findings in September 1996.

Ten years ago, the industry was on the precipice of feverish inflation and operating with gross inefficiencies. The consolidators have a chance to make it work, to plow savings into improved efficiencies that benefit patients, payers, and providers. The future looks good as they mount their resources. Driven by Med Inc. consolidators, a welcome transformation of this trillion-dollar industry is under way. We believe the next ten years will bring responsible changes that benefit Americans' health and their pocketbooks.

Epilogue

We knew that parts of this book would be out of date before the ink hit the printing press. Many of the healthcare consolidators described in these pages have grown larger in the ensuing months as they added acquisitions. In several cases, consolidators have stumbled and/or their executives departed.

While we can't note all the changes, we do feel pressed to note a significant acquisition that was announced in late 1997 and that affects two of the book's most prominent consolidators, PhyCor and Med-Partners. Both are described in Chapter Three. In a deal that shocked many industry analysts, PhyCor agreed to buy its larger competitor, MedPartners, in a transaction valued at $8 billion. PhyCor's president and CEO, Joseph Hutts, who had stuck to growing PhyCor in an evenly paced, methodical manner, said he approached MedPartners to seal what he called an "extraordinary and unique opportunity."

Post-merger, PhyCor will have annual revenues of $8.4 billion and manage 35,000 physicians. Though large, that represents just 5% of the nation's doctors.

As one can see, opportunity—for consolidators—continues to knock.

᪵ Notes

Chapter One

1. "The Economics of End-of-Life," remarks presented by Bruce Vladek, administrator, Health Care Financing Administration, at Last Acts: Care and Caring at the End of Life, Robert Wood Johnson Foundation Conference, Mar. 12, 1996.
2. Snow, C. "AHA Report: Public Beliefs Hospitals' Priorities Have Changed." *Modern Healthcare.* Jan. 13, 1997, p.3.

Chapter Two

1. Fein, E. B. "In Columbia Pact, New York City Ties Pay to Hospital Productivity." *New York Times,* Jan. 8, 1997.
2. Fein (1997).
3. "Trex Sees Mammography Sales Boom on Horizon." Reuters, Feb. 18, 1997.
4. Dalton, J. C. "Hale and Dorr Creates FDA Practice Group." *Boston Business Journal,* Feb. 24, 1997.
5. Lutz, S., and Gee, E. P. *The For-Profit Healthcare Revolution.* Burr Ridge, Ill.: Irwin, 1995, p. 101.

Chapter Three

1. "Growth of Physician Practice Consolidation Expected to Continue." Reuters, Jan. 30, 1997.
2. "Growth of Physician Practice . . ." (1997).
3. "Socioeconomic Monitoring System," American Medical Association, 1996.
4. "Outliers." *Modern Healthcare,* Apr. 21, 1997, p. 52.
5. From the website www.phycor.com
6. "PhyMatrix Puts 3Q Net Above Wall St. Views." Dow Jones News Service, Dec. 4, 1996.
7. "Cancer Facts and Figures," www.cancer.org

8. Darwin, J. "Houston Medical Firms Pursue Hot New Specialty Market." *Houston Business Journal,* Mar. 10, 1997.

9. "PPM: Key Accounting Issues Update." *Of Minds and Men—Changing Behavior in the New Physician Enterprise.* Teleconference sponsored by Salomon Brothers, Apr. 3, 1997.

Chapter Four

1. Wissner, S., and Carey, B. "Fifty Indictments Predicted for Columbia/HCA." *The Tennessean,* July 31, 1997, p. 1.

2. Eichenwald, K. "Health-Care Provider Faces Whistle-Blower Lawsuits." *New York Times,* Aug. 19, 1997.

3. Hensley, S. "Bergen Brunswig, IVAX Plan to Merge." *Modern Healthcare,* Nov. 18, 1996.

4. Eichenwald, K. "Government Blankets Hospital Chain with Search Warrants." *New York Times,* July 17, 1997.

5. Japsen, B. "Columbia's Big Ad Bucks: Giant Chain Outspends Other Hospitals on Advertising." *Modern Healthcare,* Mar. 10, 1997, p. 2.

Chapter Five

1. Japsen, B. "Another Record Year for Dealmaking." *Modern Healthcare,* Dec. 23–30, 1996, p. 37.

2. Scott, L. "Not Together Yet: Allina, Seen as System Model, Struggles to Integrate." *Modern Healthcare,* Feb. 17, 1997, p. 30.

3. Scott (1997), p. 30.

4. Perrault, M. "Giant Systems in Kansas City and Across the Nation Are Gobbling up Many of the Independents." *Kansas City Business Journal,* Feb. 17, 1997.

5. Northwest Texas Healthcare System. "Amarillo Hospital District Board Signs Letter of Intent with Universal Health Services." News release. Sept. 26, 1995.

Chapter Six

1. "Managed Care Taking Over." *Med Ad News,* Dec. 1996.

2. Pham, A. "HMOs, Fallon Community Health Hunger for Bigger Piece of the Pie." *Boston Globe,* Feb. 27, 1997, p. D1.

3. "Hospital Errors Make Falling Ill a Risky Business." Reuters, Jan. 30, 1997.

4. "Industry Taking New Look at Medical Error Casualties." *Modern Healthcare,* Oct. 21, 1996, p. 12.

5. "New HMO Ads: If All Else Fails, Lie!" *Business Wire,* Oct., 10, 1996.

6. Samuelson, R. J. "The Joy of Deregulation." *Newsweek,* Feb. 3, 1997, p. 39.

Chapter Seven

1. Briggs, L. "Mergers, Affiliations Spell Survival for VNAs." *Modern Healthcare,* Nov. 25, 1996, p. 38.

2. Vladek (1996).

Chapter Eight

1. Interview with John Hatsopoulos, *Dow Jones Investor Network,* July 30, 1996.

2. Hatsopoulos (1996).

Chapter Nine

1. *Faulkner and Gray's Health Data Directory.* Washington, D.C.: Faulkner and Gray, 1997.

2. *Faulkner and Gray's Health Data Directory,* 1997.

3. *Healthcare Informatics,* June 1996, p. ss22.

Chapter Eleven

1. Japsen, B. "Columbia's Big Ad Bucks: Giant Chain Outspends Other Hospitals on Advertising." *Modern Healthcare,* Mar. 10, 1997, p. 2.

Chapter Twelve

1. Gates, B. *The Road Ahead.* New York: Viking, 1995, pp. 9–10.

2. *Modern Healthcare,* Oct. 7, 1996, p. 94.

3. Borzo, G. "Web Technology: Coming Soon to a Hospital Near You." *American Medical News,* Nov. 18, 1996.

Chapter Thirteen

1. Wohl, S. *The Medical Industrial Complex.* Harmony, New York, 1984.

2. Pear, R. "Study Finds Administrative Costs Higher at For-Profit Hospitals." *New York Times,* Mar. 12, 1997.

3. Pear (1997).

4. "AHA Members Urged to Watch Their Ethics." Reuters, Jan. 30, 1997.

~~ Index